The Resurgence
of Populism
in Latin America

The Resurgence

of Populism

in Latin America

Robert R. Barr

LYNNE
RIENNER
PUBLISHERS

BOULDER
LONDON

Published in the United States of America in 2017 by
Lynne Rienner Publishers, Inc.
1800 30th Street, Boulder, Colorado 80301
www.rienner.com

and in the United Kingdom by
Lynne Rienner Publishers, Inc.
3 Henrietta Street, Covent Garden, London WC2E 8LU

Library of Congress Cataloging-in-Publication Data
Names: Barr, Robert R. (Robert Rennie), author.
Title: The resurgence of populism in Latin America / by Robert R. Barr.
Description: Boulder, Colorado : Lynne Rienner Publishers, Inc., 2017. |
  Includes bibliographical references and index.
Identifiers: LCCN 2017002128 | ISBN 978-1-62637-667-0 (hc : alk. paper)
Subjects: LCSH: Populism—Latin America. | Political parties—Latin America.
  | Latin America—Politics and government—1980–
Classification: LCC JL966 .B365 2017 | DDC 320.56/62098—dc23
LC record available at https://lccn.loc.gov/2017002128

British Cataloguing in Publication Data
A Cataloguing in Publication record for this book
is available from the British Library.

Printed and bound in the United States of America

The paper used in this publication meets the requirements
of the American National Standard for Permanence of
Paper for Printed Library Materials Z39.48-1992.

5 4 3 2 1

In memory of
W. Ewell Barr and William E. Barr

Contents

Tables and Figures

Tables

Figures

Acknowledgments

THIS BOOK IS THE RESULT OF A LONG-TERM RESEARCH AGENDA, THE COM-pletion of which has left me owing more debts of gratitude than I can adequately repay. Still, I would like to acknowledge at least some of those people and organizations whose assistance and support made this project possible.

A number of colleagues helped me in ways, both little and large, that contributed to the development of my ideas and the completion of the project. The thoughtful comments of Raúl Madrid and Kurt Weyland were particularly valuable to the project's early development. Additional help along the way came from discussions with and suggestions from Kevin Deegan-Krause, Carlos de la Torre, David Doyle, Tim Haughton, Kirk Hawkins, and Cas Mudde. Several anonymous reviewers provided excellent constructive criticism. Thanks go to Mark P. Jones for allowing me to cite his 2005 paper, which provided the foundation for my index of party system institutionalization. Patrick Mello provided permission to use his 2012 paper and shared another with me. His help and the advice of Claude Rubinson were key in helping me navigate the waters of qualitative comparative analysis. John Polga-Hecimovich shared advice and his data on party nationalization. I also thank Mindy Erchull for her help in deciphering the social psychology literature. Several colleagues helpfully steered me toward important research; among others, these include Cristóbal Rovira Kaltwasser, Omar Sanchez, and Selim Erdem Aytaç. My friend Anna Law advised me on the publishing process and shared important contacts. I would also like to thank Carrie Broadwell-Tkach at Lynne Rienner Publishers for her steadfast guidance through the publication process.

The many students in my seminar on political movements and organizations in Latin America, at both the University of Miami and the University of Mary Washington, have influenced my thinking on the subject of populism over the years. A few students in particular deserve special mention: Rachel Federgreen, Stephen Gregg, Elizabeth Kaknes, Kevin Kallmyer, Rachel Martin, and Caroline Wood. Another student, Tim Carroll, provided much-appreciated research assistance.

My home institution, the University of Mary Washington, has been tremendously helpful in all respects. It has provided logistical and administrative aid as well as financial assistance in the form of faculty development grants, a Jepson Fellowship, and a sabbatical. In particular, I would like to thank my department chair, Jack Kramer, for his unwavering support.

A generous grant from the Smith Richardson Foundation provided the primary financial backing for the project. With it, I was able to take time off from teaching; conduct field research in Argentina, Bolivia, and Ecuador; and attend a number of conferences. I am grateful not only for the foundation's support, but also for the understanding and flexibility of its officers, including Dale Stewart, Allan Song, Scott Boston, and Kathy Lavery. Using this funding, I researched cases and conducted interviews in Buenos Aires, La Paz, and Quito. A number of politicians, NGO officers, journalists, and representatives from international institutions and foreign governments generously shared their time and expertise with me. There are too many to name individually (and a number spoke under condition of anonymity), but I appreciate the contributions of each and every one.

Only with the support of Hilary Stebbins was this work both possible and personally meaningful—thank you.

I apologize to those I have neglected, but I appreciate your contributions all the same.

1

Populism in Latin America

IN VENEZUELA'S 1998 ELECTIONS, HUGO CHÁVEZ CAPTURED 56 PERCENT of the vote and left the country's traditional parties for dead. His victory was a watershed moment. The firebrand antagonized the elite and stirred the masses, promising a revolution on their behalf. Adding an element of old-fashioned nationalism, he liked to reference the glory and great leaders of long ago, particularly Simón Bolívar, Latin America's liberator from Spanish rule. But for many observers, Chávez's rhetoric and style brought to mind different Latin American leaders: individuals like Argentina's Juan Perón or Mexico's Lázaro Cárdenas—the classical populists of the twentieth century. And Chávez was not alone. During the first decade of the twenty-first century, four populists won elections and another half dozen competed. Once again, populism was back.

Populism first appeared after the collapse of the export-led model of economic development, in the aftermath of the Great Depression. These leaders promised political inclusion and economic benefits for society's lower classes, or the *descamisados* (the shirtless ones) to use Juan and Eva Peróns' evocative term. The most successful of these populists were enormously powerful, drawing from the support of millions of the newly enfranchised. Though corporatist systems of representation kept the mobilized masses under control, many workers gained real economic benefits in part through the use of import substitution industrialization (ISI) policies. To what extent these policies helped or hurt the population overall is a matter for debate, but either way the classical populists—even some who never took office, like Peru's Victor Raúl Haya de la Torre—had profound and lasting effects on their countries.

Although many of the first populists came with the advent of mass democracy, those in the second era came soon after its return, in the context of the wrenching economic reforms of the 1990s. Alberto Fujimori, a true

1

political outsider and novice, surprised many with his 1990 victory in Peru and then with his about-face on economic policies. The year before, Carlos Menem took office in Argentina and pulled the same trick. These, like Carlos Salinas of Mexico and Fernando Collor de Mello of Brazil, had a leadership style and oratory familiar to any student of Latin American history. But, unlike their predecessors in the first half of the twentieth century, these populists embraced neoliberal economic policies. Rather than promoting a kind of state-guided economy with broad benefits for the workers, they reduced the role of the state and its protections for the lower classes. By adhering to the prescriptions of the International Monetary Fund (IMF), the US government, and other external actors, the neopopulists embodied a more conservative version of populism. As some demonstrated (e.g., Roberts 1995; Weyland 1996), the demise of ISI did not mean the same fate for populism in Latin America, despite assumptions to that effect (e.g., Malloy 1977).

Many within the region grew unhappy with the results of the economic reforms, and the next cycle of populism veered sharply to the left. Chávez was the first of this round, taking office even before neopopulism had run its course. When he claimed a ghost was haunting the region, he "was warning the world of the anger of the millions of *latinos* who are tired of their poverty and the corrupt governments of their countries" (Demmers, Fernández Jilberto, and Hogenboom 2001a, xi). Following him were candidates like Ecuador's Rafael Correa, Bolivia's Evo Morales, and Mexico's Andrés Manuel López Obrador, all of whom promised to ease the impact of recent reforms, to restore the economic role of the state, to protect national resources, and to stop the elite from benefiting at the expense of the people. In many ways, the twenty-first-century populists are cut from the same cloth as all the others: they use the same kinds of appeals and the same kinds of personalistic, top-down connections with supporters. But their shift away from market orthodoxy distinguishes them from those of the 1990s and marks the region's third era of populism.[1]

With each iteration, the populists elected to office have had an outsized influence. Perón had such an overwhelming impact on Argentina that his legacy is still prevalent today. Fujimori and Menem pushed through constitutional changes, concentrated executive power, and altered their countries' party systems and economic landscapes. Likewise, Morales, Correa, and Chávez brought about changes in their countries' constitutions, political institutions, and economic orientations. Populists would seem to accrue greater power than most presidents, a power based not on stable partisan institutions or collaboration with the economic elite but on the backs of multitudes of supporters. In turn, they use this clout to dominate other political institutions and rearrange them to their benefit—often undermining the means of ensuring horizontal accountability that are so important to liberal democracy. In so doing, they have deeply polarized their societies. Bolivia almost split in half, with the eastern departments—the *media luna*—struggling to reject the new political framework. Venezuela experienced massive protests in 2002–2003 against Chávez and again in 2014 against his successor, Nicolás Maduro. Perhaps not coincidentally, those who highlight setbacks in the third wave of democratization or the rise of hybrid regimes typically cite these same individuals (e.g., Coppedge 2005; Levistky and Loxton 2013). The influence of these individuals is not uniform nor always so profound, of course. But the fact that the results of their leadership can be so consequential highlights the importance of understanding Latin American populism.

Goals and Contributions

In this book, I strive to contribute to the understanding of Latin American populism. To do so, I need to deal with first things first: What is populism? That the term is controversial among social scientists has become axiomatic: despite its frequent usage, many meanings have been assigned to it. Over the years, populism has referred to individuals, movements, parties, regimes, ideologies, economic policies, charisma, and so on. More recently, the two most prominent schools of thought have defined populism in either political terms (e.g., Roberts 2006, 2007; Weyland 2001) or ideational terms as a worldview or ideology (e.g., Hawkins 2010; Mudde 2007). These disputes are not about mere semantics. Depending on specifics of the definition *and* its conceptual structure, the kinds and numbers of cases of populism included can vary dramatically—so, too, can our understanding of why it emerges and what legacy it leaves.

Through a comprehensive review of the variety of conceptualizations and defining characteristics, I hope to contribute to the debate over populism's very nature. In the exploration of ways concepts can be structured, I illustrate some of the costs and benefits of each option and provide a basis for choosing the one most suited for the present purpose, an empirical analysis of populism in contemporary Latin America. Additionally, I offer a critique of the ideational views of populism. Some in this school (e.g., Mudde and Rovira Kaltwasser 2013) call for consensus around a minimal definition. Though a unifying definition is certainly appealing, minimal is not always optimal. Usefulness depends on the accuracy and utility of the content, not the complexity. Specifically, the choice of definition should be grounded in conceptual and analytical terms, and should have some continuity of meaning over time.

In the case of those using ideational definitions, their concept structure and defining characteristics have much to offer. However, as is made clear in this book, the request to have everyone use their minimal definition is to ask that we study a different phenomenon, for ideational populism is not the same thing as populism from a political perspective. In analytical terms, a gap exists between the ideational understanding of populism and the ability to study it. Scholars in this camp emphasize the role of ideas and at times even deny the importance of behavior, yet their analyses always reference actors and behavior. As such, there is a disconnect between the concept and the analysis, which raises questions about the utility of the former. This problem is unfortunate because some of the most sophisticated empirical studies of populism are found in the ideational school (see especially Hawkins 2010). Finally, to isolate discourse or ideology from all else that has been linked to populism, at least in the Latin American literature, is to cut it away from its historical roots. That said, ideational definitions still have much to offer and the emphasis on language is important. The definition I use in this book incorporates attributes found in both the ideational and political approaches but ultimately considers populism in behavioral and political terms.

A second issue I address is what populism is not. This question is not trivial. From the perspective of concept formation, a key goal is to structure concepts in a way that facilitates not only inclusion of examples but also exclusion (Goertz 2006b). In other words, a good concept should be able to tell us not only what something is but what it is not. Neglecting the latter is to invite imprecision. Indeed, in the case of populism, imprecision is a common occurrence. The evidence lies with the frequent casual linking of multiple ideas through the use of phrases like "populist outsiders" or "antisystem populists."

Three such ideas are commonly, if implicitly, tied together and tied to populism: lack of association with the established political parties, newness to politics, and the use of antiestablishment appeals. In some empirical instances these factors are linked together. Hugo Chávez is a good example: he came from outside the party system, had no prior political experience, and used an "anti" discourse targeting the establishment. Before him was Alberto Fujimori. However, counterexamples can be found in Andrés Manuel López Obrador, who was the mayor of Mexico City and a member of the Party of the Democratic Revolution (Partido de Revolución Democrática [PRD])—hardly an outsider party by 2006. Evo Morales served as a representative in the Bolivian legislature prior to running for president; Rafael Correa was Ecuador's minister of finance. Just as not all populists are newcomers or outsiders, not all outsiders or newcomers are populists. Few consider Bolivia's Felipe Quispe to be a populist, despite his newness and outsider status. The same goes for Colombia's Carlos Gaviria, who had no relationship with the established parties (though he did have political experience) and yet was no populist. So newness to politics and outsider status are not necessarily linked to populism. Antiestablishment appeals, however, are; all populists use some version of appeals based on "the people" versus the establishment, and so they sound like outsiders even if they have had previous experience or ties to parties. Still, others offer the same message, so the use of the appeals alone—by the definition used here—does not necessarily equal populism. In short, although a relationship may be found among these various ideas, they remain conceptually and sometimes empirically distinct. The fact that the literature often links them and populism together does little to advance our understanding. I attempt to make both the distinctions and the relationships clear.

Armed with an understanding of what is and what is not populism, one can then attack the question of what causes it, another key theme of this book. Observers often comment on the perpetual nature of populism in this region. This view, however, is not quite accurate. In the first place, distinct waves or eras are identifiable, as suggested earlier. In the second place, within any given era not all countries experience populist episodes, and for those that do, their experiences are not consistent. Variation can be identified not only among countries but also within them from election to election. What can account for this variation? This question taps into discussions about the relationship of populism to democracy, with some considering the former to be the mirror of the latter (e.g., Panizza 2005), and discussions about populism's relationship with politics itself, with some considering them to be one in the same (e.g., Laclau 2005a). Although populism may be inherently political and even related to democracy in some way, these factors alone cannot explain variation and so there is far more to the story.

In this book, I address the sources of populism—specifically, the reasons for the electoral success of populist candidates—in the third era. This distinct period in the region's experience with populism is of great contemporary relevance. Though recent, from the late 1990s to the present, the third era contains a high level of variation within and among the Latin American countries, though most of them share the same macrolevel features, such as experience with electoral politics under market orthodoxy, and similar opportunities and constraints resulting from globalization. The focus on the third era also allows the use of certain data that were not available previously, an opportunity that is particularly, though not uniquely, true with respect to survey data. Prior to 1996, surveys were spotty and inconsistent. Since then, however, the number and quality of public surveys have increased, thanks in part to the Latinobarómetro series. Transparency International's Corruption Perceptions Index (CPI), additionally, began around the same time. The current era of populism happens to coincide with the accumulation of information that simply is not available in any systematic, comparative way for the prior eras.

A key protagonist in this story is party system institutionalization. Since Scott Mainwaring and Timothy Scully (1995) introduced the notions of institutionalized and inchoate party systems, a number of studies have addressed their implications, including their relationship with the rise of outsiders, personalistic leaders, and populists (e.g., Flores-Macías 2012; Jones 2005; Mainwaring and Torcal 2006). In a parallel line of research, scholars have attempted to understand party system collapse, which in Latin America is typically associated with the rise of populist leaders (e.g., Dietz and Myers 2007; Morgan 2011; Seawright 2012). Among those studying populism directly, meanwhile, some assert a causal relationship between party system strength and populism (e.g., R. A. Mayorga 2006; Roberts 2006). By highlighting the role of party system institutionalization, a key theme in this book is in keeping with important strands in the literature. However, the book contains what may be the first empirical demonstration that weak party system institutionalization is a *necessary* condition for the emergence of populism. The same is not true for the rise of other kinds of political challengers.

Weak party system institutionalization is, in a sense, an opportunity. For those seeking to present themselves as some sort of alternative to the political status quo, party system weakness gives them room. This point is doubly true for populists. Populism is a political strategy involving certain kinds of appeals (antiestablishment appeals) and a way of interacting with followers (plebiscitarianism). Though unlikely, the successful use of one or the other of these, though not both, is possible in strong party systems. Where systems are weak, however, citizens do not have close ties or involvement with parties, they feel that parties lack credibility or legitimacy, they switch their votes frequently, and parties themselves are organizationally deficient. In such a context, ambitious politicians might not seek association with and support from the mainstream parties, John Aldrich's (1995) conclusions notwithstanding. Instead, they might see an opportunity to carve a new path set against those mainstream parties and linked to supporters through some direct and personalistic means. Having charisma is helpful, incidentally, but not essential.

But is it not inherently obvious that weak party systems lead to outsiders, populists, and the like? Weak party systems indeed may make it more likely that alternatives to the political status quo gain electoral support. However, a key attribute of this study is the search for both necessary and sufficient conditions, as opposed to identifying statistical likelihoods. The analysis here demonstrates the special role—the necessity—of weakly institutionalized party systems for populism. It also shows, by contrast, weak party systems are not necessary for political alternatives (i.e., outsiders, newcomers, etc.) in general.

Necessity, of course, is not the same as sufficiency. To account for populism's electoral success, one must go beyond mere opportunity. Citizens need to want it. They must be angry enough with the established parties to choose what might be considered the riskier option—the untested and unknown. Specifically, I argue that the combination of a perception of prevalent corruption *and* evidence of disadvantage, such as someone else benefiting from that corruption, can account for the public demand for populism. Whether corruption is seen as a societal ill, a norm to be tolerated, or even a good thing depends to some extent on the eye of the beholder. Research shows that the distribution of corruption's benefits has an influence on how individuals view corruption (e.g., Manzetti and Wilson 2007). Corrupt behavior like vote buying, for instance, can work (e.g., Brusco, Nazareno, and Stokes 2004; Stokes 2005), meaning that individuals will support the perpetrators of corruption when they benefit. On the other hand, perceptions of being victimized by corruption erodes political support for the system (Seligson 2006). Luigi Manzetti and Carol J. Wilson (2007) cite the telling case of Brazil's Adhemar de Barros, whose supporters said, "He steals, but delivers!" (956). When the politician steals but fails to deliver, however, that support quickly goes away. This consequence may be particularly true when the apparent beneficiaries of the corruption are members of some other group, in other words, not ordinary citizens but members of the elite or foreign interests.

The social and organizational psychology literatures explicate the linkages in this causal chain, in particular by highlighting the emotional and behavioral impact of perceived unfairness. The perception of widespread corruption is not sufficient by itself to generate this response; however, it becomes crucial when combined with the belief that someone else is benefiting. This belief is particularly potent when that someone else belongs to another group—a frame of reference that populist leaders provide. I reference psychology not to suggest that populism is about some irrational crowd psychology, with supporters mesmerized by a charismatic demagogue. Rather, I assume that vote choices reflect a level of intentionality and purposefulness. Nevertheless, I also recognize that subjective assessments, self and group identification, and emotional states can have an influence. I do not, therefore, assume that people act based strictly on instrumental considerations of material gain. In the right circumstances, populists can foster group identity, cultivate anger, and thus influence voter choice. Indeed, the aforementioned is the strategic element of populism.

In short, populism results when both the supply and the demand are present, which is the argument I seek to demonstrate. Articulating a new theory about its causes is the third contribution I hope to make, in addition

to the aforementioned discussion of its conceptual development and elabo-
ration on its relationship with closely related ideas. As already mentioned,
the role of party systems has been discussed before, and the same is true of
corruption. Three elements differ here: (1) the specific combination of factors found to be sufficient conditions for the rise of populism, (2) the identification of necessary conditions, and (3) the methods used to study it.
Most populism studies are qualitative analyses of single countries, or sometimes a handful. Only a few employ statistical analyses to determine its
causes (e.g., Doyle 2011; Hawkins 2010; Weyland 2003). None, however,
use the tools of qualitative comparative analysis (QCA) to investigate populism. In this book, I use two methodologies.

The first is a familiar qualitative method, namely, process tracing, that
I use to explore the conditions leading to the rise of populism in a single
country, Bolivia. The great advantage of this approach is the level of detail
it affords. It permits the thorough investigation of complex processes without the sacrifices of subtleties and nuance that large-N studies often require.
Within the given country, moreover, one can compare events across time
with fewer of the confounding factors that can plague cross-national studies. This approach can provide substantial leverage to make causal inferences (Collier, Mahoney, and Seawright 2004). In this instance, Bolivia
provides an opportunity to explore the changes of context that led to the
rise of its contemporary populist leader.

To bolster confidence in this theory, I go beyond the single case and
consider the region as a whole. This step is important for a few reasons.
On the one hand, because research on populism is dominated by single-
country studies, casual observers may get the false impression that populism is a virtual constant in Latin America; nearly all the studies, after
all, discuss its presence but not its absence. As careful observers of the
region know, however, populism is atypical. It may not be rare, but it is
certainly not the norm. Furthermore, some countries seem to have numerous populist candidates whereas others have none. Is there something
unique to, say, Bolivia that would pave the way for populism's rise? Why
has Chile had no populist candidates in the modern era? Without comparing across countries and, specifically, including negative instances, one
has no way to satisfactorily answer these questions. In studying only positive examples, one runs the risk that the conclusions about one instance
are merely reaffirmed, but not actually challenged, by additional studies.
Eliminating this risk is the more important reason to compare cases across
the region.

To maximize leverage in making causal inferences, negative cases
should be included alongside positive ones (Skocpol and Somers 1980). As
long as the negative cases are considered carefully (Mahoney and Goertz
2004), including both should give greater confidence in the findings. The

possibility of disconfirming evidence is greater, so confirming the argument faces a higher hurdle. Also, the researcher has the opportunity to demonstrate reasons for the outcome's presence as well as its absence. Doing so allows for understanding what is different about those countries that experience the outcome compared to those that do not. In the case of populism, incorporating a large sample of the Latin American countries allows one to understand why Ecuador, for instance, has more experience with it in recent years than Uruguay.

Beyond those instances that clearly belong in the set of positive outcomes (i.e., countries where a populist is successful) and those that clearly belong in the set of negative outcomes, moreover, are those somewhere in between. In other words, gradations can be found in levels of support for populists: just because such a candidate runs in an election does not mean victory is overwhelming or loss is complete. In Bolivia's 2002 election, for instance, the one populist candidate received only 5.5 percent of the vote. Three populists competed that same year in Ecuador; together they won about 50 percent of the vote. Venezuela's Chávez brought in almost 63 percent of the vote by himself in 2006. The existence of partial or intermediate cases—specifically, elections in which populist candidates received some, but not much, support—may present a problem for probabilistic and statistical research but reflects an inherent attribute of case-oriented work (Ragin 2000, 53).

To accommodate a multicountry but intermediate-N study, allow for complex causation, and take into account degrees of success, I use QCA (see Ragin 2000, 2008; Rihoux and Ragin 2009). QCA is a case-oriented method used to evaluate relationships among sets in a systematic way using the logic of Boolean algebra. It can be used to assess complex causal processes in which different combinations of factors are capable of producing the same outcome. Like quantitative methods, its use facilitates the comparison of multiple observations in a replicable manner, but it does not require the treatment of causal factors as variables that can have only independent effects on some outcome. Rather than provide a focus on correlations, QCA is used to consider the relationships among sets of factors to determine causal necessity and sufficiency. (More details about QCA appear in Chapter 5 and the appendixes.) Using this method, I compare all of the elections in the presidential democracies of South America and Mexico from 1996 to 2010 (an N of 35 observations). Among these thirty-five elections, populist candidates competed in fourteen (counting those individuals who received at least 5 percent of the vote). By including a range of outcomes within countries and across the region, moreover, I avoid selecting on the dependent variable. In short, this analysis provides new and powerful leverage for understanding the rise of populism in contemporary Latin America.

The Three Eras

To get a sense of contemporary populism, one should consider its roots. The first era, arguably populism's heyday, was in the 1930s and 1940s. Following the collapse of the agro-export model of development, populist leaders emerged throughout the region, campaigning against rigged political systems that benefited the few. They focused their efforts in the cities, where they could reach mass audiences through stirring speeches. These speeches typically vilified the foreign-oriented elite and praised the inherent goodness of "the people." Such distinctions were not nuances hidden in the text; instead, the rhetoric was quite explicitly Manichaean. Populists equated the elite with evil and the ordinary with purity and morality. Frequently, too, classical populists adopted elements of popular culture and folkloric customs, such as performing traditional songs in campaign events and using colloquialisms. Political rallies often had spectacle-like qualities. These rhetorical and symbolic gestures conveyed the sense that the populist leader understood and could represent the people. These charismatic leaders claimed to embody the authentic values held by ordinary citizens.

In contrast to the extant oligarchic structure, classical populists offered instead a vision of an inclusive society, in which ordinary citizens—notably but not exclusively workers or peasants, depending on the context—would gain both a political voice and a share of the country's economic wealth. Many did benefit on both counts. Argentine women gained the right to vote under Juan Perón, for instance, and countless workers gained some voice through union membership. Mexico's Lázaro Cárdenas, by reconfiguring the Institutional Revolutionary Party (Partido Revolucionario Institucional [PRI]), enhanced representation for peasants, workers, and middle-class groups, who ostensibly gained greater, even if circumscribed, influence in government. These political projects were inclusive: whether simply promising reforms to benefit sectors previously ignored by the state or fully extending political rights, classical populists helped incorporate subaltern groups into the political and economic spheres of their countries.

Economic inclusion often entailed proindustrialization and nationalist policies, along with wealth redistribution and the expansion of social rights and benefits. For example, Perón built schools and clinics, made health care a human right, extended social security benefits, and nationalized the foreign-owned railroads. His policies were not atypical: most populists took steps to create jobs, raise wages, subsidize food staples, enhance labor standards, and support education. Cárdenas took on the landholding elite and redistributed millions of acres to peasants; as a result, over 800,000 individuals gained land, often through collective ownership. He also took on foreign interests: in 1938 he nationalized oil production and proclaimed the country's economic independence. With moves like these, the state took on an interventionist role, the clearest example of which was the populists' typical embrace of ISI. Additionally, their measures benefited many groups beyond just industrial workers or rural peasants. The constituency for classical populism included multiple classes and social sectors.

Given the explicit and effective appeals to the people along with the reforms they implemented, these populist leaders developed large and loyal followings. In many cases, their support took on a cultlike or semireligious character. At the same time, however, their politics and policies represented a setback for those who had previously dominated. As such, they tended to be polarizing figures. Ecuador's José María Velasco Ibarra, for one, won five presidential elections yet finished but a single term because of coups. Víctor Raúl Haya de la Torre, a towering figure in twentieth-century Peru, created and led the American Popular Revolutionary Alliance (Alianza Popular Revolucionaria Americana [APRA]), which confronted entrenched interests. However, he was exiled and imprisoned, his party was outlawed, and, when he was finally allowed to run for office, the elections were nullified.

Similarly, whereas supporters viewed the classical populists as inherently democratic, detractors called them demagogues and autocrats. Despite their steps to incorporate the excluded, their expansion of political rights, and their embrace of electoral processes, the classical populists also disdained attributes of liberal democracy and frequently ruled in an authoritarian manner. In Cárdenas's state-controlled corporatist system, nonofficial organizations were repressed and official ones were under the thumb of the president through the PRI. In Argentina, Juan Perón, an admirer of Benito Mussolini, imprisoned his opponents, silenced opposition newspapers, and annoyed the clergy enough for them to call him a tyrant. Additionally, the mechanisms of horizontal accountability—the stuff of checks and balances—suffered under these presidents. They ignored inconvenient laws, manipulated compliant legislatures, and emasculated judicial systems. One legacy, then, of these leaders has been the debate over populism's relationship with democracy.

Marking a point of contrast with more recent populists, those of the first era also sometimes left lasting legacies in the form of stable party organizations. These parties often served as the institutional framework for corporatism and have survived well beyond their leaders. Cárdenas's PRI continues today, as does Perón's Justicialist Party (Partido Justicialista [PJ]) and Haya de la Torre's APRA. Still, not all classical populists left such a footprint. Velasco Ibarra relished his independence from parties, famously saying, "Give me a balcony and I will be president." Rather than build a lasting organization, he cobbled together various fleeting partisan coalitions for each election. Whether well-organized parties or loose electoral coalitions, populists led personalistic organizations. At the core of these organizations was neither ideology nor programmatic goals but rather an individual, with the organizations existing to elevate populists' power by mobilizing the masses on their behalf.

This first era of populism, in sum, included charismatic leaders who espoused an antielite and pro-people appeal, used top-down forms of mobilization, enhanced political and economic incorporation, embraced state-led industrialization and nationalistic economic policies, used corporatist systems of representation, and had the support of a multiclass coalition. Each of these attributes has been considered an essential component of populism at one time or another. Similarly, the distributive aspect of populism appeared to link it inexorably to clientelism and even to fiscal irresponsibility. Additionally, though the correlation between the implementation of ISI and the rise of populism was inexact, it was close enough to lead many observers to conclude that the two went hand in hand. As such, many considered populism to be a reflection of deep structural conditions and to represent a stage of development and modernization. When the debt crisis swept the region in the 1980s and conditions became hostile for interventionist economic policies, conventional wisdom suggested that populism would be a thing of the past. Under the Washington Consensus and IMF-enforced austerity, how could any politician use ISI to create jobs, extend benefits, and build the same sort of mass-backed political power as the classical populists had done some decades earlier?

The neoliberal economic policies that swept the region did indeed limit the scope of government and the possibilities for intervention. Still, a few leaders adopted very similar kinds of appeals, connected with followers in familiar ways, behaved comparably in office, and even used economic policies to benefit those most clearly left behind by the economic transformations. These leaders were the neopopulists who constituted the second era of populism in Latin America.

Some observers saw similarities in the structural conditions of the 1980s and the 1930s: deep political and economic changes produced crises and created opportunities for ambitious politicians to build support among those losing out. Indeed, the lost decade led to severe unemployment, high inflation, crippled unions, and the growth of the economically precarious informal sector in which workers lacked political clout and organized representation. These growing ranks of the urban poor became the latest group available for incorporation. At the same time, the third wave of democratization reintroduced electoral processes and opened the door once again to political contestation.

The new populists appealed to ordinary citizens, contrasting their positive and authentic values against those who would keep them down, namely, the elite and the political parties that served their interests. They toned down the nationalistic rhetoric but ramped up the "politics of antipolitics." As such, the neopopulists were more consistently hostile to partisan organizations and representative institutions than their predecessors, something that was true with respect to not only their appeals but also their own parties. Peru's Alberto Fujimori, for instance, created a new electoral label for each election, intentionally forestalling the possibility that these organizations might develop independent bases of power. Those parties that lasted across electoral cycles, like Max Fernández's Solidarity Civic Union (Unidad Cívica Solidaridad [UCS]), were still little more than personalistic vehicles. And, when neopopulists emerged through established parties, like the PRI or PJ, they manipulated or circumvented them in ways that enhanced their own influence. Carlos Salinas, for instance, undercut the corporatist-based power of the PRI by enacting neoliberal reforms, and he simultaneously used his National Solidarity Program (PRONASOL), an umbrella social program, to develop new personalistic linkages with supporters, thus bypassing multiple levels of governmental institutions and partisan organizations.

These leaders had less room for maneuver with respect to distributing economic benefits, but they could carefully target programs toward specific groups. Antipoverty programs, for instance, endured overt manipulation that directed funds away from some groups and toward others. Some also ingeniously used the proceeds from privatization to fund programs designed to benefit key groups. After a US$2 billion windfall from the sale of Peru's telecommunications utilities, Fujimori vastly increased spending on a number of public works projects, which not only provided new housing, schools, and local infrastructure but also thousands of construction jobs. The decisions about resource allocations were manifestly political in nature. Though the classical populists worked through unions and encouraged unionization, the neopopulists made efforts to further weaken organized labor. Even though unions were already on the ropes because of neoliberalism, populists viewed them as potent sources of opposition because the conservative economic platforms were detrimental to labor's interests. At the same time, favoring unorganized subaltern groups provided these leaders with a large pool of supporters from whom they could and did amass political power. Lacking unionization, these groups were arguably even more vertically tied to the populist leaders than were the supporters of the classical populists.

In office, the neopopulists tended to concentrate power in their own hands. Through compliant legislatures and constitutional revisions, the executive branch gained powers at the expense of other branches of government. The concentration of political power made them subject to accusations of authoritarian behavior similar to their classical counterparts. Fujimori went so far as to close Peru's congress in his 1992 "self-coup," an unambiguously authoritarian move. Like the earlier populists, additionally, these were polarizing figures who earned the wrath of important groups. As such, not all could gain such dominant positions. Carlos Menem of Argentina scrapped his attempt at a third term after it was ruled unconstitutional, Fernando Collor de Mello of Brazil succumbed to corruption charges, and Ecuador's congress ousted Abdalá Bucaram on charges of mental incapacity. Along with their uneasy relationship with liberal democracy and polarizing influences, the neopopulists used antiestablishment appeals, related with followers in highly direct and unmediated ways, dismantled corporatist systems of representation, embraced market-oriented economic policies, used carefully targeted economic benefits for political ends, and had support in the informal sector and among nonunionized workers. Hence, in some respects, they differed notably from classical populists, but in other, more central ways they proved to be cut from the same cloth.

The third-era populists appeared soon after the neopopulists. In fact, some overlap could be found (Fujimori was still in office when Chávez was elected, for instance), and so not all would agree that the most recent group constitutes a distinct phase.[2] However, the neopopulists came to office around 1990 (Collor de Mello and Fujimori in 1990, Menem in 1989, and Salinas in 1988) whereas, with the exception of Chávez, the third-era populists all took office after the turn of the century. Evo Morales won Bolivia's 2005 election, and Rafael Correa won Ecuador's the following year, the same year in which Ollanta Humala narrowly lost in Peru and Andrés Manuel López Obrador in Mexico. A perhaps more significant mark of distinction was the gap in their relative positions on the political spectrum. Because of their embrace of neoliberal economic reforms, the neopopulists were right of center. Given the economic conditions and international financial constraints, these presidents, like many nonpopulists during the 1990s, may have had little choice but to follow the prescriptions of international financial institutions. But then conditions changed. The impact of the economic reforms grew burdensome for many ordinary citizens, and, toward the end of the 1990s, protests became increasingly common. Benjamin Arditi (2008, 65) captures the situation well:

> Virtually everywhere—including Chile, the showcase of market-driven economic growth in the region—the excluded express their disaffection and real anger in the ballot box and in the streets. Protesters include the piqueteros [picketers] and middle-class victims of the corralito [bank deposit freeze] in Argentina, cocaleros [coca farmers] in Bolivia, sem terra [landless] in Brazil, students and Mapuches in Chile, and impoverished peasants in Paraguay. The fall of President Fernando de la Rúa in Argentina in December 2001 is the iconic moment of this backlash against politics and politicians associated with the failures of neoliberal adjustment policies, encapsulated in the chant,

"Que se vayan todos, que no quede ni uno solo" ("All of them must go, not a single one can stay").

At the same time, some countries benefited from rising demand for petroleum and raw materials. Beginning with Chávez's 1998 election, the third-era populists capitalized on this environment and helped turn regional politics sharply to the left.

That said, these populists constituted but a part of the region's turn to the left. A number of other candidates and presidents belonged to the political left but were not populists. Indeed, though the region has recently experienced a resurgence of populism, one would be mistaken to conclude that it has been the dominant regional force in recent years. The eleven countries considered in this analysis held a total of thirty-five presidential elections from 1996 to 2010. Some 126 candidates won at least 5 percent of their respective contests. Of these, only eighteen used a populist strategy (see Table 5.1). They were victorious in eight presidential elections. As in the earlier periods, these atypical individuals have had a much greater impact on the region's politics than their numbers might suggest, which is of course why they warrant attention.

Like the classical populists, third-era populists have made nationalism a significant theme, linking foreign economic interests to greedy local elite as corrupt and detrimental influences. For instance, Correa campaigned against the domestic and international forces that, he said, were exploiting Ecuador in the name of neoliberalism. In his first inaugural address, he claimed recent economic policies constituted "barbarities" that had produced "disastrous" outcomes. Despite neoliberalism's "contradiction of corruption, the need to preserve economic subordination, and the demand for service of the foreign debt," these reforms "not only were imposed, but also actively applauded by our elites and technocrats." Furthermore, he continued, "These policies have been able to sustain themselves due to deceit and antidemocratic attitudes on the part of those who have benefited from them, with the full support of multilateral organizations, which disguised as science a simplistic ideology." In short, according to Correa, "inhumane and cruel," neoliberalism "tries to convert us into markets rather than nations [and] tries to make us merely consumers rather than citizens of the world" (Correa 2007).

Antineoliberal rhetoric like this, which Chávez, Morales, Humala, and López Obrador, along with Lucio Gutiérrez of Ecuador, have shared, demonstrates the gap between the third-era populists and their neoliberal predecessors and arguably makes these more similar to the classical populists. Still, most observers agree that economic policies or ideological positions, which are typically very vague, do not constitute defining attributes of populism, in part because the classical populists included leaders with fascist leanings (e.g., Getúlio Vargas of Brazil) as well as others with socialist leanings (e.g., Cárdenas). Hence, the change from the right-of-center neopopulists to the left-wing third-era (or "radical") populists should not signal the emergence of a new or distinct political phenomenon. In fact, the recent populists share many of the same key traits with both sets of predecessors. (In this book, incidentally, I concern myself with the third-era populists, not the recent turn to the left, so I focus on the political strategy that is populism rather than populists' particular ideological positions.)

All populists, for instance, have used us-versus-them, antiestablishment appeals, and the third-era populists are no exception. They have been highly critical of their countries' elites, political parties, and legislatures. Chávez famously warned that he would make Venezuela's oligarchs squeal. Correa railed against the corrupt *partidocracia* (partyarchy) and the "sewer" that was Ecuador's congress. Humala proclaimed his pride in being "antisystem," since the system was defined by corruption. Morales said that Bolivia was divided between the "exploited" and the "charlatans" who exploited them. These criticisms went well beyond complaints of a given party or president and extended to the party system, the governing institutions, and whole sectors of society.

Although not actually revolutionaries, third-era populists have spoken of "citizens' revolutions" and "refounding" their countries in the name of the people who have been victimized by corrupt systems. As such, those who have taken office have made significant political reforms in part by rewriting their countries' constitutions. Chávez, Correa, and Morales have done so. Perhaps not surprisingly, these constitutional reforms and other changes have typically weakened institutions of horizontal accountability and enhanced the powers of the presidency. Observers often note the contrast between these populists' visions of democracy and what is characterized as liberal democracy. Indeed, the third-era populists themselves point out this contrast. Chávez claimed his participatory democracy was superior to representative democracy. Morales said he was building a new system that would supplant liberal democracy. Correa explained that in contrast to "formal" democracy, "real" democracy concerned not procedural rights but rights to substantive outcomes such as education and health. By downplaying and weakening representative institutions and formal procedures, these populists claimed to enhance the effectiveness of government: little would get in the way of the president's working on behalf of the people. Interestingly, surveys show that citizens' satisfaction with democracy has increased dramatically under populist presidents. Nevertheless, detractors accuse them of undermining democracy and crossing over to authoritarianism.

Third-era populists' relationships with supporters have followed a familiar pattern as well. Their institutional reforms, for example, suggest highly top-down or vertical connections, in which intermediary institutions that are supposed to channel voters' interests and demands have been sidelined in favor of direct and unmediated linkages. Though some variation can be found among their partisan organizations, all nevertheless have retained elements of top-down structures. Morales's party, the Movement Toward Socialism (Movimiento al Socialismo [MAS]), has been the partial exception in this regard. As is discussed in Chapter 4, his rise began on the backs of key social movements that had substantial autonomy. Over time, nevertheless, Morales carved out space with his party to connect directly with constituents. Though third-era populists still use the rallies and mass demonstrations characteristic of classical populists, both as means of communication and displays of power, they also use modern media and surveys. Polling data reflecting public support for, say, a constituent assembly or even presidential approval can signal political strength to opponents.

The third-era populists have used expansive economic policies alongside more targeted programs to help build support. Chávez, for instance, used oil revenues to fund a variety of social programs, including those channeled through the National Development Fund (Fondo Nacional del Desarrollo [FONDEN]), an entity he personally controlled with full discretion. By directing greater and greater portions of oil revenues to that fund, incidentally, he increasingly denied resources to state and municipal-level governments, which had been sources of political opposition (Rodríguez, Morales, and Monaldi 2012). Likewise, he created a series of "Bolivarian missions" to combat poverty, curb illiteracy, provide housing and food subsidies, and so on. Among these are universal, rather than targeted, programs, such as Barrio Adentro, which seeks to establish free public health care. Similarly, Correa has vastly expanded direct cash transfers to the poor and spending on a variety of programs: public expenditures more than tripled from 2006 to 2012. Such programs have been accompanied by nationalizations (or partial nationalizations) and threats thereof to gain greater shares of profits from natural resource production. These proceeds have helped fund the populists' programs. Still, their expenditures have generated familiar complaints of profligate spending and fiscal malfeasance.

In short, the third-era populists have included leaders who used antiestablishment, antineoliberal, and nationalistic appeals; mobilized followers in highly vertical ways; enhanced the powers of the presidency and weakened the mechanisms of horizontal accountability; pursued expansionary economic policies; and had a base of support centered on the underprivileged and poor. Many of these attributes are common to the populists of all three eras, but some attributes have varied. Such variation has contributed to the proliferation of definitions and lists of defining characteristics, and populism's impact on economic policy and governing institutions as well as its use of mass mobilization and specific kinds of discourse has contributed to the confusion. That is, some observers focus on populism in government and consider it to be a kind of regime, whereas others use the term *populism* as an adjective describing irresponsible economic policies. Despite differences like these, the three eras of populism have much in common, especially their appeals and their means of relating to and mobilizing mass followings. Not all populists wield these tools well enough to win office; however, those who do, for better or worse, tend to be quite consequential.

The current wave of populism may be ebbing in the region. Chávez has died, and his heir, Maduro, is facing an intractable crisis. Morales lost a referendum that would have allowed him to run for a fourth term. Right-of-center politicians seem to be gaining advantage across the region. Time will tell, naturally, whether the third era has in fact run its course. Regardless, the fact that Latin America has experienced three such periods suggests populism will return. And, until that point, the present populist leaders most likely will leave enduring marks on their respective countries, as prior populists have done. Looking beyond the region, moreover, a European version of populism is surging, and antiestablishment politicians are gaining popularity in countries as diverse as the Philippines and the United States. As such, determining just what populism is and understanding the reasons for its electoral success remain as important as ever.

Outline of the Book

The goals of the book are to elucidate the nature of populism and to explain its emergence in recent years in Latin America. Each of the following chapters contributes to these goals in a specific way, addressing populism at the conceptual, theoretical, and empirical levels. In them, I detail the attributes and boundaries of the concept, use multiple methods to demonstrate its causes, and explore its conceptual and causal distinctiveness (and thus its utility) as well as its implications.

In Chapter 2, I examine the conceptualization of populism. I make the case that the evaluation and construction of concepts should involve consideration not only of the content (the defining characteristics) but also of the conceptual structure. One could conceive of populism as one conceives of games: both chess and football are games but they have little in common. Or one could treat it like one treats chairs: the object must have not only a seat but also a back to be a chair. Though none is inherently superior to the others, the three types of concept structure—classical, family resemblance, and radial—come with certain costs and benefits. In this chapter I provide an accounting of those concept types and their applications to the study of populism. Considered as a whole, the literature leaves much to be desired in terms of clarity and empirical utility. To help remedy this condition, I advocate the use of a classical concept type. In Chapter 2, I also explore the major definitions of populism, paying particular attention to the two leading contemporary schools of thought, the political and the ideational understandings. As with concept type, the choice of defining characteristics comes with costs and benefits. Together, the concept type and defining characteristics determine what populism is, affect the utility of the concept for specific purposes, and influence the understanding of its causes. Careful consideration of each aspect is therefore of crucial importance.

These discussions lay the foundation for my definition of populism. In explaining the key defining characteristics of antiestablishment appeals and plebiscitarianism, I address the positive attributes: those features that would allow an empirical instance to be included in the set of cases considered to be populist. A thorough examination of concepts, however, should also address the negative end of the spectrum. Toward this end, I also discuss in Chapter 2 what populism is not, thus helping to separate it from closely related but still distinct concepts that are frequently linked with populism in the literature.

In the next set of chapters, I turn to the causes of populism, referring specifically to the explanations of its electoral fortunes in contemporary Latin America. In Chapter 3, I remain at a theoretical level but set the stage by examining the leading explanations in the literature. Interestingly, less disagreement can be found on this point than on the very nature of populism, but a healthy debate remains. A great number of these accounts provide rich and multifaceted arguments. Indeed, a prominent feature of this debate is not which one factor is central but which combination of factors. I continue the chapter by explaining the argument of this book in detail, drawing on several bodies of research. I share with other scholars of populism the use of a causal combination: party system institutionalization, corruption, and evidence of disadvantage. Importantly, and as with many extant accounts, the position taken here is not that each component of this combination makes an individual, unique contribution to the outcome, nor that the components combine in a linear or additive way. Instead, I point out an interactive effect among them. To put it one way, collectively these factors are greater than the sum of their parts.

The next two chapters are empirical in nature, and they include a single-country case study using process tracing as the primary methodology, and a comparative analysis that assesses causality using the QCA methodology. The hope is that by combining methodologies, I can uncover a clearer understanding of populism. A historically grounded case study illustrates the shifting political tides behind an instance of populism, whereas the multicountry study adds analytical leverage and permits at least modest generalizations regarding populism's presence and absence.

In Chapter 4, I take a careful look at modern Bolivia using standard qualitative methods and a variety of sources of data. Basing my conclusions in part on field research conducted in 2009, I explore the evolving political, social, and economic conditions of the country from the 1980s through the election of Evo Morales, with an emphasis on the last decade. The period covers several elections and thus allows for a focused comparison and the control of a number of possible confounding variables. In addition, Morales presents something of a challenging case in that some observers do not consider him to be a populist. Riding to national prominence on the backs of organized social movements, his rise had a bottom-up quality to it. Nevertheless, over time that relationship became only one part of the broader political dynamic, important and constraining but not defining. This single-country study supports the argument presented in Chapter 3.

In Chapter 5, I peer across borders, offering a comparative perspective. Specifically, I address in a systematic way the possible causes of populism region-wide, which provides a harder test for my argument and gives greater confidence in its logic. In this chapter, I examine all of the presidential elections from 1996 to 2010 in Latin America, with the exception of the smaller countries of the Caribbean basin that had a somewhat different historical trajectory and different sets of contemporary challenges, including gang-based crime and less immunity to international pressures. As such, it is a medium-N study that covers thirty-five elections and includes positive and negative outcomes, thus avoiding selection on the dependent variable. The empirical analysis provides a test of my argument alongside other leading explanations. Collectively, these explanations involve various combinations of just a few factors.

To study the relationships among them, I use QCA. Given the state of the literature, the present argument, and the size of the study, standard statistical analysis is not an ideal method to use. QCA, on the other hand, is well suited in part because it embraces causal complexity and equifinality. With this methodology, moreover, the analysis can highlight not only sufficiency but also necessity. Among the causal factors considered is the level of party system institutionalization. To measure party system institutionalization, I use a new index that can demonstrate variation not only among countries but also within them and over time. The test provides support for the argument presented in Chapter 3 and highlights, in part, the necessity of weak party systems for the rise of populism.

In Chapter 6, I provide an empirical test of a different sort. In this case, I continue with the QCA methodology to assess the distinctiveness of populism in conceptual and causal terms. In so doing, I return to topics raised in Chapter 2—namely, the conceptual and thus empirical distinctions among categories like political outsider, newcomer, and maverick—and thereby connect the broad themes of the book. More specifically, in this chapter I explore the outer boundaries of the concept and make the case that populism should not be equated, though it often is, with other kinds of "challenge politics." I also make plain two important points about concept development: first, one's choices have an impact on the empirical examples that are included and excluded, and, second, they likewise have consequences for one's understanding of causality. In making these points, I identify all of the candidates who would be considered challenge politicians and all of the candidates who would be considered populist if one were to use an ideational definition. I then explore the causes of each of these phenomena.

A comparison of the results with those from the previous chapters reveals an important distinction. Unlike the conceptual alternatives, the version of populism as presented in this book has a single necessary cause: party system weakness. In Chapter 6, I thus hope to put to rest any doubts that these same causal factors might account for any sort of political alternative or political challenger, not just populists. I then explore the reasons for the special relationship between a political understanding of populism and party system institutionalization. Collectively, these discussions demonstrate the empirical utility of this conceptualization of populism.

In the concluding chapter, Chapter 7, I continue to make this broad case about concept importance, but I turn away from causes and instead consider effects. In particular, I explore the logical consequences of the concept's attributes. This discussion includes the tendency of populist leaders to concentrate political power at the expense of other democratic institutions. In turn, I touch on the relationship of populism to democracy. On the one hand, populism promises inclusion and more effective representation of citizens, where accountability is clearly placed on the shoulders of the leader. On the other hand, however, it rejects aspects of horizontal accountability and intermediary institutions that should channel societal interests to the halls of government. Those who have high regard for liberal democracy may therefore find populism troubling. They also may find party system weaknesses troubling: as I hope to demonstrate in this book, frailties of this sort are central to the rise of populism in Latin America. For all these reasons, understanding exactly what constitutes populism and making clear the conditions under which populists are likely to be elected are important tasks for any student of Latin American politics.

Notes

1. Observers have provided a variety of names for this group, such as third-wave populism (Gratius 2007), radical populism (de la Torre 2007, 2010; Robinson 2008), and left populism (March 2007).

2. However, even some who consider the most recent populists as an extension of neoliberal populism recognize the distinctions between these two groups (e.g., Roberts 2007).

2

The Concepts of Populism

REFERENCES TO POPULISM ABOUND IN BOTH THE MEDIA AND THE ACA-
demic literature. In newspapers and magazines one reads of populist movements, leaders, parties, policies, and regimes and of left-wing, right-wing,
anti-immigrant, and economic populism. Newspapers describe the populist
leanings of politicians and candidates in the United States, France, Russia,
Argentina, and Bolivia, and their antineoliberal, antielite, anti-US, pro-
nation, procitizen, pro-people rhetoric. Reports highlight populism's fascist
and socialist tendencies, along with its inherent authoritarianism and democratic inclusiveness. Given the variety of meanings associated with the
concept, little wonder that widely disparate politicians such as Mahmoud
Ahmadinejad of Iran, Alberto Fujimori of Peru, and Marine Le Pen of
France have all carried the populist label. Further, that George W. Bush,
Barack Obama, and Donald Trump have been described as populists confirms the flexibility of the term (e.g., Frank 2004; Zakaria 2016; Zuboff
2008).[1]

Consideration of only the academic literature offers little respite from
the confusion. Some authors emphasize the discursive nature of populism
by focusing on identities centered on an us-versus-them division of society
(e.g., Laclau 1977; Panizza 2005). Others locate populism in specific historical junctures or circumstances (e.g, Malloy 1977; Vilas 1992–1993),
leading a few to conclude that it is a thing of the past (e.g., Schamis 2006).
Another group describes populism purely in economic terms, as a set of
policy outcomes (e.g., Dornbusch and Edwards 1991; Edwards 2010; Sachs
1990). Yet another argues for a purely political understanding of the term
(e.g., Leaman 2004; Weyland 2001).

These circumstances have led some analysts to call for the abandon-
ment of the concept altogether (e.g., Roxborough 1984). However, the frequency of the term's usage in the literature and the periodic reemergence of

23

empirical examples, broadly defined, make its rejection an unlikely prospect. Indeed, the occasional rise of leaders who gain tremendous personal power built on the backs of a devoted following serves as a reminder that the notion, although vague, carries some meaning. These uncommon politicians can wield enormous, even excessive, influence over a polity while maintaining significant popular legitimacy. Such examples signify something different; they are not cases of "politics as usual." As a result, they warrant distinctive categorization. The challenge has been capturing them in a way that is empirically accurate and analytically useful.

In this chapter, I explore the various strategies for conceptualizing populism with the goal of developing a definition that will be the most useful, in a comparative empirical sense, for the study of populism in contemporary Latin America. As is explored at length below, the literature on populism provides a variety of understandings that, taken together, can be applied to an enormous array of political phenomena. Collectively, in other words, the literature is guilty of conceptual stretching, where "our gains in extensional coverage tend to be matched by losses in connotative precision" (Sartori 1970, 1035). Moreover, individual strategies of conceptualization entail certain costs and benefits. I present an accounting of those concept types and their applications to the study of populism. I then examine the two predominant views regarding the concept's content: the ideational understanding of populism and the political one. Shepherding this review is the position that concepts should provide a clear guide for including *and* excluding cases, and should facilitate empirical analysis. Toward the end of the chapter comes my definition of populism. Because poor concept construction can result in vague definitions, inappropriate identification of cases, and incorrect understandings of the causes, one needs to pay careful attention to the steps of formulating a concept. Concepts and categorization are the ways one makes sense of the world; imprecision acts as an obstacle to understanding. This chapter, then, is an attempt to remove that obstacle.

The State of the Literature

Before delving into the three primary strategies of conceptualization, I wish to illustrate the state of the literature as a whole. Giovanni Sartori's (1970, 1984) work provides a useful means of evaluation. Although a handful of authors (e.g., Collier and Mahon 1993; Goertz 2006b) have made significant contributions to our understanding of concepts since Sartori's now classic works, his advice on concept evaluation and (re)construction remains useful. His guidelines identify three bases on which to evaluate concepts: "first, the *border problem* (to be settled by denotative definitions); second, the *membership problem* (precising definitions); third, the *measurability problem* (operational definitions which generally hinge in turn on the search for valid indicators)" (Sartori 1984, 34; emphasis in original). Populism, as depicted in the literature as a whole, falls short on each of them. The concept has problems with its intention ("disorganized or trivial characteristics"), extension ("undenotativeness or vagueness"), and the term ("ambiguity") (Sartori 1984, 34).

First, regarding intension (i.e., the features that constitute or define the concept), the literature insufficiently distinguishes defining properties (or what Goertz [2006b] labels "secondary characteristics"; the two terms operate interchangeably here) from accompanying properties.[2] Although the former "*constitute* what the phenomenon *is*" (Goertz 2006b, 59; emphasis in original), the latter are those characteristics that may be commonly associated with the defining features yet are in fact accidental or incidental. Distinguishing these two kinds of characteristics from each other is crucial because defining properties establish the boundaries of the concept whereas accompanying ones do not. To get a sense of the myriad characteristics associated with populism in the academic literature, see Table 2.1. The literature, furthermore, positions populism as a kind of political style, strategy, ideology, discourse, regime, policy, state of development, form of representation, and movement. Carefully distinguishing defining characteristics from accidental ones may help refine these lists and thus identify the kind of phenomenon that populism is.

Second, the concept's extension (i.e., the referents to which the concept applies) is vague, lacking sufficient linkages between the meaning of the term and the cases it means to identify (Sartori 1984). In other words, the concept as used in the literature at large does not help us identify the set of empirical examples that belong in this category. Clarity is an objective of

Table 2.1 A Partial List of Populism's Attributes in the Literature

Personalistic leadership	Exaltation of simple people
Paternalistic leadership	Defense of ordinary people
Charismatic leader	Amorphous ideology
Top-down mobilization	Challenge to the elite
Unmediated leader-follower relationship	Distrust of institutions
Unorganized following	Nationalistic rhetoric and policies
Corporatist organization	Proindustrialization policies
Large/mass following	Inclusive rhetoric and policies
Multiclass coalition	Irresponsible economic policies
Lower-class/subaltern coalition	Use of materialistic incentives
Urban coalition	Reorientation of capitalist reproduction
"Us versus them"/divisive discourse	Pursuit of governmental power
Manichaean discourse	Democratic illiberalism

any conceptualization in that the concept should have "denotational adequacy" so that one can identify its empirical referents (Sartori 1984, 28).

Third, the term itself is ambiguous in the sense that populism has many separate, though sometimes overlapping, meanings. This problem, no doubt, results from the previous two issues and leaves a term that unfortunately lacks a single accepted meaning.

Sartori wrote his guidelines from the perspective that all concepts have a classical form of necessary and sufficient conditions (discussed in more detail below). Such concepts, however, do not exhaust all possibilities, and many understandings of populism rely on different concept types. Nevertheless, his desire for unambiguity of meaning, clarity of extension, and well-organized intention is appropriate for any concept type. Concepts, after all, are a basis for knowledge in that they allow one to understand empirical reality.[3] As Sartori (1984) puts it, concepts are the "basic unit of thinking" in that "we have a concept of A . . . when we are able to distinguish A from whatever is not A" (74). In this regard, the literature on populism as a whole leaves something to be desired.

Sartori (1984) concludes, "Amidst the resulting state of noncumulability, collective ambiguity, and increasing incommunicability, it is imperative to restore or attempt to restore the conceptual foundations of the edifice" (50). Although his words are directed at the discipline of political science as a whole, they apply equally well to the specific case of populism. To overcome these problems, Sartori (1984, 50) recommends a systematic review of the uses of a concept as part of what he calls "concept reconstruction":

> Unless a reconstruction precedes the construction, [one] is not only liable to waste time and energy in rediscovering the umbrella (I mean something already discovered) but also to add a "meaning 51" to some other 50 preexisting meanings, thus adding, at best, profusion to confusion. Nonetheless, the fact remains that concept reconstruction is a means whose ultimate purpose is to provide a cleaned-up basis for construction—that is, for the formation of concepts.

Given the numerous attributes associated with populism, the confusion surrounding its conceptualization is understandable. The situation becomes even more complicated by the choice of concept type. Two analysts might agree on what populism is in ontological terms and, additionally, agree to the specific or defining characteristics, but if they choose different concept types, or ways of structuring the concept, they will not agree on the instances that belong to the category of populism. Toward the goal of clarifying the concept of populism, then, an exploration of the variety of conceptualizations within the literature is warranted.

Scholars offer several ways of categorizing the range of definitions in the literature, such as by the concept's predominant characteristic (e.g.,

Roberts 1995) or the strategies of conceptualization (e.g., Weyland 2001). In order to meet the goal of conceptual reconstruction, I group definitions by concept type: family resemblance (Wittgenstein 1953), radial (Collier and Mahon 1993), and classical (Sartori 1984). Despite the various conceptualizations, definitions of populism demonstrate a propensity toward either excessively narrow extension or overly broad extension, neither of which is empirically satisfactory for this topic. Comparative analysis depends on appropriate classification and thus on appropriately defined concepts that permit definitive inclusion and exclusion of empirical cases. "Hence part of concept-building is to think not only about the positive, but also about the negative end of the spectrum" (Goertz 2006b, 30). Having clearly defined characteristics along with a balance between intension and extension is therefore crucial. As Peter Mair (2008) argues, concepts with extension that is either too great or too small are either theoretically or empirically limited in their utility. By contrast, the middle-level concepts are the "most interesting" (188).

On Concepts

The three primary concept types or structures are family resemblance, classical, and radial. Wittgenstein's (1953) family resemblance concept uses multiple defining characteristics, yet none of them is considered necessary. The example of games is often used to illustrate this concept type: solitaire, table tennis, and basketball share few if any specific characteristics, yet each is clearly an example of a game. A standard way of specifying this concept type is the "m of n rule," in which at least m of a possible set of n characteristics need be present (e.g., any three or more of five characteristics) (e.g., Campbell 1965; Griffin 1974). The defining characteristics are related through the logical OR rather than the logical AND because none of them is necessary (Goertz 2006b, esp. 35–44).[4] For example, a family resemblance conceptualization of democracy might identify the following characteristics: universal suffrage (a), the protection of civil liberties (b), or checks on governmental power (c). If the combination of any two characteristics is sufficient (if $m = 2$), then membership could apply in the following conditions: (a AND b) OR (a AND c) OR (b AND c) OR (a AND b AND c). If just one of the three characteristics is sufficient, then membership would apply in these cases: a OR b OR c OR any combination thereof. Members of the set of democracies, then, might include a case that has only universal suffrage and another that has only the protection of civil liberties. The key point here is that since no one characteristic is necessary, the members of the category need not have all, or possibly even any, traits in common.

The classical concept type is perhaps the most familiar and is the focus of Sartori's work (1970, 1984). It relies on necessary and sufficient conditions connected by the logical AND (Goertz 2006b). A case warrants inclusion in the concept category if it demonstrates all of the identified characteristics, each being necessary and only together are they sufficient. The absence of any of them excludes the case. To use the same example of democracy, a classical conceptualization might require all three characteristics (a AND b AND c). If a country exhibited any one or any combination of two of the characteristics—but not all three—then it would be excluded. Only those examples that exhibit universal suffrage *and* civil liberties *and* checks on power would be democracies according to this definition.

These concept types have concrete implications regarding the classification of empirical examples (and, of course, regarding case selection for analysis). The family resemblance and classical concept structures are inversely related, for instance, with respect to the relationship between the number of defining characteristics and the concept's extension (Goertz 2006b). Adding new criteria broadens the extension of a family resemblance concept but narrows the extension of a classical concept. For example, by adding "an independent media" (d) to the characteristics of a democracy in a family resemblance concept, a case that exhibits only that characteristic might gain membership in the set of democracies. Using a classical definition, by contrast, raises the barriers to membership: any democracy would have to exhibit a AND b AND c AND d. Thus, the number of empirical cases considered democratic would be reduced. The reverse is also true, of course: removing characteristics decreases the extension for family resemblance concepts but increases it for classical ones.

Radial concepts occupy a space between the family resemblance and classical concept structures. The radial structure specifies necessary and collectively sufficient characteristics for only the full empirical examples (the ideal types) while allowing for partial examples or subtypes that exhibit fewer characteristics (Collier and Mahon 1993).[5] For instance, examples of "full democracies" would have to have all of the characteristics (a AND b AND c), but a "participatory democracy" might have just universal suffrage (a), a "liberal democracy" might have that along with protections of civil liberties (a AND b), and so forth. Importantly, these "diminished subtypes" are incomplete forms of the basic concept (Collier and Levitsky 1997, 2009). Often the radial concept is interpreted to require a single core-defining characteristic (e.g., Mair 2008, 193–194). That is, a radial understanding of democracy might require the presence of universal suffrage, even for the subtypes. The absence of that characteristic would rule out the example from membership in the categories of "full democracy" and any of the subtypes.

Adding new characteristics to a radial concept raises the barriers for entry only for the ideal type, and it increases the number of possible subtypes. For instance, one might add "socioeconomic equity" (e) to the characteristics of democracy. Such a change reduces the chances of finding an example of the ideal type that demonstrates e along with the other four characteristics. At the same time, including socioeconomic equity opens the possibility for a new subtype of "economic democracy" and thus increases the likely number of cases that would count as some democratic subtype. David Collier and James E. Mahon (1993) argue that one can avoid conceptual stretching in this fashion. Radial concepts, furthermore, facilitate the use of graded membership (Marsteintredet 2007). One could use the radial concept to identify those cases of democracy, for instance, that are far from or very close to the prototype. Those examples with more of the characteristics that define the full cases would be higher-order, though not highest-order, democracies, whereas those with just one such characteristic would be lower-order democracies.

To bring this discussion back to the subject at hand, consider a definition of populism with four characteristics: (1) the use of an us-versus-them rhetoric, (2) personalistic mobilization, (3) an unmediated relationship between leader and followers, and (4) a constituency drawn primarily from subaltern classes. Now imagine five hypothetical cases, among which one has all four characteristics whereas each of the others has three of the four characteristics (see Table 2.2). Depending on the concept type chosen, the number of examples classified as populist will be one (classical), five (family resemblance), or one plus four subtypes (radial). Again, the literature's collective treatment of populism is problematic enough given the number of attributes found (far more than just four), but it becomes more so when one considers concept type.

The Variety of Populisms

The choice of utilizing a radial, classical, or family resemblance concept structure comes with costs and benefits. Which is most suitable may depend on the specifics of the phenomenon in question and the goal of the research project (Collier and Adcock 1999). In the following section, I argue that for the purposes of this study, the choice of concept type should prioritize clarity in the organization of the defining characteristics. Because the waters of populism are so muddy, one may gain significant analytical value in drawing sharp, dichotomous distinctions—either a case is populist or it is not[6]—rather than allowing for a variety of subtypes or partial memberships. To facilitate the comparative analysis in subsequent chapters, furthermore, the universe of populist cases should include more than only the elusive ideal

Table 2.2 Implications of Concept Type

	Us vs. Them	Personalistic	Unmediated	Subaltern	Outcome
Classical Concept Structure					
CASE 1	Yes	Yes	Yes	Yes	Populist
CASE 2	No	Yes	Yes	Yes	Not populist
CASE 3	Yes	No	Yes	Yes	Not populist
CASE 4	Yes	Yes	No	Yes	Not populist
CASE 5	Yes	Yes	Yes	No	Not populist
Family Resemblance Concept Structure					
CASE 1	Yes	Yes	Yes	Yes	Populist
CASE 2	No	Yes	Yes	Yes	Populist
CASE 3	Yes	No	Yes	Yes	Populist
CASE 4	Yes	Yes	No	Yes	Populist
CASE 5	Yes	Yes	Yes	No	Populist
Radial Concept Structure					
CASE 1	Yes	Yes	Yes	Yes	Populist
CASE 2	No	Yes	Yes	Yes	Subtype
CASE 3	Yes	No	Yes	Yes	Subtype
CASE 4	Yes	Yes	No	Yes	Subtype
CASE 5	Yes	Yes	Yes	No	Subtype

types and yet far fewer than the everyday examples of democratic politics. A carefully constructed classical concept offers the best chances of developing just such a definition of populism. To make this case, I turn the discussion to the implications of using each concept type for the phenomenon of populism.

Family Resemblance Conceptualizations

Consider first the family resemblance version of populism (e.g., Canovan 1981; Carrión 2009; Drake 1999). The two types of family resemblance concepts are multidomain and single domain. *Domain* here refers to the general realm in which the phenomenon predominantly falls. For instance, if a central, defining feature of the concept were the demographic makeup of the constituency, the concept would fall in the societal domain. If, by contrast, a defining feature were to concern the struggle for or use of power, the concept would fall in the political domain. For the multidomain versions of family resemblance concepts, authors attempt to piece together a variety of perspectives drawn from the literature yet prioritize none. Margaret Canovan (1981) explains this approach: "We cannot hope to reduce all cases of populism to a single definition or find a single essence behind all established uses of the term. . . . If we are to characterize populism, therefore, it is clear that we shall be able to do so only in terms of a range of populisms with Wittgensteinian family resemblances between them" (7).[7] Gino Germani (1978) also offers a family resemblance definition of sorts. "Populism," he writes, "probably defies any comprehensive definition" (88). He then lists a variety of characteristics and notes "any of these elements may be stressed according to cultural and social conditions" (88).

This strategy explicitly attempts to tie together a variety of perspectives on populism and thus includes views that locate populism in a variety of realms or domains. As Kurt Weyland (2001) explains, however, drawing from a variety of domains can be problematic. Their incorporation means that the category of populism includes cases that not only share no common characteristics but also may be fundamentally different. In this formulation, for example, one case might be included in the category merely for the makeup of its social coalition, another for its ideology, and a third for its economic policies, yet the three need not have any characteristics in common. This possibility raises the prospects of having unrelated phenomena grouped together, and thus empirical analyses thereof may rest on questionable grounds. Consider the example of games, which Wittgenstein himself uses. If one is attempting an empirical analysis of, say, the physical impact of games on the participants, how useful is it to include both chess and rugby? As Mair (2008) writes of this conceptual type, "as in the film *Wedding Crashers*, anybody or anything can be claimed to have some family connection to those at the centre of the action, and hence boundaries, like wedding invitations, ultimately lose their utility" (195).

The other form of family resemblance concepts considers just a single domain. Julio Carrión (2009), for instance, restricts his definition of populism to the political domain. His characteristics include a personalistic style of leadership, an unmediated leader-follower relationship, an us-versus-them discourse, and a general distrust of institutions that might check the power of the leader. (Multifaceted definitions do not necessarily imply multiple domains; in this case these are secondary-level characteristics while the basic level is, according to Carrión [2009], the single domain of political representation.) The move to a single domain necessarily helps delimit the concept's extension, though still leaves room for a variety of empirical cases. For instance, a group that articulates an us-versus-them rhetoric might be classified as populist alongside any leader who wants no checks on personal power. Therefore, individual authoritarian leaders such as Chile's Augusto Pinochet could be included alongside groups such as Bolivia's separatist Pachakuti movement as examples of populism.

Under both single and multidomain family resemblance constructions, radically different kinds of phenomena may be lumped together. For the advocates of this approach, the inclusion of such disparate cases is exactly the point: as with the concept of games, no essential core exists that ties together various examples that nonetheless share some similarities. Canovan for one defends this approach. In the conclusion of her 1981 book, she writes, "No movement has ever been populist in all the senses identified, and indeed—given the contradictions between some of our categories—none ever could satisfy all the conditions at once" (289). On that basis, she concludes that "the various populisms we have distinguished are not just different varieties of the same kind of thing: they are in many cases different sorts of things, and not directly comparable at all" (298). This structure rejects the principle of *per genus et differentiam*, or the classification of objects in discrete groups. Depending on the nature and aims of the study, this way of constructing a particular concept can be preferable. In fact, in Chapter 6, I use it to study a variety of kinds of political challenges. For the concept of populism, however, it might not be the best choice. Given the state of the literature, the family resemblance concept structure, particularly the multidomain version, does little to rein in the confusion.

Radial Conceptualizations

Radial conceptualizations of populism (e.g., Knight 1998; Levitsky and Loxton 2013; Wiles 1969; Worsley 1969) provide a set of characteristics that define the full instance of the category and the prospects of a sub-type—specifically a diminished subtype (Collier and Levitsky 1997)—

associated with each characteristic. Adjectives associated with the basic level (e.g., *economic* populism) suggest a classification of instances lacking some of the characteristics associated with full examples. (With classical concepts, in contrast, such adjectives suggest an added dimension beyond those necessary and sufficient to classify the case.) As such, radial conceptualizations may identify the ideal type of populism and a wide variety of subtypes that need not have anything in common. For instance, Kenneth M. Roberts (1995) draws from several different domains to develop a definition of populism with five characteristics: paternalistic and personalistic leadership, a heterogeneous and subaltern social coalition, a top-down process of mobilization, an amorphous ideology, and the use of materialistic incentives to build support. He notes that prototypical cases such as that of Perón would exhibit all of the characteristics whereas subtypes would exhibit just one or more.[8] Roberts (1995) argues, "There are no clear theoretical or empirical grounds for adopting an essentialist perspective that prioritizes any single property of this multidimensional phenomenon" (88). In other words, any one of the characteristics is sufficient to classify a case as populist (albeit as a subtype), and so the party with an amorphous ideology would be included alongside the local boss who distributes patronage to build support.

Some radial conceptualizations of populism rely on a necessary characteristic to help unite the subtypes. Peter Wiles (1969), for instance, identifies a concise core characteristic. "To me," he writes, "populism is any creed or movement based on the following major premise: virtue resides in the simple people, who are the overwhelming majority, and in their collective traditions" (166). He then identifies some twenty-four secondary characteristics, all of which no empirical case will exhibit. Although he does not articulate subtypes of populism, one could use his conceptualization to identify, among many others, an urban populism, a religious populism, a racist populism, and a co-op populism. Peter Worsley (1969) also offers a radial definition. Modifying Edward Shils's (1956) definition, he posits that populism has two core characteristics: the supremacy of the will of the people and popular participation (Worsley 1969, 244, 246). "The penumbra of meanings surrounding this term need not frighten us into fearing that we have here some peculiarly spongy concept. We can always qualify it by 'Right-wing', 'Left-wing', 'pseudo-' or any other qualifiers" (Worsley 1969, 247). Hence, a variety of subtypes are possible under the rubric of populism in this case, so long as the cases exhibit these two core characteristics. Steven Levitsky and James Loxton (2013) have a similar view, though they anchor the concept in the use of antiestablishment appeals. With the use of two additional characteristics, they produce three categories of populism in the Andean region of Latin America: full populism, movement populism, and maverick populism.

Radial concepts thus have the advantage of allowing partial membership and, for those that include necessary characteristics, being able to tie together cases while still acknowledging their differences. For instance, Levitsky and Loxton (2013) can tie together the American-style phenomena that grew from the bottom up with the typical Latin American–style movements that are crafted from the top down. At the same time, however, by facilitating the inclusion of cases as some diminished subtype, radial conceptualizations can contribute to the proliferation of subtypes. This construction may therefore violate David Collier and Steven Levitsky's (1997) advice that "scholars should aim for parsimony and avoid excessive proliferation of new terms and concepts" (451). Granted, in some instances the subtypes might be useful, permitting a more fine-tuned analysis. One could study, say, the policy consequences of parliamentary democracy versus presidential democracy (rather than the policy consequences of just democracy). In the case of Latin American populism, however, one must wonder whether enough empirical examples can be identified to permit such nuance. Can the contemporary examples be divided among the categories of "movement populism," "charismatic populism," "left-wing populism," "right-wing populism," and so on ad infinitum and still facilitate comparison, or will doing so lead to the study of individual cases in isolation? Jørgen Møller and Svend-Erik Skaaning (2010) call this the "radial delusion," in which the use of radial concepts may produce empirically empty diminished subtypes.

Additionally, the radial construction requires that full cases display all of the possible characteristics, which would result in fewer full instances than instances of the subtypes.[9] By permitting diminished subtypes, then, one restricts the number of full instances while expanding the number of partial instances. The perspective of this study is that populism refers to something out of the ordinary in that it is a rejection of the status quo. Thus, although populism is perhaps not rare in Latin America, the universe of cases is relatively limited. Using a radial conceptualization, then, may result in the division of the empirical cases among a range of lightly populated categories of full populism and its subtypes.

Classical Conceptualizations

As with the family resemblance structure, classical concepts come in two versions: multidomain and single domain. For years the predominant way of understanding populism was "cumulative" (Weyland 2001), a method in which authors connected characteristics from several domains using the logical AND (e.g., Conniff 1982; di Tella 1965; Drake 1978; O'Donnell 1973). These multidimensional concepts included factors such as charismatic leadership, multiclass alliances, and antielite rhetoric. Frequently, too, they associated populism with specific developmental periods, namely, the collapse of the traditional, oligarchic regime; the collapse of the once-predominant export-led model of development; or the rise of ISI. Carlos Vilas (1992–1993), for instance, characterizes populism as a strategy of capital accumulation that was the response to the "crisis of the oligarchic order" (390). By conceptualizing populism as an integral part of a specific developmental period, this perspective limits the phenomenon historically. As a case in point, many believed populism would cease to exist in Latin America with the collapse of ISI. However, the emergence in the early 1990s of the neopopulists, who replaced ISI with neoliberal economic policies, led to a reconsideration of this understanding. Nevertheless, some dispute that this group deserves the populist classification (e.g., Drake 1991; Nun 1994; Vilas 2005). Hector E. Schamis (2006), for one, argues that "populism as a political actor is history," and that the recent examples "have been crude imitations of the original, capable of recreating its rhetoric and rituals but unable to reproduce its substance" (32). A more common response, nevertheless, has been to adjust the notion of populism so that it is not delimited to historical periods (e.g., R. A. Mayorga 1995).

In this work, I concur that a historically limited definition may be analytically limiting as well. Empirically, the many similarities among the early or classical populists, the neopopulists, and those of the third era beg for comparison. Theoretically, one can reasonably question the logic of limiting the application of a concept to specific time periods as opposed to the specific contextual qualities. For instance, can one find greater analytical utility by defining populism as a response to an economic transformation that took place in a certain period or as a response to any economic transformation that the people find disruptive? The latter route may prove advantageous for the analyst. Should new circumstances replicate some of the same features prevalent in earlier periods, the concept that is not era-specific may remain useful. At the same time, however, for the concept to carry meaning from one time period to another, some continuity of understanding must be present, a point discussed in further detail later.

Not all multidomain concepts are historically contingent, however. Nevertheless, by tying together characteristics drawn from the realm of politics (meaning the struggle for and exercise of power), economics (the distribution of resources), and society (the demographic characteristics), the multidomain concepts may leave the analyst wondering what populism is. What constitutes its core? Single-domain definitions attempt to answer this question. In so doing, they facilitate empirical analysis (R. A. Mayorga 2006, 134).

There are few types of single-domain, classical conceptualizations of populism. The debate among these is not about concept structure but about content. One is the economic definition, which considers populism as an economic or fiscal outcome (e.g., Dornbusch and Edwards 1991; Edwards 2010; Sachs 1990). This perspective defines the phenomenon simply, usually along the lines of fiscally irresponsible policies. It associates the phenomenon with the cases of free-spending leaders whose policies contribute to both the spread of mass consumption and the rise of inflation. The very simplicity of this conceptualization becomes problematic in that it has an unbounded extension: a strict interpretation would label as populist any government that has greater expenditures than revenues. Consider Jorge Basurto's (1999) view, which emphasizes economic redistribution. He argues, "populists spoke for government action to achieve a more equitable distribution of wealth" (75). As a result, only by adding secondary characteristics would one avoid including as populists any European politician supportive of social democracy, any Democrat in the United States supportive of welfare, and so on. At any rate, this perspective is not common in the contemporary political science literature. Two other types—the ideational and the political—are far more common. The following sections are concentrated on these two perspectives.

The Ideational Approach

According to advocates of the ideational approach (e.g., Abts and Rummens 2007; Canovan 2002; Hawkins 2009; Pauwels 2011; Stanley 2008), populism is limited to a set of ideas based around the division of society into two camps.[10] Some describe these ideas as ideologies, others as worldviews. For instance, Cas Mudde (2004) defines populism as "a thin-centered ideology that considers society to be ultimately separated into two homogenous and antagonistic groups, 'the pure people' versus 'the corrupt elite,' and which argues that politics should be an expression of the *volonté générale* (general will) of the people" (543). Kirk A. Hawkins (2009), to some extent, takes issue with this approach: "Unlike an ideology, populism is a latent set of ideas or a worldview that lacks significant exposition. . . . It has a subconscious quality that manifests itself primarily in the language of those who hold it" (1045). Despite the disclaimer, he defines populism in very similar terms as those using the ideological definition and evaluates cases based on the language employed.[11] Some consider the language-based and ideological views as distinct schools of thought (e.g., Gidron and Bonikowski 2013), but given their similarities as well as their positivist underpinnings, they are treated together here as variants of the ideational approach. The ideas they describe are indeed crucial to understanding populism, yet an exclusive focus thereon becomes problematic in both empirical and analytical terms.

With its focus on ideas, manifest and identifiable in language, this approach in some ways enhances empirical analysis, facilitating cross-case and cross-regional comparisons (see especially Hawkins 2010; Mudde and Rovira Kaltwasser 2012). Defining populism this way means that one readily can find examples in many circumstances; there are no organizational, institutional, or other attributes to complicate matters. Advocates of the ideational approach highlight the value of a simple, or minimal, definition. Cas Mudde and Cristóbal Rovira Kaltwasser (e.g., 2011, 2012) in particular encourage its use, in part to bring well-needed consensus to the discipline.

Still, the plea to use a single-characteristic definition can mean, and even require, the researcher to study different things. As discussed, this implication is true with any concept that has a narrow intension: the extension is expansive. Using this approach, all examples of divisive language could be taken to be populist, regardless of the speakers' characters, their goals, and so forth. Though one could draw from any number of cases in Europe, Latin America, and beyond, meaningful comparison would be in doubt.

Consider Hawkins's (2009) conceptualization of populism as a set of ideas manifest in "a Manichaean discourse that identifies Good with a unified will of the people and Evil with a conspiring elite" (1042). This conceptualization is appealing since its simplicity offers clarity, but that same simplicity also results in denotational shortcomings. Illustrating the point, Hawkins (2009) finds that George W. Bush, along with the usual suspects, used populist language. In fact, Bush's score was almost as high (where higher means more populist) as that of Juan Perón, and higher than the scores for the likes of Lázaro Cárdenas, Getúlio Vargas, and Carlos Menem. He suggests, though, that this outcome should be considered a measurement error, and he offers several qualifying factors, thus narrowing the concept's extension, that help separate Bush from other populists.[12] The necessity of this step suggests the ideational definition, by itself, is inadequate to distinguish positive cases of populism from negative ones.

One can find ways to avoid this issue, of course. Greater specification of the ideological or linguistic attributes could both improve the concept's denotational adequacy and balance the extension.[13] Even so, an important point to highlight is that this approach ties together potentially discrete kinds of political phenomena so long as populist ideas are present. If one is interested in ideas alone, then an ideational concept makes sense. On the other hand, if one is interested in political movements or strategies or parties, then an ideational definition might be a poor fit: the empirical cases included might not be the ones of interest. For this book, the concern is not the presence or absence of ideas but instead concentrated political power, so the focus is on individuals and behavior.

The ideational perspective, nevertheless, considers a focus on political behavior to be misplaced. Hawkins (2010) offers an explanation: "It is unclear why we need to impose a behavioral standard. . . . We do not worry about a charismatic movement or even bad economic policy in the same way that we worry about the universal suffrage and freedom of speech that constitute modern democracy" (39). Many analysts would disagree; bad economic policy, for instance, concerns a great number of people. I am not arguing in favor of a universal standard, but there are reasons why so much of political science concerns political behavior. Ideas become important in a political sense not by their mere existence but when they are manifest in some concrete way. Nevertheless, Hawkins (2010) continues to argue, *"Behavioral attributes are products of the underlying set of ideas. A pop-ulist worldview is the motivating force that lies at the heart of every pop-ulist movement"* (39; emphasis in original). A common and long-standing understanding holds that an opportunistic and charismatic leader is at the heart of populism. The strict ideational approach would deny the role of such a person—deny the possibility that an ambitious actor might attempt to manipulate citizens through the use of appeals with which he or she does not fully agree. Perhaps populists are motivated by a specific worldview. However, is making an a priori assumption about their beliefs safe, particu-larly one that holds politicians to a high standard of sincerity? Clearly polit-ical behavior can reflect much more than ideas; it can reflect, among other things, personal ambition, group economic interests, psychological factors, resource availability, political opportunity, and any number of structural conditions.

Given the concern for ideas over actors, the ideational definition leaves undefined the protagonist in the drama. It emphasizes the notion that soci-ety is divided between competing camps, rather than look at who creates those divisions in the first place and for what reasons. In this perspective, "the people" as an identifiable group *is created* and only then becomes a political actor in its own right. But cannot the latter be the result of an intentional, political process? In other words, some person or persons may attempt to gain power by developing an antagonistic relationship between two groups and do so independently of the content of the ideas expressed. Much of the literature on Latin American populism concurs that the role of an individual politician is important, hence the frequent citation of some "personalistic" character of populism.

Mudde and Rovira Kaltwasser (2012, 10) attempt to reclaim the impor-tance of political leaders and behavior within their ideology-based approach:

> Populist leaders are indeed very relevant. They not only try to mobilize the
> electorate but are also one of the main protagonists in the process of defining

the morphology of the populist ideology. However, an excessive focus on leadership narrows the analysis to the supply-side of the populist phenomenon, generating a kind of modern version of Carlyle's "great man theory," which presupposes that the leader is the main and almost only factor that explains political development.

They continue by asserting that populism "depends on skilful political entrepreneurs and social groups" (10). Nevertheless, they define populism as a "thin-centered ideology." It has certain secondary characteristics, namely, that the ideology depicts society as divided into two antagonistic camps and that politics should be an expression of the general will. Yet no actors or behaviors are part of this definition. Logically, then, the exclusion of leadership and political behavior from the definition means that these traits are not necessary components of populism but instead are incidental. If the excessive focus on leadership presents certain risks, would not the excessive focus on ideas do the same?

With respect to comparative analysis, furthermore, those utilizing this perspective have difficulty measuring ideas without reference to actors and behavior. Indeed, every empirical study that uses an ideational definition focuses on actors and behavior: the election of Europe's right-wing parties, the rise of the radical left leaders in Latin America, the consequences of populist leadership, and so forth. Hawkins (2010) captures the reasons behind this apparent conflict: "I define populism in terms of worldview and discourse, and I change the word into an adjective—'populist movement,' 'populist leader,' and so on—when I want to refer to *actual* instances of populism" (41; emphasis added). Matthijs Rooduijn, Sarah L. de Lange, and Wouter van der Brug (2014), using an ideological definition, position populism as a "property of a message rather than a property of an actor sending the message" (564), yet they go on to study the parties that use that message. Similarly, Mudde and Rovira Kaltwasser (2011) apply their ideological definition to the cases of Jörg Haider, Jean-Marie Le Pen, Hugo Chávez, and Evo Morales: "In conclusion, all four actors meet our ideological minimal definition of populism" (9). Their empirical discussion, in other words, deals with populist leaders—individuals behaving in a certain way—not ideas. Though the proponents of this approach define populism in ideational terms, they can only study it in behavioral ones.

One consequence is that this approach is forced to study subtypes—and *only* subtypes—of populism. Because it cannot empirically assess the ideas by themselves, it must deal with instances where the ideas are associated with some kind of political behavior, such as politicians articulating the ideas or mass movements responding to the ideas. With classical concepts, when cases exhibit all of the necessary and sufficient conditions plus additional ones, they may be grouped in subtypes. Importantly, these are not diminished subtypes; they are full members that have one or more additional characteristics. These additional characteristics, however, may have consequences. According to the ideational perspective, each of these is a full member in the category of populism and thus, by extension, must be comparable in empirical terms. The underlying ideas may be the same, but can one be confident in the empirical analysis that compares "populist parties" with "populist presidents," "populist movements," and "populist regimes"? As these are different kinds of political phenomena, such an analysis would seem to rest on a weak foundation.

All of the above is not intended to suggest that the ideational perspective is unimportant. Indeed, these accounts highlight crucial themes of populism. The key point, instead, is that the conceptualization that relies only on ideas has certain deficiencies, most importantly the empirical and analytical difficulties resulting from a focus on ideas at the expense of political behavior. Naturally, all concept types and specific conceptualizations have their limitations; for the present analysis, nevertheless, useful alternatives exist. Considering these ideas in the form of political appeals (and in conjunction with other factors), as argued below, proves beneficial.

Before leaving this discussion of ideas and language, another treatment of populism warrants attention: the discourse analysis school exemplified by the work of Ernesto Laclau (1977, 2005a, 2005b). Despite the similarities to the ideational approach, Laclau's poststructural approach is antipositivist and normative and thus may be considered distinct. He and others in this school (e.g., Barros 2005; Groppo 2009) draw from different traditions and have different objectives than the ideational scholars and yet confront similar obstacles.[14]

In his earlier work Laclau (1977) offers the following definition of populism: "Our thesis is that populism consists in the presentation of popular-democratic interpellations as a synthetic-antagonistic complex with respect to the dominant ideology" (172–173). Here he highlights antagonism to a dominant ideology likely to occur in a generalized social crisis. In his later work he further specifies these notions, concluding with this formulation:

> The emergence of the "people" depends on the three variables I have isolated: equivalential relations hegemonically represented through empty signifiers; displacements of the internal frontiers through the production of floating signifiers; and a constitutive heterogeneity which makes dialectical retrievals impossible and gives its true centrality to political articulation. We have now reached a fully developed notion of populism. (Laclau 2005a, 156)

At the risk of oversimplification, his understanding centers on the process of creating these sets of antagonistic identities. As such, he does not offer a definition of populism per se, at least not in a reductionist sense of the word. Rather, for Laclau, populism is about the logic of constructing social relations. Consider, for instance, that his view of populism does not assume a priori the content of the "empty signifiers," the symbolic nodes that draw diverse groups together. These symbols, instead, can be of any sort. The central idea is the creation of a symbolic representation of a diverse set of interests that comes into contrast with some "other."

Although the consideration of identities and identity formation is both interesting and important, this specific configuration can present certain challenges (Stavrakakis 2004, 263–265). Beyond the issue of providing little operational guidance, the primary concern is that of the concept's unbounded extension. Because Laclau's concept deals with the creation of political divisions, one must wonder if populism is distinct from virtually any other kind of political discourse. Indeed, he explicitly states that it is not. He writes, for instance, that populism is not "some kind of marginal political phenomenon, but . . . the very essence of the political" (Laclau 2005a, 222). Even more definitively, he asks whether populism could be synonymous with politics and responds unambiguously: "The answer can only be affirmative" (Laclau 2005b, 47). Because Laclau answers positively, one must wonder what analytical utility can be derived from this view of populism. Even the more accessible adaptations of this approach strike the same obstacle. Panizza (2005), for instance, identifies one defining characteristic of populism: discourse that divides "the people" from "the other." This one characteristic is simultaneously necessary and sufficient; other factors, including political leaders and leadership, may be logically accidental but not conceptually necessary. As a result, the range of empirical cases of populism would be expansive, a point of which Panizza is clearly cognizant. He notes, for instance, "almost every political speech appeals to the people or claims to speak for the people, which could make it impossible to distinguish populist from non-populist political entities" (Panizza 2005, 5).

This conceptualization leaves the analyst with little capacity to differentiate those phenomena that belong in the category of populism from those that do not. As with the ideational approaches, the empirical and analytical implications do not facilitate the comparative, empirical study of populism, at least of the kind attempted here. And this point leads to a discussion of the remaining single-domain approach.

The Political Approach

The other single-domain classical conceptualization of populism is focused on the mobilization of masses by personalistic leaders (e.g., Conniff 1999; R. A. Mayorga 2006; Roberts 2006; Weyland 2001). The literature frequently labels this approach simply the "political" perspective (e.g., Leaman 2004; R. A. Mayorga 2006).[15] The conceptualizations in this camp almost invariably include multiple secondary characteristics of various sorts, such as discursive or rhetorical elements alongside individual, institutional, and constituency characteristics. Weyland (2001, 14), for example, highlights the strategic aspect of populism and includes four secondary characteristics: a personalistic leader, pursuit or exercise of governmental power, unmediated and uninstitutionalized support, and a large but unorganized following. Roberts (2007, 5) offers a related definition with the characteristics of top-down mobilization, a personalistic leader, a challenge to the elite, and defense of "the people." These and other examples recognize an individual's pursuit of power—political intentionality—in addition to the support based on mass mobilization.

These definitions bring out the political nature of populism and the behavioral aspect that the ideational approach shuns. As such, they are more in line with the historical meaning of the concept. Most early assessments of populism included, among other aspects, a certain kind of political leadership in which the development of a mass following was central to winning and exercising power (Weyland 2001, 5). Schamis (2013, 146–147) warns of the perils of uprooting a concept from its original usage, which can lead to conceptual stretching and homonymy, and advocates anchoring concepts in their historical meanings. His point is well taken: to the extent that concepts can be redefined at will, they lose all utility. To be sure, many of the contemporary political definitions of populism are structured differently than the classical definitions, which used multidomain concepts of a variety of types. That said, the more recent variants retain essential components of the earlier ones while stripping them of nonessential, temporally specific aspects. The works of Roberts (1995) and Weyland (1996), written in response to the rise of populism in unexpected circumstances, persuasively explain the logic of this step. Hence, although these definitions are not the same as those originally used, a clear lineage remains. The ideational perspective has a more difficult time in claiming such an ancestry.

The inclusion of political intentionality, or goal-oriented political leadership (Pappas 2012), also helps avoid the pitfalls of an exclusive focus on the ideational. In particular, as important as ideas are, they cannot fully explain political behavior. Just as Mudde and Rovira Kaltwasser's (2011, 2012) caution against an overemphasis on leadership, the same point can be made against an overemphasis on ideas. The political perspective includes the behavioral component and often, though not always, includes the ideational component as well. For instance, Carlos de la Torre pays a great deal of attention to discourse, to the point that some (e.g., Hawkins 2010, 8–9) consider him a discourse analyst. However, de la Torre (2010) defines populism in this way: "I see populism as a style of political mobilization based on strong rhetorical appeals to the people and crowd action on behalf of a leader" (4). The political intentionality is clear from this statement: discourse here is considered in behavioral terms. Unlike the strict ideational approaches, this view deals with the *use* of ideas and does so at the conceptual level.

The multifaceted nature of most of the political conceptualizations of populism is a double-edged sword. On the one hand, for the classical concept construction, adding defining attributes helps to narrow the extension, bringing it to a more manageable level compared to the minimal definitions. On the other hand, however, if too many attributes are included, then the extension may become too narrow. Each additional attribute raises the threshold for membership in this concept type, so moving from, say, three to four criteria necessarily reduces the number of cases that can be included for membership.

Some argue, moreover, that the political definition may be somewhat limited in its ability to account for the broad diversity of populist experiences. Given the emphasis on personalistic or top-down mobilization, one may question the extent to which this definition can apply to the nineteenth-century movements in the United States and Russia, to the right-wing political parties of contemporary Europe, or even to select instances in Latin America. Those in the ideational camp, meanwhile, defend their position by highlighting the broad applicability of their minimal definition, allowing for interregional comparisons. Indeed, the strategy of using a minimal definition does have this advantage. Nevertheless, as discussed earlier, a minimal definition also presents the challenge of including very different kinds of phenomena under one umbrella category. The desire to use the concept for empirical analysis (the goal in the present study) is not necessarily advanced in this way. Hence, if the political definition fails to accommodate other kinds of phenomena that may not be comparable, that should not be seen as a strike against it.

The logic of using a minimal definition so that regional differences can be accommodated raises an additional question, which is whether one should assume a priori that these regional differences could only be accommodated by an expansive, minimal definition. Are the European examples of populism so different from the Latin American cases that only the rhetoric ties them together? Admittedly, Europe has had fewer examples of the truly massive movements with transformative effects that seem to characterize populism in Latin America. But could this fact simply be a function of the institutional and socioeconomic environment in which European populism exists rather than a difference in kind? Compared to the highly centralized presidential systems of Latin America, the parliamentary systems of Europe arguably provide different incentives for potential populists. And with a significantly higher standard of living, perhaps the audience for the appeals of European populists is smaller. These are speculations, but the point is simply that a minimal definition might not be necessary in order to conduct cross-regional comparisons, though such a discussion is beyond the scope of the present study.

Defining Populism

In this book, I use a single-domain, classical concept structure to define populism. Specifically, populism is a means of building and/or maintaining political power based on the mass mobilization of supporters through the use of antiestablishment appeals and plebiscitarian linkages. In one respect, populism represents a challenge to those who wield power, on behalf of ordinary citizens and embodied by an individual. Yet it is not merely the idea that the status quo must change. It is instead a strategy of enhancing the power of an individual. A populist is someone who uses this strategy as a primary, though not necessarily only, means of generating support. Populists seek to develop (and successful ones do) a mass movement as a basis of power.

This definition is located squarely in the domain of politics, and its two defining characteristics are collectively necessary and sufficient to classify a case as populist. The first defining characteristic is a kind of appeal: the reasons politicians offer about why citizens should support them. As I use the idea here, antiestablishment appeals represent a challenge by "the people" directed against those who wield power, the "establishment." The appeals are not based on opposition just for the sake of opposition but for the sake of ordinary citizens. One could describe them accurately as "people versus the establishment" appeals. This message goes beyond being merely "pro-people," a virtually universal characteristic in democratic politics. Instead, the idea of "pro-people" is elevated to an "us versus them" struggle between groups. Important themes in Rafael Correa's appeals, for instance, included the slogan "Ya Basta!" ("Enough already!") and the claim that he was leading a "citizens' revolution." Exactly who belongs to each group is a function of rhetorical framing: the populists' appeals help to shape the outlines of this struggle. Correa claimed, "Power is controlled by economic interest, the banks, the *partidocracia*, and the media connected to the banks" (cited in Conaghan 2008, 47). Hugo Chávez excoriated the "Pontius Pilates," the "creole oligarchs that utilize the military as Cerebrus to assail against their own people and care for the grotesque privileges of the dominant elites," and claimed his Bolivarian Revolution would open "the door to a new national existence" (cited in Hawkins 2010, 62–64).

Language is crucial in these appeals, but symbols can play a role as well. Visual clues, behavioral traits, and the like can demonstrate aspects of these appeals, perhaps most notably that the populist is not a member of the establishment. Evo Morales famously wears sweaters instead of the business suits of Bolivia's white elite. Abdalá Bucaram embraced the moniker El Loco (the Crazy One) and conducted rallies like spectacles where he danced and sang while wearing jeans and guayaberas.[16] Pierre Ostiguy (2009, 5–6) refers to this type of display as a low sociocultural appeal on what he terms the "high-low axis":

> On the low, people frequently use a language that includes slang or folksy expressions and metaphors, are more demonstrative in their bodily or facial expressions as well as in their demeanor, and display more raw, culturally popular tastes. Politicians on the low are capable of being more uninhibited in public and are also more apt to use coarse or popular language. They appear—to the observer on the high—as more "colorful" and, in the very extreme cases, somewhat grotesque.

Ostiguy goes on to compare politicians on different ends of the axis: "Carlos Menem with his huge sideburns, flaunting his raw sexual tastes, riding on top of a garbage truck in the slums or galloping on horseback dressed in a poncho . . . versus the rather stiff, 'proper,' and 'respectable' Civic Radical Union Radicales Eduardo Angeloz or Fernando De la Rúa" (6).

Canovan (2002), along with a number of other scholars, argues that populism's central message is that politics has escaped popular control and that citizens "have been shut out of power by corrupt politicians and an unrepresentative elite" (27). This argument is not, however, the exclusive domain of populists. Others can and do use versions of antiestablishment appeals. Noemí Sanín, despite being a former member of Colombia's Conservative Party, and thus the establishment, attempted to portray herself as a challenger of the corrupt political class (Posada-Carbó 2005). The extent to which the appeal worked is a separate question from its use. Additionally, others may use antiestablishment appeals from time to time, but this definition of populism requires that they constitute a major (though not the exclusive) theme in a politician's effort to build power and are expressed with some regularity.

This focus on appeals creates some overlap with the ideational definitions of populism. The message identified above has much in common with, say, the focus of Hawkins's research. Yet the understanding of appeals differs: rather than remaining exclusively in the realm of ideas, the appeals become an aspect of political behavior. Recall that Hawkins views populism as a latent worldview that exists at the subconscious level, thus denying intentionality. By contrast, the perspective offered here is that politicians use appeals to build support. Therefore, the ideas are not latent; they are explicit and intentional. Their impact or effectiveness depends on whether citizens agree with the value of challenging the establishment and the notion that the populist leader is the one to lead the charge. Both the ideational and economic definitions largely neglect this intentionality and thus also neglect an important part of the politics associated with populism. As Taggart (2002) notes, however, the identification of who constitutes "the people" becomes a significant and powerful weapon when directed against some group, which populists invariably do. The use of such a weapon, then, reveals its strategic aspect.

The other defining characteristic of populism is plebiscitarianism. This term typically evokes "the powerful imagery of Roman emperors and French authoritarians who governed on the basis of popular adoration, with the masses giving their noisy consent to every course of action" (Lowi 1985, xi). Somewhat more generally, plebiscitarianism deals with leaders' pursuit of public affirmation of their authority. As Max Weber (1978) writes, "the leader (demagogue) rules by virtue of the devotion and trust which his political followers have in him personally" (268). The "personal" aspect is central here, in that the leader, whether already elected or seeking election, takes issues directly to the mass of supporters, as opposed to working through layers of intermediaries. Plebiscitarianism therefore has a highly top-down and unmediated character, and followers have the impression of a direct and personal connection with the leader. Some scholars use the terms *personalist mobilization* and *personalistic leadership* to express essentially the same idea. As is discussed later, however, personalism can suggest a variety of meanings, so in this book, I use the term *plebiscitarianism* instead.

As conceived here, plebiscitarianism is a kind of linkage. In general, linkages are interactive connections between two units (Lawson 1980). Specifically, they are the means by which political actors and constituents exchange support and influence.[17] Although they may and often do take the form of formal institutions, linkages also can be informal. Plebiscitarianism can come in either form. In formal plebiscites, citizens give an up or down vote on a specific topic in the form of a preformulated choice. A referendum on rewriting the constitution is an apt example, and one the Latin American populists have used several times in recent years. More frequently, though, one finds examples of informal linkages such as mass demonstrations.[18] These call to mind the rousing speeches of, say, Juan and Eva Perón from the balcony of the Casa Rosada to countless throngs packed into the Plaza de Mayo. At times the informal and formal go hand in hand. Rafael Correa, for instance, "mastered the art of mobilizing public opinion via polls, the media, and the streets in order to disorient, demoralize, and disorganize political opponents" in his successful drive to change Ecuador's constitution (Conaghan 2008, 47). In either case, the interactive aspect is the leader's request for and the public's demonstration of support. As a result, plebiscitarianism need not be artificially confined to governance, since mass demonstrations are standard tools of both populists in office and those seeking it.

Populists are not the only ones to use this linkage. As with antiestablishment appeals, nonpopulists can and do use plebiscitarianism. What distinguishes populists is the use of a strategy that combines both, and the combination of these features gives populism its prototypical character (see Figure 2.1). When either or both stop being part of the individual's political strategy, then the classification of populism would no longer apply. For instance, should clientelism replace plebiscitarianism as the predominant linkage, which happened in the case of Alberto Fujimori, then by this definition the case would no longer be classified as populist.

Use of this particular definition has advantages, at least for the present study. First, using a classical concept structure located in a single domain helps analysts identify what populism is in an ontological sense. This concept type requires the identification of necessary features: actual instances either exhibit them or they do not. Family resemblance concepts, as a point of contrast, have a more forgiving structure with lower requirements for inclusion. As such, using the classical single-domain concept reduces the risk of grouping together or analyzing unrelated occurrences. Compared to other concept types, then, classical ones can facilitate the evaluation and classification of empirical examples. The single-domain approach also aids in eliminating accidental features of populism that may be present only in isolated contexts, thus providing the concept with enough flexibility to travel from one period or place to another, thus facilitating comparisons across time and space. Using two defining characteristics, furthermore, should contribute to a balanced extension, resulting in fewer referents than

Figure 2.1 Venn Diagram of Populism

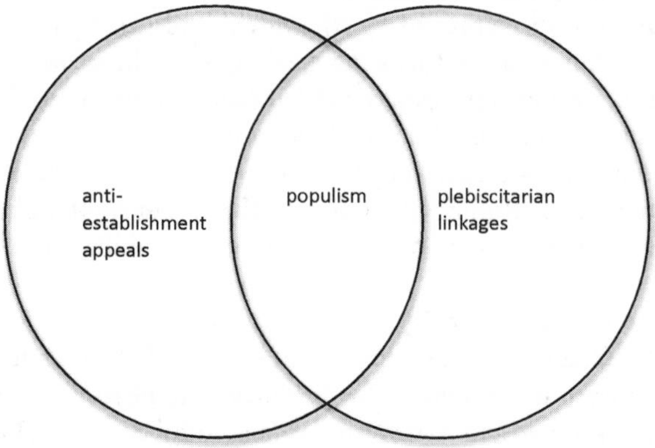

a minimal definition might, but more than the highly complex definitions. The result is enhanced analytical utility.

Finally, this definition also taps into a commonsense and historical usage of the term: what makes episodes of populism so interesting to many observers is the accumulation and use of political power by an individual that is based on the support of large numbers of followers. Early understandings of the concept tapped into the same theme. Torcuato di Tella (1965, 47), for instance, describes populism in this way: "It may be defined as a political movement which enjoys the support of the mass of the urban working class and/or peasantry but which does not result from the autonomous organizational power of either of these two sectors. It is also supported by non-working-class sectors upholding an anti-status quo ideology." Although di Tella and others of his generation did consider the social constituency as a defining characteristic of populism, that constituency was nonetheless broad and flexible: the working class, the peasantry, and the nonworking class. More to the point, di Tella begins by noting populism's political nature. And, like so many others, he notes the importance of ideas—the "anti-status quo" ideology—but ideas occupy a secondary conceptual position, not a primary one. In other words, his view is that populism is not an ideology. Hence, at least compared to other contemporary understandings of the term, the present definition maintains a continuity of understanding over time.

Incidental and (Mis)associated Characteristics

This conceptualization has a number of implications regarding characteristics that have been associated with populism in the literature. Some of these, by the terms of this definition, are incidental characteristics and others have been inappropriately tied to the concept.

Consider first the target of the rhetorical and symbolic challenge. At times in Latin America the focus has been against the economic elite, the political elite, foreign interests, or some combination thereof. The anti-establishment appeals as described here implicitly recognize that the specifics from one case to another will vary, even while the nature of the process is the same. Rather than specify the target of the challenge, for instance, "the establishment" can be economic or political, domestic or foreign. The selection depends on the context. These appeals, though, go beyond those often offered by a loyal opposition that criticizes current officeholders. Instead, they are directed at the established centers of power. In contemporary Latin America, for instance, one hears complaints of the political class, referring to a modern-day oligarchy of sorts. Hugo Chávez, for instance, demonized Venezuela's domestic oligarchy but then changed the target of his criticism to the US government. The logic, though, was the same: these powers were counterrevolutionary forces attempting to hold back the will of the people. Importantly, through its criticism of the political status quo, this appeal "explicitly or implicitly invokes criteria for assessing the performance of a political system" (Scarrow 1996, 301), and, thus, advocates prescriptions for change.

If the context shapes the target of the challenge, the conclusion should follow that context would also shape the audience of the appeals (populism's constituency). The literature frequently associates the phenomenon with a certain constituency, although which one depends on the author at hand. Some highlight a multiclass composition (e.g., Roberts 1995), whereas others argue for the primacy of rural workers (e.g., MacRae 1969), urban labor (e.g., Hennessy 1969), or the marginalized masses (e.g., Mouzelis 1985). However, one cannot expect the audience to remain static across time and space; indeed the empirical record shows that it does not. Hence, whether, or to what extent, the populist movement is a multiclass movement and whether the primary constituency consists of workers, peasants, or the informal sector are functions of context. In contemporary Latin America, those who find the appeals most attractive are largely found in the informal economic sector of unregulated, self-employed workers. However, in Argentina of the 1940s, the audience was the urban workers. In Louisiana of the 1920s, rural people liked the language of Huey Long. What is common among these cases is the appeal, not the audience. "Artisans as well as peasants make excellent populist material" (Wiles 1969, 169). Even di Tella (1965) admits the following of populism's supporters: "Their social situations are different, but what they have in common is a passionate hatred of the status quo" (50). Put differently, populism's social constituency is a function of where the construction of the us-versus-them conflict will most likely take hold. The present definition, then, eliminates the need to offer superficial or secondary characteristics concerning the nature of the social constituency.

The focus on appeals also may shed light on a third characteristic frequently associated with populism: charisma (e.g., Conniff 1999; de la Torre 2010; Wiles 1969). Certainly the most successful populists have had tremendous personal charisma, but there have been notable noncharismatic populist leaders as well (e.g., Peru's Alberto Fujimori). Charisma is a useful resource for any politician, helping build support no matter the type of appeal. It may be particularly useful, nevertheless, for populists. Since the populist leader attempts to represent the people, charisma helps instill confidence in the leader's capacity to perform. Although charismatic personalities have a natural advantage in generating support, they do not seem to be necessary and thus do not belong as a defining characteristic. In a sense, charisma serves a similar supporting role sometimes assigned to crises: it facilitates mobilization (Roberts 1995, 113–114). In addition, charisma is a notoriously vague concept, as even its supporters acknowledge (e.g., Conniff 1999, 19). Using a vague concept to illuminate another vague concept is of little use.

Another frequently cited characteristic is personalism (e.g., de la Torre 2010; R. A. Mayorga 2006; Roberts 1995; Weyland 2001). The issue with this term is not that it is necessarily misplaced but that it has multiple meanings and thus does not help clarify matters. Scholars varyingly use the word to convey personal ambition, bases for loyalty, or vertical organization. For instance, Roberts (2006) writes, "The essential core of populism is the political mobilization of mass constituencies by personalistic leaders seeking to challenge established elites" (127). This view implies that populism centers on an individual's ambition. "In the fashion of Argentine populists," according to Joel Horowitz (1999), "Perón pulled power to himself and refused to share it" (33), and "in what can be called populist style, Menem amassed power, stretching the constitution" (42). Associating populism with an individual's political ambition is logical given the plebiscitarian linkages. Inherent in these linkages is significant individual responsibility to the people. As such, ambitious personalities may be the ones that seek out such individualistic configurations of power. Naturally, though, populism is neither the only outlet for personal political ambition nor the only form of personalistic authority (Ansell and Fish 1999).

Another view of personalism concerns organizational characteristics, specifically unmediated representation (e.g., Stein 1980). For example, Weyland (2001) states, "Since under populism the ruler is an individual, that is, a personalistic leader, the connection between leader and followers is based mostly on direct, quasi-personal contact, not on organizational intermediation" (13). Personalism here is merely a derivative or perhaps descriptive feature of the plebiscitarian linkage. As mentioned, the very idea of this linkage is that a leader embodies the will of the people—that representation need not get bogged down in multiple layers of institutions (occupied by the political class) that are likely to misconstrue, ignore, or delay effective representation. Hence, plebiscitarian linkages lead to personalism in this sense of unmediated representation, and thus including both as central features of populism is repetitive.

Personalism is also associated with loyalty to individuals rather than to ideologies, platforms, rules, or any other impersonal factors (Ansell and Fish 1999, 286). De la Torre's (2010) description of Ecuadorian populism fits this notion: "Ideologies or concrete electoral proposals were not important; what mattered was the role of personalities as the embodiment of different social classes and lifestyles" (91). Similarly, Roberts (2006) describes populist movements as "umbilically tied to dominant personalities" (128). In this perspective, then, personalism concerns the reasons why citizens support a given political actor. The problem is that constituent loyalty may stem from multiple sources. For instance, the distribution of patronage, which is highly dependent upon personal connections, can secure bonds of loyalty as easily as an individual's specific message or a powerful personality. Thus, personalism in the sense of loyalty could result from the benefits received (via clientelistic linkages), the individual's message (appeal), or the individual's personality (charisma). Because of the lack of clarity associated with personalism, the term is best dissociated from the concept of populism.

A fifth such characteristic concerns the organizational features of populist phenomena, a minor debate in the literature. Many analysts emphasize populism's general lack of institutionalization (Weyland 2001) or the absence of organizational intermediaries (Mouzelis 1985). Others, however, take a different view. David Laycock (1990) states, "The development of these populist 'systems of narration' owes a great deal to the organizational breadth and depth of particular populist movements" (18). Roberts (2003), meanwhile, suggests that "any number of organizational outcomes is likely to emerge" from a populist movement (2). Nevertheless, the extent to which the organization is "thick or thin" (Gunther and Diamond 2003) and the degree of contingency (Roberts 2002) certainly vary.[19] Examples range from Alberto Fujimori's highly ephemeral electoral coalitions (*party* seems too strong a term) to the "thick" organization of Juan Peron's PJ, with Canadian Preston Manning's Reform Party perhaps somewhere in between.

Perhaps, then, delinking populism from any specific organizational form would be best (Ostiguy 2009; Roberts 2003, 2006), albeit within the parameters set by plebiscitarianism. A variety of organizational characteristics may be supportive of such a linkage. Following scholars as far back as di Tella (1965), however, the crucial component here is the absence of group autonomy within the movement. Autonomy would suggest the power to influence, something that would be more consistent with participatory linkages than plebiscitarian ones. As Nicos Mouzelis (1985) argues, "even in cases of populist movements with strong grass-roots organizations, in so far as the rank and file's allegiance is centered on the person of the leader, local or intermediary cadres are left without a structural basis for establishing some degree of political autonomy vis-à-vis that leader" (334–335). The point to highlight here is that populism can be associated with a variety of specific organizational types as long as they share one common feature: absence of autonomy within the movement. Rather than a defining characteristic in its own right, however, this feature results from the nature of the linkage.[20] Although the specific organizational features may help distinguish one populist from another, they do not help distinguish populists from nonpopulists.

Incidentally, the absence of autonomy in populism is an interesting point to consider. Some mass movements use antiestablishment appeals but have a grassroots or bottom-up nature (they use different linkages). Some observers label these as populist because of their appeals. However, their internal dynamics are dramatically different from those of populist organizations as understood here. For instance, the agrarian movements in the United States in the late 1800s had a decidedly bottom-up development trajectory. They began with farmers' cooperatives that promoted participatory linkages through which individuals would work together to solve common problems (Canovan 1981, 17–58). The movements coalesced in the form of the People's Party, which nominated William Jennings Bryan, the charismatic orator, as its presidential candidate in the 1896 elections. Although commonly described as a populist, Bryan did not create the movement that supported him; rather, the movement chose Bryan. This relationship suggests a balance of power between the leader and the supporters that tilts in favor of the latter. Indeed, the People's Party rejected Bryan's choice of running mate and nominated another. Bolivia's Evo Morales is another, albeit partial, example, having emerged in the context of the powerful *cocaleros* (coca growers) movement. (His relationships with supporters changed over time, as is discussed in detail in Chapter 4.) By contrast, top-down movements created by a leader in support of his or her political ambitions suggest a different internal dynamic. Because the archetypical examples of Latin American populism exhibit top-down traits, this definition emphasizes the role of leaders in these movements.

A sixth characteristic sometimes associated with populism is the use of clientelism. Politicians and parties frequently use multiple kinds of linkages simultaneously. However, the predominant one should be used for classification purposes. Populists, for instance, typically use clientelistic linkages alongside plebiscitarian ones once in power. Because of the nature of the appeals they offer, they face the challenge of improving the lives of their supporters and frequently use the distribution of patronage for this purpose. However, clientelism should be excluded from the conceptualization of populism for several reasons. First, where a politician predominantly relies on clientelism, one is more likely to speak of machine politics or neopatrimonialism (Bechle 2010).[21] These patronage-based organizations typically have internal dynamics quite distinct from populist movements (Mouzelis 1985). The former usually rely on a cascading series of intermediaries, for instance, quite unlike the direct connections found in populist movements. In addition, the leaders of these organizations are often replaceable. The organization can continue to exist as long as the material benefits continue to flow. In populist phenomena, by contrast, the leader has a more central role; this figure is seen to be indispensable for the continued operation of the movement. This indispensability results in part from the absence of intermediaries in any populist organization: there is no "vice" populist, no second in command with an independent legitimacy who could replace the leader should the need arise.[22]

Furthermore, since the use of clientelism at some level is virtually a political universal, highlighting its use in a populist scenario does little to help clarify the distinguishing characteristics of such phenomena. Also, clientelism typically involves the distribution of state resources, which limits it to those in office. If one were to include clientelism as a defining characteristic, populism could not exist outside of elected office. The fact that leaders can and do use antiestablishment appeals and plebiscitarian linkages and develop enormous, dedicated followings as private citizens suggests that restricting the concept of populism to those in office would not be appropriate (Ostiguy 2009). Finally, limiting populism to its clientelistic linkages would be a mistake because the nature of the relationship would be missed. As Weyland (2001) explains, "where proliferating clientelism transforms the relationship of leader and followers into a purely pragmatic exchange, political rule based on command over large numbers of followers eventually loses its populist character" (14).[23] Should clientelism become the principal linkage, one could no longer consider the phenomenon populist.

Finally, one must consider the characteristic of political "outsider." Politicians, including populists, frequently describe themselves as outsiders, not beholden to vested interests and not corrupted by national politics. However, statements along these lines can mask relations or experience with the political establishment. For the sake of clarity, outsiders may be best understood in relation to politicians' actual experiences with the party systems, as opposed to their efforts at framing themselves (see Kenney 1998). If insiders are those politicians experienced with a country's competitive parties, then an outsider is someone whose political experience, if any, is as an independent or in association with a new or marginal party. This location vis-à-vis the party system says nothing, technically, about either the kinds of appeals or linkages a politician might use. One can find examples of well-connected politicians who nevertheless broadcast antiestablishment appeals. Outsider status, however, clearly enhances the credibility of those claims. Likewise, many outsiders may have an incentive to use plebiscitarian linkages, as they may lack significant organizational or institutional support. For this reason, populists, particularly the successful ones, are very often outsiders, and many scholars link outsider status with the concept of populism (e.g., Roberts 2012). Nevertheless, the use of antiestablishment appeals and plebiscitarianism does not require the absence of association with the party system. As such, outsider status should not be considered a defining characteristic. In Chapter 6, I return to this discussion of outsiders.

Conclusion

In this chapter, I demonstrate that in addition to the disputes about populism in ontological terms and its defining characteristics, disagreement also arises over which concept structure to use. The disputes of the former type are problematic enough, but the devil is often in the details: two scholars who agree on populism's character could use different concept structures and thus disagree on what constitutes a case of populism. Based on the literature as a whole, populism may be the jelly of political science concepts—it is hard to pin down. The desire of some to drop the concept from the lexicon of social science is understandable but misplaced. Difficulties in capturing a phenomenon in conceptual and definitional terms do not equal impossibility. And the fact that the idea of populism continues to capture the attention of so many observers and scholars is telling: there is something distinctive about it and thus it warrants the effort to understand it.

Reaching a consensus on its defining characteristics and conceptual structure may be, in many respects, an admirable goal. On the other hand, the various perspectives allow researchers the flexibility needed to capture their specific subjects in a way most suited for their own analyses. Too much of either consensus or flexibility, however, could be a bad thing. The good news in the development of populism studies may be that the range of concept types appears to be narrowing in the recent literature. A number of prominent studies have forcefully advocated for the benefits of using a classical concept type (e.g., R. A. Mayorga 2006; Mudde and Rovira Kaltwasser 2012; Weyland 2001). Furthermore, the dispute regarding the defining characteristics appears to be narrowing down to two primary strands: the ideational and the political. To what extent this trend will continue, of course, is up for debate. Indeed, some recent works challenge the dominance of the ideational and political approaches (e.g., Edwards 2010; Levitsky and Loxton 2013).

In this book, I take the perspective that a good concept is a useful one, not only for identifying constitutive elements of a phenomenon but also facilitating empirical analysis. The conclusion follows that a relationship exists between the kind or goal of study and the choice of concept. The selection of course has parameters: one should avoid conceptual stretching, maintain some consistency with the historical meaning, and so forth. Within these limits, nevertheless, a concept's analytical utility is of obvious importance. Given the present study's goal of determining the reasons for the electoral success of contemporary populists in Latin America, a single-domain, classical concept structure that embodies a political understanding of populism is well suited. Nevertheless, broader reasons not confined to a specific study can be identified to adopt this perspective on populism. Among them are the benefits of clarity that classical concepts bring; the empirical benefits of being able to directly study concrete examples of the concept, as opposed to only indirectly studying it through subtypes; and the historical legacy of the political approach. Importantly, I am not trying to suggest that classical concept structures and a political behavioral approach are universally preferable; that is not at all the case. The point is specific to the case of populism, the emergence of which I investigate in the following chapters.

Notes

1. Bale, van Kessel, and Taggart (2011) provide a useful analysis of the print media's use of the term in the United Kingdom.

2. Goertz (2006b) considers concepts to have three levels. The basic level reveals the object's essence and is used in theoretical propositions. The secondary level contains the elements that constitute the basic level. The indicator level provides for the operationalization of the concept.

3. This conclusion is valid from either Sartori's semantic viewpoint that emphasizes precision in naming things or Goertz's (2006b) ontological perspective of identifying what things are.

4. However, some argue that the logical AND still plays a role. If membership requires three of five characteristics, then those three characteristics are connected by the logical AND (e.g., a AND b AND c). Nevertheless, if m equals just 1, then there is no necessary combination of factors, so the logical AND would play no role. As such, characterizing the family resemblance concept as requiring only the logical OR seems most accurate.

5. Collier and Mahon (1993) use the term *secondary categories* (see especially pp. 848–850).

6. This perspective leaves room for success and failure. Those who use a populist strategy but fail to gain significant electoral support would still be populists.

7. Interestingly, though, she divides populism into two types and then subdivides these into seven subtypes. Although this step could suggest a radial conceptualization, Canovan (1981) explicitly denies the possibility of a case exhibiting all of the characteristics, thus eliminating the prototype basis of radial concepts.

8. Roberts (1995) uses the term *family resemblance*, but the logic expressed is consistent with radial conceptualizations: "By disaggregating, it is then possible to identify populist subtypes that share a 'family resemblance' and manifest some but not all of the core attributes" (88). A true family resemblance structure would consider these cases to be full instances, not subtypes.

9. As a result, such cases could be considered ideal types, which would have extremely limited extensions. "It is an *ideal* type because it never or rarely can be found in practice" (Goertz 2006b, 83; emphasis in original).

10. One might consider the ideational perspective as a kind of political approach since those who use it invariably highlight the political dimensions of populism. Hawkins (2010), for instance, points out that populism involves "political ideas"

and beliefs about "the nature of the political world" (5). In this view, ideas foster antagonistic relationships between groups struggling for influence. Because power is inherently about relations (e.g., Dahl 1991; Lasswell and Kaplan 1950), the division of society into competing camps is the very basis of politics. Nevertheless, because of this perspective's immediate concern for the ideas themselves, and not political behavior, this perspective belongs to a separate domain from the political.

11. Indeed, Hawkins has coauthored with Mudde and adopted the ideological definition of populism (e.g., Hawkins, Riding, and Mudde 2012).

12. These include the rectification of past injustices, a revolutionary or reformist platform, and the demonization of a Muslim elite (Hawkins 2009, 1058).

13. Stanley (2008) steps in this direction by using an ideological definition with four distinct components: the idea of popular sovereignty, the existence of two "units of analysis" (the people and the elite), an antagonistic relationship between the people and the elite, and a positive valorization of the people with a corresponding denigration of the elite. Given the tight overlap among the last three of these, their separate categorization may add little compared to other ideational definitions.

14. For instance, Mudde draws from Freeden's morphological understanding of ideology (e.g., Freeden 1996), whereas Laclau draws from Althusser's materialist understanding (e.g., Althusser 1971). My thanks to an anonymous reviewer for highlighting this point.

15. Others call it political strategy (e.g., Weyland 2001) or the political-institutional approach (e.g., Hawkins 2009).

16. See de la Torre's (2010) excellent analysis of Bucaram.

17. Linkages are distinct from appeals because the latter lack the aspect of exchange or interaction. A clientelistic linkage, for example, involves the exchange of material benefits for political support, whereas an electoral linkage involves the exchange of votes for adequate representation (Lawson 1988).

18. Public opinion polls can serve as a proxy for the mass demonstration.

19. Gunther and Diamond's (2003) "thick or thin" notion is akin to Roberts's (2002) "level of association."

20. Lawson (1988) suggests that organizational form follows from the dominant linkage.

21. As an example, Levitsky (2003) gives an account of how clientelism became the predominant linkage in Argentina's Peronist Party, turning it into a machine party. This transformation was crucial for its electoral success. If this account is correct, then Carlos Menem—the maverick who made the transformation—would not be considered a populist, contrary to some accounts (e.g., Roberts 1995), but rather the head of a hierarchical patronage-based party.

22. The struggle of Nicolás Maduro as Hugo Chávez's replacement is a case in point.

23. For a similar discussion, see also Knight (1998, 231–232).

3

Explaining the Third Era

PRIOR TO HUGO CHÁVEZ'S FIRST VICTORY IN 1998, VENEZUELA'S ECONOMY was not in good shape. For the five preceding years, the average annual inflation rate was over 61 percent. The size of the economy was shrinking at the same time: per capita gross domestic product (GDP) had an average annual growth rate of –0.53 percent. Perhaps unsurprisingly, voters rejected the political establishment and threw their support behind a populist alternative. Rafael Correa's election in Ecuador, on the other hand, came during improving economic circumstances. Though the five-year average inflation rate was over 12 percent, in the year before his 2006 election, it was but 2.4 percent. The five-year average growth rate, meanwhile, was almost 3 percent, and unemployment had fallen to 7.7 percent from over 11 percent two years earlier. One might not call this improvement an economic miracle, but Ecuador was far from being in crisis. Yet, as in Venezuela, the voters elected a populist. What might these examples have in common that could explain a similar outcome?

Contrary cases like these have plagued the search for an explanation of populism's causes and have spawned a lively debate. Among the most frequently cited causes are shortcomings of the party system or representation crisis (e.g., Carrión 2009; Mainwaring, Bejarano, and Leongómez 2006; Panizza 2000; Roberts 2007), lack of trust or confidence in democratic institutions (e.g., Doyle 2011; Seligson 2007), public distaste for corruption (e.g., Hawkins 2010), unacceptable economic conditions (e.g., Roberts 2006; Walker 2008), and economic structural changes (e.g., Conniff 1999; Demmers, Fernández Jilberto, and Hogenboom 2001b).[1] Certainly a list of factors like this one fails to do justice to any of these works included as examples; many of these sources contain nuanced and multifaceted explanations. Indeed, perhaps the majority of studies of populism employ some combination of factors in explaining its emergence, though the combinations vary. Roberts (2007), for instance, argues that the transition to neoliberalism and the crisis of political representation resulted in populism, whereas Hawkins (2010) posits a combination of corruption and "other policy failures such as economic crisis" (160). Perhaps those searching for causes should not attempt to identify the impact of a single variable but to determine instead those combinations of factors associated with populism's rise.

Using just such a combination, I offer an explanation for the third era of populism. The argument is that party system weakness, the prevalence of corruption, and perceived harm from that corruption can account for the electoral support these candidates have received in recent years. In so doing, I also offer explanations for both the supply of and the demand for populism. Both sides of the equation, so to speak, are required for a full understanding. A supply of populist candidates is a necessary precondition, obviously, for citizens to have the opportunity to grant them support. Unlike some accounts, my argument is not built on the assumption that such candidates will appear automatically. I also recognize that, even when present, the candidates will have no great electoral fortune if insufficient numbers of voters want this kind of alternative, which highlights the importance of demand.

I also pay attention to the psychological microfoundations of behavior. Rather than treat public support for populists as the result of either objective rationality or pathological irrationality, I take seriously insights from the fields of social and organizational psychology. These lessons can help make sense of the causal pathways connecting voters' perceptions to their behavior. What follows is, first, a review of the literature on the causes of populism and, second, an explanation of the argument that will be demonstrated in the chapters that follow. Also discussed are the relevant findings from the psychological literature and the implications thereof.

Existing Explanations

A great number of the arguments about populism's causes address, in one way or another, the public's discontent with the status quo. The general idea is that when voters endure some kind of hardship or deprivation, they seek out redemptive solutions (Canovan 1999). One identified source of hardship is economic, though the specifics vary among scholars (e.g., Conniff 1999; Roberts 2006). Panizza (2005), for instance, argues that populism can arise from an economic crisis that breaks down the social order. Ignacio Walker (2008) highlights the role of rising social needs alongside failed economic reforms and institutional problems. Panizza and Romina Miorelli (2009) write, "Unmet social needs and heightened economic insecurities, for instance, provide raw materials for the articulation of political grievances" (42). Writing of the African context, Danielle Resnick (2015) argues that reduced job opportunities and insufficient service provision contribute to populism's emergence. As should be evident, these accounts typically are not simple models of economic voting but more complex theories involving social or political changes stemming from shifting economic circumstances. And they can draw from cases that are consistent with the argument. Alberto Fujimori's rise, for instance, came in the context of a hyperinflationary episode: in August of 1990 Peru's annualized inflation rate topped 12,000 percent. This economic crisis, plus the growth of the Shining Path (Sendero Luminoso) insurgency, created a breakdown in social order and uprooted society's connections with the political establishment. As such, the combination provided fertile ground for the election of an antiestablishment challenger.

In some ways this contemporary explanation is similar to the structuralist explanations that dominated the early literature (e.g., di Tella 1965; Germani 1974; Vilas 1992–1993). These often highlighted the disruptive changes resulting from the collapse of the export-led development model and the "revolution of rising expectations" associated with modernization. As di Tella (1965) writes, "the moment the lid is unscrewed from a traditional society, no one can predict the amount of pressure which will force its way out" (49). Peronism in Argentina, by this account, would reflect not necessarily an acute crisis of the Peruvian hyperinflationary sort, but a crisis nonetheless, and one in which economic changes created status incongruence and pressures that the existing system could not contain. As logically follows, one could explain the neopopulists of the 1990s as a result of the collapse of state-led industrialization, resultant debt crises, and the lost decade of the 1980s. Further, the third era could be explained as the result of globalization, which asked its losers to endure too much. Writing of the political left in Latin America, for instance, Susan C. Stokes (2009) argues that the trends of globalization and declining social spending help account for its recent electoral successes. These, then, could be considered critical junctures that open up new political possibilities (see Roberts 2013).

Together, these accounts therefore include immediate crises and deep structural changes, which might be understood as proximate and distal causes, respectively. Despite the several good empirical examples that seem to demonstrate each set of causes, many others seem to defy the arguments. As others note (e.g., de la Torre and Arnson 2013, 19; Knight 1998), populism has also emerged in times without crises and at noncritical junctures. Mexico's Andrés Manuel López Obrador almost won the 2006 election, for example, despite a low unemployment rate of 4.7 percent, a modest but positive per capita GDP growth rate of just under 2 percent, and an inflation rate of 4 percent. These indicators suggest the country was neither in economic crisis nor at a critical juncture. Moreover, one can find instances of countries that were in acute crises or at critical junctures that failed to produce populist outcomes. Consider the Bolivian example: in 1985 its inflation hit a staggering 25,000 percent rate, its vital tin industry collapsed, and early elections were called. This moment was certainly a crucial one in Bolivia's modern history and an economic emergency. The winner of the 1985 elections was Víctor Paz Estenssoro, founder of the Nationalist Revolutionary Movement (Movimiento Nacionalista Revolucionario [MNR]), already a three-time president, and in no way a populist. Looking broadly across cases, in short, suggests that economic conditions of this sort are neither necessary nor sufficient to account for populism.

A second general strand of thinking about populism emphasizes political and institutional sources of discontent. These accounts emphasize the frailties of political institutions and citizens' lack of trust in them (e.g., Carrión 2009; Doyle 2011; Seligson 2007). Regardless of the reasons, where citizens distrust "the traditional political institutions of liberal democracy," voters will "be attracted to candidates who adopt electoral strategies that portray them as crusading outsiders, railing against the established political order" (Doyle 2011, 1467). For some, institutions are broadly conceived, including political parties along with courts, legislatures, and means of policy implementation: not only the means of representation and interest mediation but also the mechanisms of governance and guarantors of the rule of law.

One variant on this line of thinking discounts, at least implicitly, the distal causes, or the sources of distrust of the political institutions (esp. Doyle 2011). The focus instead is on the proximate causes: distrust leads to popular demand for a populist alternative. An advantage of this approach is its flexibility in that citizens could lose faith in their democratic systems for a variety of reasons. Once trust is lost, nevertheless, support for a populist candidate is likely. Another variant, however, argues that the shortcomings of state capacity lead to discontent and the rise of outsiders and populists (e.g., Mainwaring 2006b; Paramio 2006). For instance, R. A. Mayorga (2006) suggests that "grave deficiencies in state capacity," which led to problems of governance, contributed to a crisis of representation and "brought about favorable conditions" for the election of populists and anti-system actors (162). Scott Mainwaring (2006b) explains that this factor is not about a temporary or onetime problem of governance or of a government, nor necessarily about a political crisis at a critical juncture, but instead involves a long-running, chronic underperformance of a range of state institutions.

For each of the two versions above, the immediate evidence of a problem of discontent is the perception among the citizenry. However, the empirical record in ways challenges the theory, at least in terms of necessity and sufficiency. For instance, one can cite examples of extremely low trust in political institutions that fail to result in support for populism. Among the data used in Chapter 5 is an index of the Latinobarómetro survey results for confidence levels in various institutions: political parties, congress, and the judiciary. Based on this data set, none of the observations analyzed shows positive levels of confidence.[2] In other words, a lack of trust in political institutions could be considered a constant, rather than a variable, in Latin America. That said, there is a difference between a score of 46 percent (for Uruguay prior to the 2009 elections) and 7.5 percent (for Argentina prior to the 2003 elections). But the two lowest scores are from cases where populists did not receive substantial electoral support. And of the bottom third, fewer than half showed substantial support for populists. From a comparative perspective, trust in political institutions may not have the explanatory power some give it.

A third general variant of the argument for public discontent as a cause of populism focuses on corruption. Although a number of studies highlight public concern about corruption in an individual case or populists' rhetoric lambasting corrupt politicians, Hawkins (2010) provides the most thorough corruption-based argument. He posits that voters turn to populist alternatives because of normative concerns, specifically regarding the breakdown of the rule of law as represented by corruption. The redemptive character of populist discourse, he suggests, has a strong appeal in these circumstances. Indeed, as measured by Transparency International's CPI, concern over corruption was substantial in every case of contemporary Latin American populism. However, substantial concern over corruption could also be seen in a number of countries where populism was not supported. Interestingly, Hawkins's own findings cast some doubt on the individual impact of corruption. He notes that the perception of corruption is "a crucial precondition" for the emergence of populism—a necessary factor—yet "neither perceived corruption nor any of our other indicators considered in combination are sufficient conditions for the emergence of populist movements; many other countries also experience conditions of widespread corruption and policy failure without seeing populists come to power" (Hawkins 2010, 160).

Herein lies an important consideration, which is the distinction between the impact of an individual factor and its potential role in a combination of factors. Although Hawkins finds that corruption is not sufficient by itself, some additional factor or factors, together, must be able to explain populism. As has been often noted, trying to establish simple correlations between populism and a single causal factor proves vexing or, worse, misleading (e.g., Bermeo 2009; Weyland 2003). To be fair to the scholars cited above, many take multifaceted views. Consider those who highlight the role of parties or the quality of representation. Mainwaring (2006b), for instance, ties state deficiencies to crises of representation. Roberts (2013) argues that populism "is a permanent possibility where representative institutions are weak" (38), but the likelihood of populism's rise increases during the critical junctures of political and economic transformations. David Doyle (2011), despite emphasizing the role of trust in institutions, explains that the level of party system institutionalization matters as well. Moving beyond the role of parties, one can find explanations like Carlos de la Torre and Cynthia J. Arnson's (2013); they suggest a combination of weak political institutions and socioeconomic privation or exclusion leads to populism. Walker (2008) explains contemporary populism as the result of three factors: "the failure of the neoliberal economic reforms of the 1990s, the decomposition of traditional institutions and elites, and the new social demands of these emerging social sectors" (13). The general point, in short, is that many if not most explanations of populism's causes use some combination of factors to establish sufficiency. Just which factors make up the combination is perhaps the key question.

Returning to Hawkins (2010), his search for corruption's accomplices leads him to consider supply-side factors: those conditions that would prompt a candidate to use a populist strategy in the first place. This search leads to an important wrinkle, especially since the Latin American literature, by and large, pays little explicit attention to issues of supply. The arguments described above all deal with the demand for populism. Rather than discuss, say, the impact of institutional weaknesses on the incentives and calculations of candidates or prospective candidates, the causal impact is usually confined to voters. Consider Roberts (2013), who makes the case for the importance of critical junctures. These are periods of realignment that make populists' activation of support among nonparticipants and conversion of those who had previously supported other parties more likely. This logic, sound though it may be, simply assumes the presence of the populist candidate. The question of supply, in other words, is taken for granted.

The European literature has paid more attention to supply, highlighting in particular the role of spatial competition dynamics (e.g., Ignazi 1992; Mudde 2007). These accounts, however, are better in explaining the ideological positioning of parties than the decision to use antiestablishment appeals and plebiscitarian linkages. Hawkins (2010) suggests that the appropriate supply-side factor to consider is the availability of extraordinary leadership, which may be a fair assessment. Some political skill must be involved in a populist strategy; not everyone can pull it off. The role of individual leadership is also something that political science has a poor record with, but not without good reason. This sort of factor is notoriously difficult to study, at least in a comparative empirical way, and may be nonfalsifiable. As a result, the explanations become case-specific and ad hoc, ultimately defying generalization. But these criticisms should not be construed as arguments against the search for supply-side explanations. In fact, the opposite is true. Logic suggests that a full understanding of populism's emergence must consider both sides (see Mudde 2007; Norris 2005).

Explaining Contemporary Populism

In this book, I argue that populism's causes—specifically, the reasons for populists' electoral success—are a combination of factors that account for both the supply and the demand sides of the equation. In brief, populists' electoral success can be explained by the presence of three factors: (1) a weakly institutionalized party system, (2) the perception among voters that corruption is rampant among the political class, and (3) evidence of an unfair, disadvantageous outcome of that corruption. Before I explain the argument in detail, I should note that the position here is that these factors do not necessarily have independent effects on the likelihood of populists' electoral success, but that they interact in a way that creates propitious conditions for populism. In other words, causal factors do not always add together in some mechanistic or linear fashion. Instead, the whole can be greater than the sum of the parts, and, as such, the combination itself is more important in understanding the outcome than the individual factors. As is discussed below, this point may be particularly evident in the association of the second and third causal factors.

The Supply Side

The first factor, a weakly institutionalized party system, addresses the supply of populist candidates.[3] This side of the equation has received less attention, on the whole, in the Latin American literature on populism than in the European literature. The former overwhelmingly focuses only on the demand side.[4] Hawkins (2010), for one, suggests that the strictly demand-side analyses ignore half of the story.[5] Party system institutionalization, however, helps in this regard. Though it does not address agency-level aspects like charisma or leadership qualities, which is a limitation, it contributes to the understanding of the supply-side forces at work.

The concept of party system institutionalization comes from Mainwaring and Scully (1995). Arguing that the level of institutionalization has an impact on democracy, they conceptualize it along four dimensions: the stability of interparty competition, the extent of party roots in society, the legitimacy of parties and elections, and the level of party organization. Subsequent research has demonstrated multiple effects of party system institutionalization, for instance, the foci of party competition, the effect on economic policy, and the impact on democratization (e.g., Flores-Macías 2012; Jones 2005; Mainwaring and Zoco 2007; Moser 1999, 2001; Stoner-Weiss 2001; Torcal, Gunther, and Montero 2002). Some also see the rise of outsiders, antisystem politicians, and populists as effects of weakly institutionalized systems (e.g., Mainwaring and Scully 2008; Mainwaring and Torcal 2006).[6] Indeed, even if the specifics vary significantly, weak parties and weak representation are widely cited causes of populism (e.g., Mainwaring, Bejarano, and Leongómez 2006; Panizza 2000; Roberts 2006, 2013). Though the present argument finds much support in the literature, a key difference concerns the role of party system institutionalization as one of three factors in a causal combination.

Specifically, the level of party system institutionalization affects the incentives to use the populist strategy and thus affects the supply of populism. In countries where party systems are well institutionalized, citizens are connected to parties, they believe in the legitimacy of the parties (and elections), parties themselves are well organized and stable, and competition among them is stable. For a candidate to use antiestablishment appeals in these circumstances might prove unwise. Voters in these circumstances are not terribly likely to be receptive to the message that the political establishment is immoral or corrupt when the voters believe in the legitimacy of the establishment to which they feel connected. The populist strategy would face significant challenges here, and so the incentives to use it are negligible. By contrast, in weakly institutionalized, or inchoate, settings, the incentives may be reversed. Parties in these circumstances are not connected to voters, are not well organized, experience volatile electoral results, and may not be seen as legitimate. Simple logic suggests that, at a minimum, the risks of a populist strategy are low and that the payoff might be high.

Party system institutionalization has a similar effect on plebiscitarianism. In well-institutionalized systems, a candidate who attempts to connect to supporters through plebiscitarian linkages will be competing against entrenched organizations that can count on voter loyalty and substantial institutional resources. Indeed, in such circumstances, candidates have a strong incentive to join parties in order to benefit from those resources and the parties' positions as known quantities (Aldrich 1995). In other words, party organizations have a level of influence and power that individual candidates want to tap into rather than challenge. Although parties can use a variety of linkages with supporters, plebiscitarianism involves the direct and top-down connections between leader and followers, which necessarily de-emphasize the role of organizations, institutional platforms, and the like.[7] Where party systems are strong, to use plebiscitarian linkages would be to reject those party-based benefits. Perhaps for this reason the countries with the strongest party systems, Uruguay and Chile, have had no populists in the third era.

Where party systems are weakly institutionalized, however, all of these conditions are turned around and plebiscitarianism may prove advantageous. What had been sources of strength and power are now weaknesses and liabilities. The political incentives are thus reversed, and politicians may find that emphasizing personalistic characteristics and abandoning party organizations make for a better path to political power. As an example, Steven Levitsky and Maxwell A. Cameron (2003) found this dynamic in Peru under Alberto Fujimori. This logic, moreover, is supported by the research: in well-institutionalized party systems, parties tend to compete on programmatic grounds (Jones 2005), whereas in weakly institutionalized party systems, competition centers on either clientelism or personalism (Mainwaring and Torcal 2006).

A related reason that a weakly institutionalized party system contributes to the supply of populism is that it enhances the need, or at least the utility, of this strategy as a route to political power. Weyland (2001) explains the principal power capability of populism in terms of numbers of supporters, as opposed to economic clout or military might. For instance, unlike patrimonialism's reliance on economic advantage or caudillismo's reliance on force, populism relies on support from large numbers of people. Party government in democratic settings depends on supporters, too, of course, but not at every turn. Disciplined parties with deep pockets do not need to mobilize supporters for each piece of legislation. In weakly institutionalized party systems, by contrast, public support takes on added significance. One option in these environments for candidates looking to win office is to develop the means of mobilizing citizens—first for the election and then as part of governing. Absent the institutional and organizational backing of strong parties, in other words, a reliance on the repeated mobilization of supporters becomes a viable path to power and rule (at least for those skilled enough to do it). One can see the impact of an inchoate party system in Ecuador, where recent leaders have sought a variety of sources of power. Alfredo Palacio attempted to ally with well-organized social movements, Lucio Gutiérrez sought the support of social movements and the military, and most recently Rafael Correa has used the direct mobilization of citizens.

This emphasis on the impact of party system institutionalization on the supply of populism does not mean that it can have no impact on the demand side. Of course, some overlap is possible. When party systems become weakly institutionalized, citizens may lose their partisan loyalty and begin to see parties as illegitimate, among other results. In addition to providing incentives to use a populist strategy, these circumstances may affect voter choice (i.e., citizens may demand some alternative). Jason Seawright (2012), for instance, argues that eroding partisan identification and poor ideological representation lead citizens to vote for political alternatives.

This effect may be seen in part by the higher levels of electoral volatility in weak party systems (e.g., Roberts and Wibbels 1999). Nevertheless, situating this factor primarily on the supply side seems apt, given its direct role in creating opportunities for political alternatives to compete. That it might have an additional role on the demand side does not alter its importance on the supply side.

If weakly institutionalized party systems can explain the presence of populists, then this condition should be considered a necessary causal factor. Without the supply, citizens would have no populist candidate to support. Of course, a political actor might interpret a certain public mood as a kind of demand for populism and, in turn, choose to use a populist strategy despite the presence of a strong party system (more on this effect later). However, such a situation is likely to be exceptional and the politician's effort unsuccessful. Obviously, supply alone cannot account for public support, and so this factor is not individually sufficient to explain populism. To reach sufficiency, the demand side must come into the equation.

The Demand Side

On the demand side are the factors that cause citizens to feel angry about the status quo and thus inclined to vote for a candidate who uses antiestablishment appeals and plebiscitarian linkages. These factors are the perception that the political class is corrupt and information that can be construed as evidence of disadvantageous effects of its behavior (i.e., indicators that some other group, foreign or domestic, is receiving benefits at the expense of ordinary citizens). This combination generates a sense of unfairness, which causes voters to become angry with the political establishment and, in turn, willing to vote for populists. A few of these points require explanation.

With respect to corruption, one should note that the perception of its existence, by itself, is insufficient to lead voters into the arms of populists. At first glance, some might find this assertion surprising, especially since a large literature demonstrates the corrosive effects of corruption on the likes of trust, collective action, and political legitimacy (e.g., Mishler and Rose 2001; Morris 1991; Seligson 2002). That the perception of corruption would erode legitimacy might seem sufficient to lead citizens to cast their votes for political alternatives. However, studies that examine the impact of the perception of corruption on voting behavior show that although corruption may lead to the loss of support for incumbents (e.g., Welch and Hibbing 1997), it does not necessarily lead to higher support for challengers (e.g., Chong et al. 2011; Seawright 2012). Instead, citizens may simply withdraw from electoral participation. Declining electoral support for ruling parties therefore may be matched by declining support for all competitors (e.g., McCann and Domínguez 1998).

Furthermore, citizens often support corrupt politicians. A number of studies, for instance, show how clientelism can help politicians generate or maintain political support (e.g., Bratton and van de Walle 1994; Clapham 1982; Rundquist, Strom, and Peters 1977), even in systems that use the secret ballot (e.g., Brusco, Nazareno, and Stokes 2004; Stokes 2005). The logic is simple: corruption may provide parties or politicians with the means to incentivize voter choice. In exchange for material benefits, citizens may return the favor in the form of political support. Hetherington's (2011, 49) description of Lino Oviedo's spin on corruption in Paraguay is instructive:

> Oviedo used a different meaning of corruption, accusing political leaders of reneging on private promises to followers. In using this strategy, Oviedo understood that if people believe in his charismatic aura enough, and trusted that he would direct resources toward them, he would be impervious to the accusations of corruption that he slung at his opponents.

In other words, corruption would be construed negatively only when politicians failed to distribute the proceeds. The lesson is that one should not expect the perception of corruption, alone, to cause citizens to vote for populists.

This conclusion begs the questions of why and when corruption would affect populism. First, one needs to realize citizens' concern about corruption competes with other issues and does not automatically trump them. Voters weigh considerations of corrupt activity against partisan and policy preferences (e.g., Peters and Welch 1978). Their preferences, additionally, may be more intense for things beyond honest government (Rundquist and Hansen 1976). One such issue may involve the receipt of material rewards. Research shows that citizens will support governments they believe to be corrupt if they receive tangible benefits (Manzetti and Wilson 2007). On the other hand, political support "declines considerably" if the corrupt governments fail to distribute rewards (Manzetti and Wilson 2007, 963). Put somewhat differently, the receipt of benefits mediates the impact of corruption.

Several recent studies add important nuances to this story by revealing further mediating factors, including corruption victimization and the kinds of corruption (e.g., Klašnja, Tucker, and Deegan-Krause 2014; Seligson 2006). For instance, Daniel W. Gingerich (2009) finds that low levels of exposure to corruption (victimization) have no impact on political behavior, but the opposite is true for high levels of exposure where responsibility is clear. In these circumstances, individuals are motivated to protest. Adding still more nuance, Marko Klašnja, Joshua Tucker, and Kevin Deegan-Krause (2014) divide corruption into pocketbook and sociotropic kinds: the former involves personal experiences and the latter involves perceptions of corruption on society. The impact of the two kinds on voting depends on the level of certainty about the corruption. Certainty is high in the former case because pocketbook corruption involves personal experience. Sociotropic corruption does not, however, and so its impact on voting behavior can vary. The authors find "that sociotropic corruption voting may require credible or very strong signals" (Klašnja, Tucker, and Deegan-Krause 2014, 23). Their work builds on research demonstrating that information about corruption influences voters' decisions (e.g., Chong et al. 2011).

These findings help answer the question of when corruption might play a role in the rise of populism: with the right combination of mediating factors, corruption can have an impact. Specifically, it can have an effect on individuals' voting behavior even if they are not personally the victims of corruption but see credible signs of corruption. However, these signs must demonstrate some disadvantage resulting from the corrupt activity; as highlighted above, corruption by itself is insufficient and corruption that produces benefits can generate or maintain political support. Therefore, for evidence of corruption to have an impact, it must demonstrate some resultant disadvantage.

Different kinds of information may be interpreted as credible evidence of disadvantageous outcomes. Any of the following could be seen as evidence of corruption: a high level of foreign economic influence suggesting the country is being "sold out" to international interests, high-profile judicial proceedings against politicians accused of embezzling tax revenues,[8] or even negative evidence in the sense that the political system provides little or nothing for ordinary citizens. Evidence comes in two general forms, nevertheless: information that seems to indicate that someone else is the beneficiary, and information that suggests simply that the concerned individual is not the beneficiary. In either case, a reasonable conclusion is that the corrupt system is producing outcomes that are to a particular voter's relative disadvantage, and the result is a perception of unfairness.

How does one know that a combination of factors affects the vote and not the disadvantage by itself? The reason comes from the studies showing objective deprivation alone is not sufficient to affect behavior. For instance, studies on the correlation of socioeconomic status and voting suggest political disengagement among the poor rather than action to effect change (e.g., Leighley and Nagler 1992; Lijphart 1997; Lipset 1960). In addition, abject conditions such as poverty do not necessarily lead to collective protest (e.g., Tarrow 1998). Recent research, moreover, indicates that declining economic circumstances in either objective or subjective terms did not lead to the "left turn" in Latin America but rather improving circumstances or assessments (e.g., Remmer 2012). The political salience of any other form of deprivation depends on the presence of other conditions, whether availability of resources, organizational capacities, or opportunities. This line of reasoning lends support to the notion that the combination of corruption and disadvantage is associated with changes in voting behavior.

Still unaddressed is the causal linkage between these factors. Why would corruption and evidence of disadvantage cause a change in voting behavior? One might posit that the answer is simple self-interested rationality: corruption's victims seek a change to remedy the material disadvantage. As indicated above, however, objective deprivation is insufficient by itself to cause a change in behavior. As such, there is more to the story than material concerns, and so a strict rational choice assumption is not appropriate here. Instead, the argument is that emotions play a role: a corrupt system that disadvantages ordinary people is seen as unfair. This assessment makes people angry and can influence their voting behavior.

Though no direct indicators can be found to demonstrate the level of anger among the voters of Latin America,[9] the literature contains ample support for making these links. Research shows, in the first place, that assessments of fairness have an impact across a range of evaluations and behaviors (e.g., Albin and Druckman 2012; Gibson 2002; Mutz and Mondak 1997). Ethan B. Kapstein (2008), for one, argues that issues of fairness are crucial for social cooperation, to the extent that great powers "sometimes eschew narrow, self-interested maximization strategies" in negotiating international agreements (245). Numerous studies also show the connections between emotions and political behavior (e.g., Brader 2006; Goodwin, Jasper, and Polletta 2001; Huddy, Feldman, and Cassese 2007; Marcus and MacKuen 1993; Rudolph, Gangl, and Stevens 2000). Ted Brader (2005), for instance, finds that emotionally evocative ads "change the manner in which voters make choices" (402), and he concludes that emotions have a causal role. As another example, Elisabeth Jean Wood (2003) argues that participation in El Salvador's rebellion by campesinos, who did not stand to gain materially, can be explained by emotional considerations. Additionally, anger has an impact. Many studies show that anger, as opposed to fear or anxiety, leads citizens to engage in political activity, including demonstrations and mobilizations (e.g., Best and Krueger 2011; Smith, Cronin, and Kessler 2008). This wealth of political science literature is helpful indeed, but to get an even better handle on the reasons for these connections, I turn to the discipline of psychology.

Microfoundations

The social and organizational psychology literatures provide microfoundations that support the previous explanation for populism, both for individuals' emotional response and their resultant behavior. With respect to voters' feelings of being treated unfairly, a central tenet of equity theory is that the perception of an injustice produces emotional distress (Adams 1965; Austin and Walster 1974).[10] As J. Stacy Adams (1965) writes, "there can be little doubt that inequity can result in dissatisfaction, in an unpleasant emotional state" (283). Emotional reactions, in turn, can shape how people make decisions (e.g., Damasio 1994; Eagly and Chaiken 1993; Lerner and Keltner 2000, 2001). For psychologists, this phenomenon is hardly surprising, but it can run against assumptions of self-interested rationality. Individual attitudes and behavior often defy expectations generated by rational choice models. I do not wish to suggest that self-interest is irrelevant but instead that one's understanding of self-interest can be shaped, mediated, accompanied, or subsumed by other factors. In short, emotional states play key roles in shaping attitudes and behaviors, and they do so in predictable ways.

Two important schools of thought further the understanding of the evaluations and effects of inequity (see Tyler and Smith 1998). The theory of distributional justice, for one, suggests that satisfaction and behavior are linked not to objective standards but instead based on a comparison between outcomes received and those judged to be equitable (e.g., Adams 1965; Greenberg 1982; Walster, Walster, and Berscheid 1978). Simply put, those who feel underbenefited deem the outcome to be unfair and become upset as a result. Individuals evaluate outcomes using a variety of distributive justice principles and criteria. One, and perhaps the most important, involves social relations (e.g., Deutsch 1975). In other words, the nature and quality of the relationship—and not a strict view of material self-interest—can shape whether or to what extent the outcomes are considered fair.

Another school of thought, procedural justice theory, emphasizes not the outcomes per se but the judgments about the decisionmaking process that produced them (e.g., Leventhal 1980; Thibaut and Walker 1975; Tyler, Rasinski, and McGraw 1985). Much of this literature deals with workplace settings and issues of dispute resolution, but some also extends to the realm of politics. Tom R. Tyler (2001), as an example, argues that legitimacy is almost entirely shaped by perceptions of procedural fairness. As with distributive justice, individuals use several criteria to judge procedural fairness. Among the most cited are consistency in how decisions are reached, the suppression of personal biases in decisionmaking, compatibility with moral and ethical values, and the trustworthiness of the authority (see Tyler 1988). Where decisionmakers appear to be inconsistent, biased, unethical, or untrustworthy, individuals will likely consider the process to be unfair. From this perspective, the process is more important than the outcome, including self-interested material gain.

Though some debate exists about the relative influence of individuals' judgments of decisionmaking processes and outcome fairness, many highlight the interaction between them (e.g., Cropanzano and Ambrose 2001). Perceptions of procedural justice, for example, can influence evaluations of the equity of the distribution (e.g., Tyler 1990). Additionally, Howard M. Weiss, Kathleen Suckow, and Russell Cropanzano (1999) show that happiness has to do entirely with outcome; that is, those who receive a positive outcome even from an unfair system report being happy. Weiss, Suckow, and Cropanzano (1999) also show, however, that anger is the result of the combination of an unfavorable outcome and a biased procedure. That people make distributive and procedural justice evaluations at the individual, group, and social or macro levels also bears noting (e.g., Azzi 1993; Brickman et al. 1981; Wenzel 2004). In other words, individuals make these judgments not only when the processes and outcomes affect them on a personal level but also on a group or even societal level. In short, and to put this in terms of the theory advanced here, when people benefit, individually or as a group, from corruption they are unlikely to feel distressed even if the process is unfair. By contrast, when they, individually or as a group, are disadvantaged by a corrupt system, they will be angry.[11]

Does the anger or distress over perceived unfairness affect behavior? Again, equity theory suggests that it does: the distressed emotional state motivates individuals to work toward restoring justice (Crosby 1976; Mark and Folger 1984). This tendency applies to both those that are unfairly advantaged and those unfairly disadvantaged. Those that are advantaged may resort to psychological strategies of restoring equity by justifying their status (e.g., Lerner 1981; Taylor and Moghaddam 1994). At times, though, they may also attempt to restore actual equity, which can involve a sacrifice of material self-interest (e.g., Montada 1991).

The disadvantaged are a more complicated group, perhaps especially since they often do nothing to restore equity (e.g., Major 1994; Martin 1986). According to John T. Jost and colleagues (2003), those who suffer the most are the least likely to challenge the injustice, and "members of disadvantaged groups are even more likely than members of more advantaged groups to provide ideological support for the very social system that is responsible for their disadvantages" (30). These scholars argue that a kind of dissonance accounts for their findings. This line of research is consistent with the work in political science demonstrating that poverty or objective deprivation alone does not affect behavior.

Nevertheless, several factors mediate this tendency. Among them are two relevant for the present argument: the clarity of the injustice and the perceptions of how the injustice was produced (e.g., Lind et al. 1993; Taylor and Moghaddam 1994). The disadvantaged, in other words, are more likely to act if the reality of the injustice cannot be distorted—the evidence is plain to see—or if the decisionmaking procedure that produced the outcome is considered to be unjust. These findings support the corruption literature that shows behavioral responses to be influenced by not only the perception of corruption but the clarity of evidence thereof.

The behavioral response can take a number of forms. The most likely "active" response is to seek redress from the person responsible for the injustice and, if that step proves insufficient, to turn to a third party for help (Tyler and Smith 1998). Jerald Greenberg (1987) also finds that individuals are more likely to take action when the procedural source of the injustice is not an individual but a broader entity, such as an organization. In what would seem a logical further conclusion, where a single politician is corrupt, behavioral responses to an injustice are unlikely, but when the political class or political system is to blame, a behavioral response is likely. This response, moreover, can take the form of collective action. Ursula Dibble (1981), for instance, finds individuals will act collectively to restore equity when they believe both that a procedural injustice has taken place and that they personally suffered from the outcome. Heather J. Smith and Daniel J. Ortiz (2002) argue collective action results when individuals identify as part of a group and that group perceives an injustice. The point is that either individual or collective assessments of injustice can produce behavioral responses.

The psychological literature, in short, helps explain why the perception of corruption or the status of objective deprivation, individually, may be inadequate to cause a change in voting behavior. It also helps explain why the combination will affect behavior. When individuals receive a positive outcome from an unfair, corrupt process, they will not be angry. However, a negative distribution and clear evidence of an injustice do cause anger and are likely to affect behavior, both individually and collectively. Finally, as has been demonstrated in the political science literature, angry voters are likely to try to oust those responsible by choosing candidates not associated with the political establishment (Kostadinova 2009; Seawright 2012). The wealth of research should provide confidence in this mechanism linking causes to outcomes, even if it cannot be demonstrated directly.

Why Choose a Populist?

The judgment of unfairness and the emotional response of anger lead people to change their voting preferences, but why would they choose a populist? First, recall that this argument considers the supply side as well. In other words, for the present purposes one should not view the impact of corruption and disadvantage in isolation from the impact of party system institutionalization. The combination of these factors can explain electoral support for populism. Hence, when this combination occurs, citizens will have the opportunity to choose a populist. In some cases, however, other kinds of political alternatives are also present, whether newcomers, outsiders, or mavericks, as is explored in Chapter 6. Under these circumstances, voters will typically abandon the political establishment, which they hold responsible for the unfairness. So all of the political alternatives will likely benefit electorally, at least to some extent.

Still, populists may be particularly well situated to gain because of the combination of antiestablishment appeals and plebiscitarianism. First, these appeals are well suited to generate support in these circumstances. Markus Wagner (2014) finds that individuals are likely to get angry when they hold an external actor responsible for some crisis or problem; that effect is enhanced when that actor was supposed to care for the individuals' welfare. This conclusion can be applied to political parties, charged with representing citizens' interests. Recall, too, Greenberg's (1987) findings that citizens are more likely to take action when the blame lies not with a single individual but some broader entity. Herein lies the genius of the us-versus-them appeal: populism blames a group (the political establishment) for failing to take care of the needs of ordinary citizens. According to the literature, this message is tailor made to tap into the emotional state of angry voters, but not all outsiders, newcomers, and other political challengers use appeals of this nature.

Additionally, part of populism's appeal is reformist in nature. Antiestablishment appeals criticize the political class as having failed to tend to the needs and interests of ordinary citizens and, in turn, imply that changes are necessary. Not coincidentally, these appeals are often accompanied by grand promises of greater inclusion, economic empowerment, and so forth. The rhetoric of "refounding" the nation so common to the recent populists is indicative of this point. Combined with plebiscitarianism, this message suggests an enhanced level of responsibility (and accountability) for improving the lives of ordinary citizens. The top-down and personalistic nature of these linkages leaves little doubt that resolution rests in the hands of a single individual, not a party or group. To put it slightly differently, the reformist message of populism is not set in the passive tense: "Things can be fixed." The message instead is "*I* can fix them." (See Chapter 7 for further discussion of this point.)

This pairing of antiestablishment appeals and plebiscitarianism is the core of populism, and it sets populists apart from other kinds of political alternatives. When voters are angry at the perceived unfairness of the status quo, they turn to third parties for help. Candidates considered alternatives because of their newness to electoral politics or lack of association with established parties do not use the same combination of antiestablishment appeals and plebiscitarian linkages. As such, they do not offer the same sort of solution. When voters consider the political options, then, the populist candidate may appear to be the best-suited "third party" to resolve the unfairness that generated their anger in the first place.

This line of thought suggests another reason why angry voters would turn to populists: populists are the ones that cultivate and amplify these emotions. If they benefit from voters' emotional state in the first place, by enhancing that emotional state, they are likely to benefit even more. Their appeals place blame for problems, often especially corruption, at the feet of the political class, thus framing the context. In so doing, they enhance the saliency of both the problems faced by ordinary citizens and the responsibility of the established parties.

A wide body of research shows the impact of framing on public opinion (for discussions see, e.g., Chong and Druckman 2007; Kahneman and Tversky 2000). Studies also show that exposure and media coverage of corruption increase its saliency and do so independently of the actual level of corruption (e.g., Grigorescu 2006; Rose and Mishler 2007). Additionally, whereas corruption alone can lead to withdrawal from participation, the identification of responsible actors helps increase the likelihood of action (e.g., Gingerich 2009; Tavits 2007). Populism takes advantage of these dynamics. The antiestablishment appeals serve as framing techniques, calling attention to unfair processes and outcomes and clearly identifying the responsible group. These steps will raise the saliency of these issues and thus likely enhance the emotional and behavioral responses. As the ones calling attention to the problems and offering a solution, the populist candidates would be well positioned to benefit.

Mass Movements

Perhaps tangentially, the psychology literature and attention to populists' framing techniques may also help account for the mass movement character of some cases as well as their political potency. Put somewhat differently, one can understand why the most successful cases of populism (but not all of them) could be described as social movements—examples of collective action. The research shows, firstly, that group identification can affect a range of individual attitudes and assessment, including issues of fairness and equity (e.g., Azzi 1992; Clayton and Opotow 2003; Wenzel 2002). This conclusion applies to both assessments of distributive and procedural justice. Writing of the latter, Tyler and Steven Blader (2000) argue that concerns about the fairness of group decisionmaking procedures have an impact on personal motivations, and those "procedural justice judgments have more influence on people's attitudes and behaviors than do their assessments of their personal self-interest" (10). When individuals identify with a group, furthermore, group-level assessments can have greater impact on attitudes and behaviors than individual-level assessments (e.g., Brewer and Kramer 1986; van Zomeren et al. 2004). Behaviorally, the impact includes participation in forms of collective action. When the disadvantage or inequity is understood as a group phenomenon, people "may be more willing to challenge the inequity. Not only might people feel less devastated by a disadvantage they interpret in intergroup terms, they may actually feel more empowered to deal with it" (Smith and Ortiz 2002, 111).

The psychological research also shows an interesting interaction between group-based anger and collective action, thus supporting related findings in the political science literature. That anger makes people optimistic about risk estimates and more willing to engage in risk-acceptance behavior is well known (e.g., Lerner and Keltner 2001; Lerner et al. 2003). When accompanied by group identification, this effect may contribute to the likelihood of collective action. Multiple lines of research in psychology, including relative deprivation theory, social identity theory, and intergroup emotion theory, predict collective action on the grounds of group-based assessments (see van Zomeren et al. 2004 for a discussion). Collective disadvantage drives collective action because anger leads to action.[12] As Diane M. Mackie, Thierry Devos, and Eliot R. Smith (2000) write, "anger is a potent predictor of offensive action tendencies" (613). Importantly, this group-based anger leads to actions that challenge the status quo (or the outgroup responsible for the disadvantage), including forms of protest, like demonstrations and mobilizations (e.g., Mackie, Devos, and Smith 2000; van Zomeren et al. 2004). Smith, Tracey Cronin, and Thomas Kessler (2008) find that group-based anger increased the likelihood of collective protest even among faculty members in response to pay inequities. In sum, both group identification and group-based anger contribute to collective action, including forms of which that challenge the status quo.

These points relate to populism through the influence of framing. Specifically, the us-versus-them dynamic of populist appeals not only chastises the political establishment but also lionizes the people. These appeals thus identify and help create an in-group (victims who should be angry) and an out-group (those responsible). Among its effects, framing can influence self-perception and collective identity formation (e.g., Brewer and Gardner 1996; Hunt, Benford, and Snow 1994). As the discourse approach to populism highlights, a key aspect of the phenomenon is the creation of antagonistic identities (e.g., Laclau 2005a; Panizza 2005). In short, the populist strategy taps into these interactions of identities, judgments, emotions, and behaviors identified by the psychology literature. Hence, the most skilled populists can generate group-based identities and group-based anger, thus propelling their supporters to engage in collective action. For this reason, populism is often (and rightly) associated with mass demonstrations and "crowd action," and thus is sometimes defined as a movement. Examples like Perón and Chávez, who could gather hundreds of thousands of people in enormous and public displays of support, appear to uphold this view. Though other factors may lead followers to engage in this sort of activity, the psychological literature explains an important part of it.

Not all populists are so successful at building large and loyal follow-ings. One can find the likes of perennial candidate Álvaro Noboa, who has run for Ecuador's presidency four times but has yet to gain a large enough following to propel him into office. Furthermore, there are the likes of lit-tle-known candidates such as Bolivia's Ivo Kuljis, or the many populists who never go beyond local or regional politics. The strategic understanding of populism recognizes these individuals as members of the category; they are simply less successful than some of their better-known counterparts. Incidentally, the agency-level factor of political or leadership skill is most pertinent here: generating a mass movement requires an unusual level of talent. Skillful politicians may be able to do so and, as a result, also develop an enormous amount of political power. The ability to stage mass demon-strations is a visible display of that power and one that can make opponents think twice. The prospect of having supporters rewrite and approve consti-tutions is a level of strength that can overwhelm institutional and other con-straints. In other words, populism can result in enormous power held by a single individual, and this potential potency is exactly why many find it so interesting.

Conclusion

In this chapter, I present an explanation for the electoral support of Latin America's third-era populists. The combination of three factors—weakly institutionalized party systems, prevalence of corruption, and evidence of disadvantage—can account for both the supply of and demand for pop-ulists. The level of party system institutionalization affects the incentive and opportunity structure for politicians. When party systems are weak, candidates stand to gain by distancing themselves from the political estab-lishment and using means of linkages that highlight personal connections and pinpointed accountability.

The dual perceptions of corruption and disadvantage, meanwhile, trig-ger assessments of unfairness and a desire to rectify it. The psychology lit-erature provides substantial support for this relationship. It shows that indi-viduals judge distributions and procedures in ways independent of strict self-interested calculations, that assessments of unfairness cause anger, that anger leads to action, and that these effects are amplified when conceived in group terms. This explanation is not, strictly speaking, a simple story of haves and have-nots or of subaltern groups seeking improvements to their absolute conditions. Instead, the process involves emotional reactions to corrupt practices that come at the relative expense of one's group. Voters are likely to challenge the political establishment in these circumstances. And because populism is inherently reformist and helps to frame these issues, voters may support the populist candidate as a means of resolving the unfairness.

Though populism in other eras or regions may result from a similar dynamic, the scope of this argument is limited to recent cases of Latin American populism. One may expect, nevertheless, that any instance of populism in an electoral context emerges because of both supply and demand factors. Additionally, a full understanding of voters' motives in other contexts may require an examination of psychological dynamics. A wealth of studies from the organizational and social psychology literature, not to mention sociology and political science, highlights the role of subjective assessments and emotions and thus casts doubt on the utility of rational choice assumptions. Although predictions based on rational choice assumptions sometimes turn out to be accurate, their unbounded application is not warranted. In short, context matters (Druckman 2004). In contemporary Latin America, many countries have experienced persistently high levels of perceived corruption, party system weakness, and other representational shortcomings, as well as other issues such as inadequate social spending and the perception of excessive foreign economic influence. This, then, is the context in which the present argument makes sense, but circumstances can change. For instance, one may speculate that even if anger is always a key component in the demand for populism, the causes of that anger may vary. Even in the present context, the argument is that corruption and some evidence of disadvantage can account for the demand side, but what constitutes evidence may vary.

These possibilities highlight an assumption of equifinality. In this study, in other words, I recognize the prospect that more than one path may lead to populism. By acknowledging this assumption, I also must acknowledge that equifinality is possible not only among eras or regions but also within them. Most of the studies in the populism literature include multiple factors in explaining the emergence of one or more cases of populism. Perhaps this phenomenon does in fact have multiple causes. Still, if one reduces explanations to unique circumstances, then little if any knowledge is gained; some level of generalization is necessary even if it requires simplification. The method used in Chapter 5 is well suited in this regard. QCA facilitates modest levels of generalization, and it does so by testing not only individual factors but also all of their possible combinations. In this way, it can account for the leading singular causes identified in the literature as well as the many causal combinations the literature also offers. This analysis, nevertheless, offers support for the one causal combination presented in the present chapter. First, though, I turn to the case of Bolivia. A careful investigation of its dynamics shows exactly how these factors developed and interacted and thus led to the rise of Bolivia's case of contemporary populism.

Notes

1. Excluded are the many studies of the classical populist period that highlighted the level or stage of economic development as the primary cause (e.g., di Tella 1965; Germani 1974; Vilas 1992–1993). The emergence of neopopulism in a distinct developmental stage largely, though not entirely (e.g., Schamis 2006), put this view to rest (see Roberts 1995; Weyland 1996).

2. An observation is an election in a given country, and the data have a one-year lag to illustrate conditions in place prior to the election (i.e., 2006 data will be analyzed for a 2007 election).

3. Recall that the term *populist candidate* refers to a politician who relies primarily on the strategy of populism.

4. Exceptions include Roberts (2007) and Weyland (1999). Of the neopopulist wave, Roberts (2007) writes, "The combination of social exclusion and institutional frailty re-emerged to provide both incentives and a favorable political opportunity structure for new populist movements" (9). He goes on to explain, however, that there have been diverse political responses to the contemporary context, not all of them populist. This point reintroduces a supply-side question: What explains the presence of populist alternatives in some cases but not in others? Weyland (1999) highlights institutional characteristics as supply-side factors but limits their role to that of permissive conditions, not causes.

5. He goes on to suggest that extraordinary leadership is the supply-side factor that helps explain successful populist movements (Hawkins 2010). Conaghan (2011) similarly emphasizes agency when she explains the importance of Correa's effective campaigning.

6. Others suggest that the rise of populists can be the death knell of party systems, as appears to have happened in Peru and Venezuela. To be clear, though, the sequence put forth here is slightly different: first comes weakness of party systems, and then come the incentives to use a populist strategy. Whether the election of a populist subsequently kills the party system is a topic beyond the scope of this study.

7. As noted in an earlier chapter, I am not suggesting that populists have no organizational backing; many have. Rather, whatever level of organization exists, it serves the populist leader by facilitating these linkages (or at least the appearance of them). It does not, in other words, have an autonomy or independent identity apart from the populist.

8. Klašnja, Tucker, and Deegan-Krause (2014), however, find the impact of corruption scandals on voting behavior is often overstated.

9. Researchers typically illustrate the public's mood through qualitative indicators, though some use data on protests and demonstration (e.g., Bellinger and Arce 2011). Still, no means have been discovered of directly demonstrating society-wide emotional conditions.

10. The terms *inequity* and *injustice* are treated synonymously.

11. These theories are closely related to that of relative deprivation, and all may be considered members of the field of social justice (see Tyler and Smith 1998). A key distinction, though, is that relative deprivation theory concerns outcomes relative to an individual's or group's expected outcomes. The logic articulated here does not necessarily concern expectations but rather revealed inequities. For recent reviews on relative deprivation, see Walker and Smith (2002), and Smith et al. (2012).

12. The sociology literature also highlights the role that emotions play in social movements. For a discussion, see Jasper (2011).

4

Populism in Bolivia

EVO MORALES'S ASSUMPTION OF THE BOLIVIAN PRESIDENCY IN 2006 WAS a watershed moment for the country for multiple reasons. Not only was he Bolivia's first indigenous president, despite the country's having a majority indigenous population, but also he was the first candidate in modern times to receive a majority of the popular vote.[1] Additionally, he was the country's first modern populist president. His rise is the subject of this chapter.

In some respects, Bolivia might seem a most likely case for populism, given its enduring poverty (the poorest in South America) and historic political instability (on average heads of state have served for less than one year). Since its tumultuous transition to democracy in the 1980s, moreover, the country and its voters have endured a number of troubles. It had the hemisphere's worst case of hyperinflation in 1985, when the inflation rate surpassed 20,000 percent. In an unfortunate coincidence, this change came on the heels of the collapse of the international price of tin, Bolivia's dominant export since 1900.[2] Some 20,000 miners lost their jobs. The response was the New Economic Policy, a version of shock therapy inspired by Jeffrey Sachs. In order to implement the policy, the government declared a state of siege, suspending constitutional guarantees. Though the New Economic Policy ended the hyperinflation, it caused other hardships for many and sparked series of social conflicts. Meanwhile, the major political parties converged around a neoliberal consensus, leaving voters of the political left and those formerly included through corporatist structures in uncharted waters. As the 1990s came and went, continued neoliberal policies and attacks on the domestic coca industry still failed to dislodge the traditional parties and pave the way for a populist to take office. The election of December 2005 changed that. In a context where no winning candidate since 1985 had received more than 36 percent of the vote, Morales's tally of 54 percent was staggering. He has repeated the feat twice since then, taking both the 2009 and 2014 elections with more than 60 percent of the vote.

If the tumult and difficulties of the 1980s and 1990s were insufficient to lead to a populist's election, what changed in the 2000s? What factors can account for populism's emergence starting in 2005? In brief, Bolivia's middling party system weakened over time, entering a crisis in the early 2000s and creating an opportunity for populists to present a serious challenge to the traditional parties. Voters, meanwhile, were dismayed not only with continued political corruption but also with economic deals that seemed to prioritize international actors' interests over the needs of ordinary people. Politicians, in other words, seemed to be selling out the country, and everyday Bolivians were paying the price. The appearance of political corruption at the expense of the people caused eruptions of anger, as illustrated by the water war of 2000 and the gas wars of 2003–2005, which led to the resignation of two presidents. By the election of 2005, the conditions were right for both the supply of and demand for populism.

In this chapter, I explore the causal factors leading to Morales's first victory. The chapter represents a single-country, qualitative study that uses a variety of kinds of data, including elite interviews. I try to place the 2005 election in its appropriate historical and political context and, in so doing, illustrate the logic articulated in the previous chapter.

Bolivia's Party System

With Bolivia's transition to democracy, three parties became the central players in the country's party system. The MNR, Bolivia's oldest, dates to the 1940s and began as a reformist movement created by Víctor Paz Estenssoro and Hernán Siles Zuazo. It played a central role in the 1952 revolution. Paz Estenssoro held the presidency three times prior to the authoritarian interlude (1964–1982) and took it again in 1985 (see Table 4.1, which lists the posttransition presidencies). The second-oldest party, the Revolutionary Left Movement (Movimiento de la Izquierda Revolucionaria [MIR]), appeared in 1971 under the leadership of Jaime Paz Zamora. Paz Zamora was its presidential candidate for most of the posttransition period, winning office in 1989. As for the Nationalist Democratic Action (Acción Democrática Nacionalista [ADN]), Hugo Banzer founded it in 1979, soon after the end of his dictatorship and as a part of the "democratic opening." Like Paz Zamora, he was his party's perennial candidate and he took office once, in 1997. However, he resigned in 2001 due to declining health and died in 2002.

These three parties had electoral competitors, but collectively they received a majority of the vote in each general election from 1985 through

Table 4.1 Bolivian Presidents

Years in Office	President	Party	Share of Vote (%)
1982–1985	Hernán Siles Zuazo	UDP	39 (1980)
1985–1989	Víctor Paz Estenssoro	MNR	30
1989–1993	Jaime Paz Zamora	MIR	22
1993–1997	Gonzalo Sánchez de Lozada	MNR	36
1997–2001	Hugo Banzer	ADN	22
2001–2002	Jorge Quiroga	ADN	N/A
2002–2003	Gonzalo Sánchez de Lozada	MNR	22
2003–2005	Carlos Mesa	None	N/A
2005–2006	Eduardo Rodríguez	None	N/A
2006–2010	Evo Morales	MAS	54
2010–2015	Evo Morales	MAS	64
2015–present	Evo Morales	MAS	61

1997. However, they lost this position beginning with the 2002 contests. Additionally, since earning a congressional majority was unheard of, they often formed governing coalitions, leading some to describe the political system as "parliamentarized presidentialism" (e.g., Centellas 2008). For instance, the MNR held the presidency in 1985 but teamed up with the ADN in the so-called Pact for Democracy. The ADN held the presidency in 1997 but had a coalition member in the MIR. These three, in short, defined Bolivia's party system.

Though not particularly well institutionalized, the party system not only had clearly defined components but also was reasonably stable. Nevertheless, Mainwaring and Scully classify it as inchoate in their 1995 volume. They argue Bolivian "party organizations are generally weak, electoral volatility is high, party roots in society are weak, and individual personalities dominate parties and campaigns" (Mainwaring and Scully 1995, 20). Strong personalities did dominate the parties' internal dynamics, especially in the cases of the ADN and MIR since their founders continued to lead them. Though the same could be said initially of the MNR, leadership did pass to a new generation (namely Gonzalo Sánchez de Lozada) after Paz Estenssoro's last presidency (1985–1989), suggesting some level of organizational stability. Additionally, the MNR was relatively well organized by comparison, and in 1990 it instituted internal democratic procedures.

Bolivia's parties were also seen to be relatively detached from society. Prior to 1997, citizens cast a single, closed-list vote for the presidency and both houses of the legislature. (From 1997 onward, one-half of the lower house has been elected from single-member districts where voters choose specific candidates.) Because none of the parties were internally democratic before 1990, the leadership decided who would occupy the party's proportion of the congressional seats. Representatives, as a result, owed their allegiance to the party elders, not to an electoral constituency. Consider that as late as 1995, according to a survey by the Centro de Investigación del Congreso, only 34.1 percent of congressmen believed their principal role (among multiple possible responses) was to represent their constituency; 90.7 percent assumed it was legislation (cited in Eyzaguirre Ll 1999, 88). This perspective, moreover, was not lost on the public. A 1990 survey, for example, showed that a mere 5 percent of Bolivians believed that political parties represented their interests (Gamarra 1994, 46–47). The implication was that politicians were free to operate according to the rules of clientelism, and citizens complained of inadequate representation.

In fact, the representational role of parties was always circumscribed. The 1952 revolution ushered into power the first mass-based party, the MNR, yet because of a formal power-sharing agreement, representation was largely the responsibility of the lead labor confederation, the Bolivian Workers Central (Central Obrera Boliviana [COB]). The arrangement between the MNR and COB became the basis for a division of labor, of sorts, with popular representation (albeit limited to workers) in the hands of the COB and state management in those of the political parties (Gamarra 1994, 65). Subsequently, years of instability and military rule thwarted the development of parties' representative role.

Nevertheless, one can dispute the conclusion that Bolivia's party system should be categorized as inchoate, at least prior to the early 2000s. R. A. Mayorga (1997), for one, makes the case that Bolivia's party system has been misclassified. He argues, first, that volatility in Bolivia was lower than in Brazil, Ecuador, and Peru, and, second, that most of the volatility could be found within blocs: the centrist bloc of the three main parties and a bloc of two outsider parties challenging the system (R. A. Mayorga 1997, 153). As Figure 4.1 illustrates, the three traditional parties collectively gained over 70 percent of the vote during the elections of the 1980s, over 50 percent during the 1990s, and then slipped to 42.2 percent in the first election of the 2000s, presaging their collapse in 2005. Despite the steady decline, their collective share of the vote was reasonably steady, certainly by regional standards.

R. A. Mayorga (1997) goes on to argue that despite the somewhat personalistic nature of Bolivia's parties, they were not removed from society: "The ADN and MNR have strongly personalized and authoritarian leaderships, but both have shown the ability to integrate distinctive social, economic, ethnocultural, and regional demands. Both, moreover, have displayed an extraordinary level of discipline in congress" (154). Similarly, Eduardo A. Gamarra and James M. Malloy (1995), in their contribution to the original Mainwaring and Scully volume, note that most of the political problems in Bolivia "hinge on the dynamics of the parties. As a result, par-

Figure 4.1 Decline of the Traditional Party System

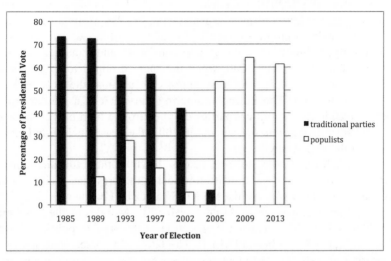

Notes: Traditional parties include vote totals for MNR, MIR, and ADN. It excludes Jorge Quiroga's campaigns with PODEMOS and PDC. Populists include vote totals for Carlos Palenque (CONDEPA), Max Fernández (UCS), Ivo Kuljis (UCS), Johnny Fernández (UCS), and Evo Morales (MAS).

See the List of Acronyms for the full names of these parties.

ties have always been in effect the main source of the problem of governance in Bolivia, and at the same time the only real source of any potential solution" (421). The parties, collectively, could tackle significant issues, including the hyperinflation of the 1980s, the privatization of state-owned industries (including the capitalization policy lauded by the World Bank), and decentralization (Morgan 2011, 227). In addition, when faced with the rise of the UCS and Conscience of the Fatherland (Conciencia de Patria [CONDEPA]), direct challengers to the establishment, the party system was strong enough to co-opt them by drawing them into governing coalitions and thus undermining their outsider credentials. As imperfect as the party system was, in other words, its members remained indispensible. Though not terribly strong, Bolivia's party system prior to 2000 was hardly on the verge of collapse. Indeed, for much of the posttransition period, it was "showing increasing levels of institutionalization" (Sanchez 2008, 323).

After the turn of the century, however, Bolivia's party system weakened substantially, a process of "decomposition" in R. A. Mayorga's (2006) telling. The country's scores on the party system institutionalization index used later in this book (see Chapter 5 and Appendix 1) confirm this impression. Briefly, the scale is an extension of Mainwaring and Scully's

(1995) index in that it captures changes over time, and the data for the region from 1996 to 2010 range from 27.1 to 75.3, with higher scores representing greater levels of institutionalization. In 1996, Bolivia's score was 51.37, narrowly earning the classification of an institutionalized party system. It dipped slightly the following year to 50.41 and remained between 50 and 51 until the year 2000, when the score dropped to 47.18. From there it continued to decline, reaching 40.79 in 2004, the year prior to Morales's election. The Latinobarómetro's survey tells a similar story: public confidence in political parties dropped from a high of 21.6 percent in 1997 steadily down to 6.4 percent in 2003, the year Sánchez de Lozada resigned the presidency.[3]

More telling are the electoral results. In 2002, the traditional parties came the closest since the transition to losing the presidency. The results were a virtual three-way tie: the MNR's Sánchez de Lozada received 22.46 percent, barely above the 20.94 percent for Evo Morales of the MAS and the 20.91 percent for Manfred Reyes Villa of the New Republican Force (Nueva Fuerza Republicana [NFR]). The latter candidates were not only appearing in their first presidential contests but also representing new parties.[4] With no candidate receiving a majority, Bolivian electoral law required the newly elected Congress to decide between the top two candidates. Morales had previously announced that he would not negotiate with any other parties to form a government, which gave Sánchez de Lozada an edge in the congressional negotiations. After difficult talks, Sánchez de Lozada secured the votes through a coalition with the MIR and UCS (Singer and Morison 2004). According to Armando de la Parra, a former representative from Cochabamba, the results and the somewhat odd coalition were the clearest signs to date that "the old system was dying" (interview with author, July 7, 2009). Still, an old party held on to power—at least temporarily.

The following year, President Sánchez de Lozada resigned his post in the face of intractable social conflicts. The position passed to his vice president, Carlos Mesa, who held no party affiliation. For this reason, some argue the government's collapse marked the "end of the traditional parties" (Senator Tito Hoz de Vila, interview with author, July 8, 2009). Mesa, the new president, faced the same sort of resistance, and, in 2005, he, too, resigned. Early elections were held in December of that year, when Morales received 53.74 percent of the vote—the first majority in the popular vote since the country's transition to democracy. His closest competitor was Jorge Quiroga from the new party Social Democratic Power (Poder Democrático Social [PODEMOS]), which garnered 28.6 percent.[5] The MNR, meanwhile, received 6.5 percent of the vote, and neither the ADN nor the MIR appeared on the ballot. The party system had effectively collapsed (Morgan 2011).

Sources of Decline

The dramatic decline in the condition of Bolivia's party system at the turn of the century had several causes. The cumulative effect of persistent governance problems (R. A. Mayorga 2006), along with programmatic decline (Morgan 2011), widened the gap between parties and those they were supposed to represent. As noted, the parties did implement a variety of significant policies and handled serious issues during the posttransition period. Nevertheless, these steps failed to resolve fundamental problems. Data from the World Bank demonstrate the broad point: from the late 1990s until 2005, the Bolivian government's effectiveness rating declined rapidly, from a high of –0.06 in 1998 to a low of –0.68 in 2005 (see Figure 4.2).

Ineffective governance becomes problematic for a party system when poor performance extends beyond a single administration and governing party and involves a variety of state functions, such as maintaining security or management of state resources. Key among these concerns are socioeconomic conditions. Although Bolivia's economic problems may have deeply rooted historical and structural sources, the failure of the state to remedy them in any significant way contributed to the declining confidence citizens had in their representatives. According to the World Bank, Bolivia is the poorest country in South America with a per capita GDP of US$1,020 in

Figure 4.2 Bolivian Government Effectiveness Scores

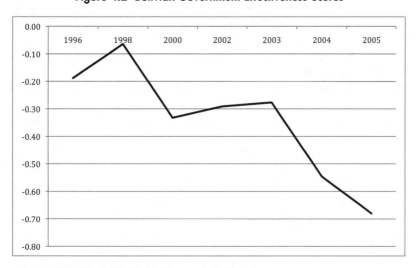

Source: World Bank, Worldwide Governance Indicators.
Note: The data range from –2.5 (least effective) to 2.5 (most effective). A value of 0 indicates the average of the world sample.

2005, the year of Morales's first election. This figure had hardly changed since 1980, when it was US$845. In fact, only after Morales's election has the country experienced any substantial per capita economic growth. At least by this measure, the Bolivian majority's standard of living was static for most of the posttransition period. By regional standards, additionally, the country appeared to be doing slightly worse over time: its per capita GDP was approximately one-third the value of the regional average in 1978; by 2006 it had dropped to 27 percent of the regional average. More specifically, what modest growth the country experienced in the early 1990s eroded around the turn of the century. Per capita GDP grew by slightly over 2 percent per year between 1994 and 1998, but declined by 1.65 percent in 1999. From that year through 2003, the average growth was –0.074 percent.

Meanwhile, more and more citizens had to find work in the informal sector. In 1996, when urban unemployment was 3.8 percent, the share of workers employed in the informal sector was 56.9 percent, according to the International Labor Organization (ILO). That portion rose to 64.3 percent in 1999 and has remained above 60 percent since then, averaging 64.8 percent from 1999 to 2005 (ILO 2014).[6] In addition, Bolivia's inequality and poverty indicators worsened through the 1990s. In terms of inequality, its Gini index, as estimated by the World Bank, in which a score of zero represents perfect equality and 100 represents perfect inequality, was a modest 42.04 in 1993 but deteriorated to 63 by 2000. It improved slightly after that, but stood at 58.47 in 2005, second to only Honduras in all of Latin America, the most unequal region of the world. Over 60 percent of the population lived under the national poverty line in 2005, and 28.2 percent lived on less than US$2 per day. These numbers were a slight improvement from 2000, but poverty had worsened dramatically through the 1990s, from a rate of 19.2 percent living on less than US$2 per day in 1990 to 37.6 percent in 2000. The situation was significantly worse for the country's indigenous population. One estimate puts the 2002 indigenous poverty rate at 74 percent, compared to 53 percent for the nonindigenous population (Jiménez Pozo, Landa Casazola, and Yañez Aguilar 2005).

These economic conditions existed despite the promise of neoliberal reforms. In response to a hyperinflationary episode in 1985, Paz Estenssoro initiated a draconian austerity program, dismantling the state-led economy he helped create decades earlier. The so-called New Economic Policy, which was issued by presidential decree (Decree no. 21060), immediately floated the exchange rate (bringing the rate from 67,000 bolivianos per US dollar to 1.1 million bolivianos per dollar), froze public sector wages, increased public sector prices, reduced spending on public investment, and implemented other budget austerity measures (Morales and Sachs 1990, 238–240). Subsequent measures included the elimination of price, wage, and interest rate controls; reductions in labor rights; and substantial reform to the tax code, policies encouraged by the IMF and other international actors. Collectively, these reforms were the most radical in the region, save for those in Chile (Kohl 2006, 305). Initiating this shift to neoliberalism required a state of siege and efforts to break the unions, such as sending labor leaders into internal exile. Despite organized labor's resistance, the longer-term result was the loss of political power and influence. Neoliberalism thus ended the virtual guarantee of stable employment for Bolivian workers as well as their means of corporatist representation in government (Barr 2005; Silva 2009, 109).

Despite the social and economic costs of the New Economic Policy, the three major parties all adopted neoliberal economic policies (Domingo 2001). The general market orientation remained steady under the administrations of the MNR (1985–1989, 1993–1997, 2002–2003), MIR (1989–1993), and ADN (1997–2002). Pressure from the IMF and other institutions played a role in this development, particularly as declining tax revenues left the state in greater need of assistance, thus increasing these outside institutions' leverage (Lopez Montaño 1997, 78). Consider that between 1980 and 1999, Bolivia was one of the top twenty recipients of IMF adjustment loans, receiving seventeen of them (in Latin America, only Mexico and Argentina received more), yet the annual per capita growth averaged –0.4 percent (Easterly 2005, 5). Still, the country's elite was committed to the new Washington Consensus. As Benjamin Kohl (2006) describes the situation, a neoliberal hegemony emerged in Bolivia "that balanced the demands of [international financial institutions] with those of a local elite committed to neoliberal ideology" (313).

Given the lack of progress for most Bolivians, voters became increasingly disenchanted with both the neoliberal policies and the parties responsible for them (Madrid 2011). In the eyes of many, the parties pursued these reforms despite their negative impact on ordinary Bolivians. In other words, the party system prioritized the wishes (demands) of international interests like the IMF over the needs of its own constituents. As Jana Morgan (2011) describes, the convergence around neoliberalism contributed to the party system's programmatic decline. In conjunction with the loss of corporatist forms of inclusion, a representational vacuum of sorts appeared. This lacuna presented an opportunity for political entrepreneurs.

Contributing to the programmatic decline and party system weakening was the government's push to eradicate coca, the source material for cocaine. As with neoliberal reforms, international pressure led traditional parties to adopt policies that were inconsistent with the interests of many ordinary Bolivians (Morgan 2011). The cultivation and consumption of coca (chewing the raw leaves, brewing tea, etc.) is a traditional part of life for Andean indigenous cultures. Coca also grew in importance during the

1980s and 1990s, when participation in the coca economy replaced many of the jobs lost during the economic restructuring. The collapse of Bolivia's tin industry in the mid-1980s, for instance, resulted in the migration of many former miners to the Chapare region to grow coca.[7] As the economy continued to shed formal sector jobs, more workers turned to coca.

In response to the growth of the coca agricultural sector, the United States began to pressure Bolivia to help fight its war on drugs. All of the posttransition governments felt this pressure and worked with the United States at least to some extent. For instance, the administration of Siles Zuazo created the Mobile Rural Patrol Unit (UMOPAR), a US-funded and trained police unit dedicated to drug interdiction. The Paz Estenssoro government followed up by participating in Operation Blast Furnace, in which US troops and military equipment supported Bolivian efforts to shut down coca processing. Bolivia's Congress had not authorized the presence of foreign troops, however, so the operation set off widespread complaints about the violation of Bolivian sovereignty (Ledebur 2005, 149).[8] The subsequent administration of Paz Zamora continued to support US eradication efforts: the president secretly approved direct US funding for the Bolivian army to fight narcotics trafficking. Next was Sánchez de Lozada, who adopted a plan called "zero option," which called for the full eradication of all surplus coca. His efforts toward this end resulted in massive protests from *cocaleros*, and he bowed to the domestic pressure and stopped actively eradicating coca (Thoumi 2003, 335).

However, Hugo Banzer and his vice president Jorge "Tuto" Quiroga, who finished out Banzer's term after he resigned for health reasons, gave no mixed signals regarding eradication. And, paradoxically, in this one area, the Bolivian government was quite effective. Banzer enacted his Dignity Plan to eliminate illegal coca production in five years and followed through by pursuing eradication much more vigorously and forcefully than his predecessors. His efforts against drug trafficking included the creation of the Expeditionary Task Force, supported by US funding. This unit was separate from the existing military and police structures, prompting some to label it a group of mercenaries. The Expeditionary Task Force was implicated, furthermore, in a number of human rights violations in its short lifespan (2001–2002). However, to the surprise of many, the program was largely successful: the government eliminated over 30,000 hectares of coca in the Chapare region alone, bringing the country close to the goal of zero coca (Ledebur 2005, 154–155).

In the 2002 campaign to elect Quiroga's successor, candidate Sánchez de Lozada indicated that he opposed forced eradication and the militarization of Bolivia's drug policy. However, the United States threatened the withdrawal of aid and he backtracked. On October 23, 2003, Larry Rohter reported in the *New York Times* that Sánchez de Lozada had met with President George W. Bush asking for financial assistance to help the coca farmers who would lose their livelihood because of eradication. Otherwise, he said, "I may be back here in a year, this time seeking political asylum." Bush responded by saying that all heads of state have problems, and he wished his Bolivian counterpart good luck.

Collectively, these successive administrations, involving all three of the traditional parties, pursued antinarcotics policies that, in the eyes of many Bolivians, appeared to benefit the United States more than their own country. This "low-intensity war" against the producers of coca had an impact that extended far beyond the *cocaleros* and affected a broad segment of Bolivia's population (Quintana 2005, 12). Banzer, especially, underestimated the impact of his policies on ordinary citizens. The majority of coca production remains in the hands of independent family farms—roughly 70,000 of them—while another 300,000 Bolivians work in some aspect of the coca-processing industry. By some estimates, 10 percent of Bolivia's workforce was employed in coca-related activities in the 1990s (Williams 1999, 5). In addition to these groups are the perhaps millions who consume legal forms of coca. According to a former Bolivian congressman, when Banzer closed two important markets for coca leaf, the price rose 250 percent, harming most acutely the poor consumers. The same observer noted that because of the horizontal, small-scale nature of the industry and the widespread consumption of the product, the attempts to eradicate coca affected a broad swath of Bolivian society across roughly 70 percent of the country's territory (Representative da la Parra, interview with author, July 7, 2009). Moreover, the efforts to eradicate coca led to daily conflicts between the Mobile Rural Patrol Unit and the family farmers (Stefanoni and do Alto 2006, 35). The economic costs of these efforts were significant. Some estimates indicate that during the Banzer-Quiroga years, the country lost from US$600 million to US$900 million in revenue and more than 50,000 jobs (Hylton and Thomson 2007, 101). Not surprisingly, eradication policies were a frequent catalyst of social conflict.

Failures of effective governance, worsening socioeconomic problems, and policy preferences at odds with large portions of the population contributed to the decline of the country's party system. Along with the collapse of corporatist inclusion, citizens had fewer satisfactory means of formal representation. The response was both the proliferation of new organizations, including neighborhood associations, unions of informal sector workers, and the *cocaleros* union, and also an increasing tendency to express demands through informal channels (Barr 2005, 83). Among these groups were indigenous organizations. As indigenous peoples in Bolivia tend to value collectivist identities and interests and frequently demand greater local autonomy and control of resources, the collective platform of Bolivia's party system left indigenous organizations with few outlets for representation. Because some 60 percent of the country's population is indigenous, this was no small matter. Though the rise of groups like the Unitary Syndical Confederation of Peasant Workers in Bolivia (Confederación Sindical Única de Trabajadores Campesinos de Bolivia [CSUTCB]) and the politicization of indigenous identity stem from a variety of factors (R. A. Mayorga 2006; Yashar 1999, 2005), one cause was the programmatic decline of the party system. As Donna Lee van Cott (2007) explains, the "meteoric rise of indigenous movements and parties should be understood in the context of the collapse of the political left in the late 1980s" (134).

Not surprisingly, another response was the appearance of political entrepreneurs seeking to take advantage, something that began as early as 1989 when Carlos Palenque challenged the established parties in the presidential contests. His new CONDEPA party tapped into Palenque's popularity, particularly within the Aymara community, as a television personality (Madrid 2012, 48). He received 12.2 percent of the vote. The results were slightly better in the next election, when he won 14 percent. Max Fernández of the new UCS joined the competition that year, taking 13.7 percent. Both of these candidates, using antiestablishment rhetoric and plebiscitarian linkages, appealed to informal sector workers and marginalized groups, including indigenous populations (F. Mayorga 2003; R. A. Mayorga 2006, 154–155). The two took steps like incorporating indigenous sayings and symbols (like the *wiphala* flag), promoting indigenous schools and the recognition of Aymara as an official language, and including indigenous candidates on their party lists (Madrid 2012, 48). The UCS and CONDEPA found enough supporters to gain some national significance, but nevertheless remained minority parties during the 1990s.[9] Less than a decade later, though, conditions became much more advantageous for populism.

In short, the collective ineffectiveness of the country's political parties to address deep-seated economic issues clearly was detrimental to the party system. And, by pushing what seemed to be international interests (neoliberalism, coca eradication) over domestic interests, Bolivia's parties became increasingly distant from the voters, who in turn grew ever more frustrated with the political elite. As a result, the party system weakened to the point of collapse in the first few years of the new century, thus presenting a fruitful environment for populism.

Angry Voters

As the party system weakened and the quality of representation languished, citizens withdrew somewhat from the political system. Citizens' confidence in parties declined, falling from 21.6 percent in 1997 to 6.4 percent in 2003,[10] as did their attitude toward democracy itself. Latinobarómetro surveys report citizens' support for democracy declining steadily from 64 percent in 1996 to a low of 45 percent in 2004.[11] It rose slightly the next year, to 49 percent, and then dramatically to 62 percent the year Morales took office.[12] This attitude was not limited to the electorate; even political actors agreed. A series of Instituto Interuniversitario de Iberoamérica surveys asked representatives whether elections were the best means of expressing policy preferences; those who agreed "very much" fell steadily from 68.4 percent in 1993 to a minority of 40.5 percent in 2002. This attitude appears to have depressed voter turnout as well. As a percentage of registered voters, with voting being compulsory, turnout was a healthy 81.97 percent in 1985 but it declined steadily over the next decade, bottoming at 71.36 percent in 1997 and rising very slightly in the next election to 72.06 percent (International Institute for Democracy and Electoral Assistance 2015). This malaise nevertheless failed to result in significant electoral returns for any populist candidate until 2005. In that year, voter turnout soared to 84.5 percent and climbed even higher in 2009, to 94.6 percent, helping Morales dominate those contests. A key factor in this change concerns the mood of the electorate, a shift from frustration to anger.

Although government ineffectiveness and the prioritization of policies favoring international over domestic interests created a distance between constituents and representatives, the continued pursuit of internationally oriented policies against a background of corrupt political behavior ignited a series of intractable conflicts. The rising frequency and severity of social conflicts serve as good, if indirect, indicators of the changing mood. Figure 4.3 illustrates the increasing number of protests over a twelve-year period,

Figure 4.3 Conflicts by Administration

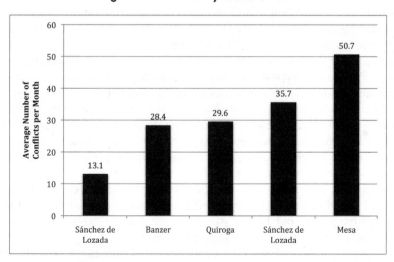

Source: Laserna, Ortego, and Chacón (2006).

rising from an average of 13.1 conflicts per month during the first Sánchez de Lozada administration to more than fifty during the Mesa administration in 2004–2005. The scope and impact of these episodes also heightened, beginning around the turn of the century with the so-called water war.

Protests over Disadvantageous Policies

In 2000, Cochabamba erupted in protests in response to the privatization of the city's water utility. The national government had signed the contract with an international consortium, Aguas del Tunari, after a single-bidder, closed-door process in 1999 (Shultz 2003, 35). Upon taking control, the new owners hiked the prices for water consumers by as much as 200 percent. Though the local elite could bear the cost easily, most could not. A new citizens' group, the Coalition for the Defense of Water and Life (the Coordinadora) headed by Óscar Olivera, emerged and helped coordinate demonstrations and general strikes. It "succeeded in focusing pent-up anger and social unrest" (Olivera and Lewis 2004, 54). Tens of thousands of people from the lower and middle classes took to the streets in January, again in February, and most dramatically in April, clashing with the 1,200 security forces that President Banzer had deployed during a formal state of siege (Shultz 2003, 35).

The price of water was not the protesters' only, or even major, concern. They objected to the government's privatization and commoditization of natural resources where ordinary citizens would bear the costs. Some 40 percent of those in Cochabamba lacked access to water via the utility, and thus were unaffected, and yet many of these individuals participated. Moisés Arce and Roberta Rice (2009) describe the protests as "outrage against the blatantly unreasonable terms of the privatization deal, which granted the consortium control over all of Cochabamba's surface and sub-terranean water source" (91–92). Olivera explained that people were struggling against the agreement that would benefit the wrong group. He said they "fight so that the water is not privatized, they fight so that the [water] company might not fall into the hands of the transnationals, they fight so that the [communal] water networks do not become property of the transnationals, they fight for the *usos y costumbres* [traditions and customs] of the campesinos, but these are people who do not manage nor enjoy [access to] water" (cited in Perrault 2006, 159). "Water is life" was the ubiquitous slogan of the demonstrators, but more threatening slogans could be heard, like "power to customary uses—long live water, die privatizers!" (Perrault 2006, 156). Note that protestors directed their anger not specifically at the foreign businesses but instead at the domestic actors who gave foreign companies control over such fundamental resources.

Another of the protesters' concerns was the manner in which deals like this one were conducted: they were upset with government corruption. As

Willem Assies and Ton Salman (2003) describe, the water protests were not only about the contract but also due to the "deceit about the tariff hike and beyond that to the lack of transparency in the negotiations in a context of widespread government corruption" (28). President Banzer's administration was noted for its ineptness and corruption (Salman 2007, 120), so the secrecy of the negotiations fit the public narrative, and his initial response to the protests reinforced it. After the January 2000 demonstrations, Banzer agreed to review the rate increases but then changed course, resulting in another round of protests and his declaration that they were illegal (Shultz 2003, 35).

The protests quickly expanded as additional groups began making their own demands. First the local police joined in, striking and demanding higher salaries, and then the protests spread to teachers, university students, informal sector workers, and so on (Barr 2005). After the April protests, the Banzer administration rescinded the contract but could not fully placate the public, and so social convulsions erupted again that September. Again a variety of groups pressed their own demands: coca farmers wanted to increase the legal acreage for raising coca; teachers demanded a 50 percent increase in their salaries; campesinos wanted the repeal and modification of several laws that affected their costs of agricultural production; and university students, transport workers, and informal sector workers all had demands of their own. Protesters seized Cochabamba for a full twenty-six days and, collectively, virtually crippled the country by halting all ground transportation.

The situation worsened during the second Sánchez de Lozada administration. In February 2003, the country erupted in response to a proposed tax increase. The president was seeking another IMF loan to help deal with fiscal problems, but the IMF demanded a reduction of the deficit. Sánchez de Lozada's response was a 12.5 percent increase in income taxes for even fairly low-wage workers and low-salary earners (Assies and Salman 2003, 60). Police were among the first to protest the tax bill while also demanding higher pay. They were joined by teachers, and then by students, farmers, pensioners, and others, all of whom not only denounced the tax policy but made additional demands. The tax policy, which put demands of the IMF ahead of the concerns of ordinary Bolivians, was just the spark for a more generalized outburst. Not coincidentally, during these demonstrations, protesters targeted the headquarters of the established political parties (Hylton and Thomson 2007, 109). The president called in the military to control the situation, and more than thirty people died in the clashes (Silva 2009, 134).

Later that year, the country exploded yet again in response to plans to have another international consortium, Pacific LNG, export natural gas to North American markets via a route across Chile. The discovery of hydrocarbon reserves in the late 1990s and early 2000s made Bolivia home of the second-largest gas reserves in South America. By 2003, natural gas had become the country's largest export. Despite this abundance, energy consumption in Bolivia is exceptionally low, even by regional standards. Bolivia's per capita electricity consumption is less than 25 percent of the per capita average for South America, and its per capita energy consumption is roughly half that for South America. This statistic is not a function of conservation; rather it is a product of the limitations of infrastructure. Roughly 75 percent of rural and 20 percent of urban Bolivians lack access to electricity (IMF 2006, 34). Meanwhile, the foreign companies that would exploit the gas were to receive generous deals: they would pay 18 percent royalties and a 12 percent tax based on the value of the gas at the "pit." These fees were low compared to many arrangements in other countries, and the value of the gas in this deal was roughly half of the cost of gas being exported to Brazil (Assies and Salman 2003, 62–63).

Not surprisingly, the impression grew among the population that the government was exploiting Bolivia's natural resources to the benefit of international actors and at the expense of ordinary citizens. The political establishment in La Paz was giving foreigners greater access to the country's natural gas than its own disadvantaged citizens. "Gas for Bolivians" became the rallying cry, reflecting the view that national development and social welfare should be the priorities of any plans to exploit the country's natural resources (Perrault 2006, 168). Protests began in El Alto and La Paz, cutting off a highway that isolated a group of tourists near Lake Titicaca. The government responded with a rescue attempt that resulted in six dead and spurred further protests. Again, a variety of groups were involved. Leading figures in 2003 included Jaime Solares of the COB; Óscar Olivera and his new group, the Coalition for the Defense and Recuperation of Gas; Evo Morales and the *cocaleros*; Aymara leader Felipe Quispe of the CSUTCB; and El Alto councilman Roberto de la Cruz. "Protestors and their leaders clearly directed their fury at persistent economic and political exclusion and repression" (Silva 2009, 140). As with the water wars, despite the absence of a single leader, the protests spread nationwide, effectively shutting down economic activity for a while. As this proceeded, the calls to defend the country's gas were joined by calls for the president's resignation. Not only those from lower socioeconomic groups participated; many members of the middle class did, too (Hylton and Thomson 2007, 116).

The response to the growing unrest was force, even to the point of sending tanks onto the streets (Assies and Salman 2003, 65–66). Clashes with security forces in early October left scores of protesters dead. "Rage at the killings and indifference to the suffering of the popular sector," however, stiffened the protesters' resolve (Silva 2009, 141). In the midst of the turmoil, Sánchez de Lozada proposed holding consultative referenda in the country's departments on hydrocarbon policy. The move came too late; seeing no feasible alternatives, on October 17, Sánchez de Lozada resigned his post and flew to the United States. In the end, this gas war resulted in some seventy deaths and the collapse of the government. The president's resignation, however, resolved little: similar conflicts involving hydrocarbon and water policies led to the resignation of Carlos Mesa in 2005.

Mesa took over the presidency with a promise to take a number of steps, such as reviewing the capitalization process (which was the basis for the gas laws), changing hydrocarbon legislation, creating a constituent assembly to rewrite the country's constitution, and holding a referendum on gas export policy. The first of these was to address the widespread suspicions of irregularities associated with the privatization law (Assies and Salman 2003, 67). The referendum took place in 2004, and among its questions was the possibility of raising royalties or taxes or both up to 50 percent of the value of the gas extracted. Following the approval by the voters, Congress then took up the task of rewriting the law. After much delay, it produced legislation keeping royalties at the current 18 percent but raising taxes to 32 percent. This measure was highly controversial, opposed by many in the eastern departments where the hydrocarbon deposits are located and by the indigenous, labor, and other groups who by this point wanted full nationalization. Mesa allowed the law to pass, though without his signature. Once again the country was paralyzed with massive protests. In June, facing some 500,000 demonstrators in the streets, Mesa followed his predecessor into early retirement. With new elections now looming, many Bolivians continued to face the fear that the country's elite and foreign interests would continue to commandeer the nation's resources (Singer 2007).

The cycle of protests from 2000 through 2005 can be understood as a coherent whole, despite the proliferation of separate groups and specific demands involved. At least initially, the demands of the various groups involved were of a bread-and-butter sort, such as calls for salary increases and relief from taxation or high prices. Yet these had in common the complaint that the government was failing in a basic way: the market-oriented reforms designed to appease international interests were hurting Bolivian citizens. Despite acting independently of one another, each would attempt to magnify the impact of its protest or demonstration by overlapping its efforts with other groups. The result was a larger, more impactful collective action (see Silva 2009).

Importantly, each major disturbance began in response to an arrangement with an international actor: Aguas del Tunari, Pacific LNG, or the IMF. And, as the cycle of protests continued, they began to take on a broader meaning when the various demands were framed in more fundamental terms about indigenous rights and national control over natural resources. Still, these protests were not nationalist along the lines of Bolivia versus some foreign incursion or oppressor. Instead, they concerned the reaction of ordinary citizens to a domestic elite who acted against their interests: the government should give citizens of the country priority access to Bolivia's natural resources, not their international friends.

As with the original water war, the sources of the escalating cycle of protests were the conduct of governmental authorities and the nature of the international deals. Research on the relationship between foreign economic involvement and protest activity supports this point. For instance, David G. Ortiz and Sergio Béjar (2013) establish a correlation between IMF programs and collective action in Latin America and argue that participation in an IMF program leads to protests because people "perceive a loss of legitimacy and question the sovereignty of their domestic governments" (492). Arce and Rice's (2009) statistical analysis of the sources of the Bolivian protests offers additional support for this conclusion. They find that the level of per capita foreign direct investment had a positive effect on protest activity. "At the heart of the water and gas wars was a deep-seated rejection of neoliberalism as a form of neocolonialism and the special place that these resources hold in the history of Bolivia" (Arce and Rice 2009, 96).

Thomas Perrault (2006) adds a helpful perspective here, noting that the Bolivian protesters had two basic concerns: "First, protestors demanded *procedural* justice, calling for greater participation and transparency in decisions over the management of natural resources. Secondly, protestors demanded *distributive* justice, calling for more equitable distribution of the benefits deriving from the exploitation of natural resources" (154; emphasis in original). As the psychology literature indicates, the dual perceptions of an unfair outcome and a biased decisionmaking process are particularly combustive (e.g., Weiss, Suckow, and Cropanzano 1999), and this theory is consistent with the scale and severity of the protests Bolivia experienced.

With respect to procedural justice, citizens indeed were widely skeptical of the decisionmaking processes at the governmental level. The Latinobarómetro began asking respondents in 2004 whether they believed the powerful governed the country for their own benefit or for the benefit of all the people. In that year, 76 percent said the country was governed for the benefit of the elite. In the year of the worst protests, 2005, the number jumped to 81 percent. (It plummeted, though, the year Morales took office, falling to 57 percent.) The prior discussion mentions specific incidents, such as the bidding process during the water privatization and the problems associated with gas policy's foundational law (capitalization), but the source of this perception goes deeper, to the prevalence of corruption.

The Role of Corruption

By any number of measures, Bolivia has consistently ranked among the most corrupt countries in Latin America, a region already notorious for its corruption. On Transparency International's CPI, for instance, Bolivia ranked 106 in 2003, the year of the gas war. Within the Americas, only Ecuador, Paraguay, and Haiti ranked lower.[13] In 2005, Bolivia's global ranking declined to 117. Another measure, the World Bank's control of corruption index, shows similar results, with Bolivia ranking among the worst in the region and getting worse. On a 100-point scale, Bolivia's score dropped from 51.2 in 1998 to 17.6 in 2002. It remained low through 2005, when it was 25.4, but jumped after Morales's election to 42 in 2006. These considerations are not just abstract, moreover. Mitchell A. Seligson (2006) finds that Bolivians are frequently victimized by corrupt practices, such as having police, public employees, and others solicit bribes. His study shows Bolivia has the worst level of corruption victimization (among El Salvador, Honduras, Guatemala, Ecuador, Peru, Bolivia, and Paraguay). As a point of comparison, Bolivia's level of corruption by this measure is more than four times that of El Salvador (Seligson 2006, 390).

Since the time of the transition, citizens' perception of corruption among the political class has been widespread and growing. With greater freedom of the press after military rule, reports of unlawful activity among politicians became increasingly common. This perception, moreover, had a solid foundation in that Bolivia's political system has traditionally been highly clientelistic; parties were widely known to be little more than means of patronage distribution (Gamarra 1994; Malloy 1991). Corruption of public administration followed, becoming especially conspicuous during the Jaime Paz Zamora government. His administration was flooded by charges of corruption stemming from the lack of transparency in the privatization process, leading many observers to describe the process as a free-for-all for party insiders (Gamarra 1994, 41). Even the privatization law itself was suspect: it was passed in the wee hours of the morning without the requisite quorum present (Gamarra 1994, 57).

The decentralization and privatization reforms passed by his successor, Sánchez de Lozada, arguably should have curbed corruption by reducing executive discretion over at least some funds and providing citizens with a stake in the privatization process. Nevertheless, corruption continued to be a problem, with allegations following Sánchez de Lozada's administration, and he himself was eventually charged with human rights violations after leaving office. The Banzer administration had a terrible reputation; during his time, public administration was "plagued with corruption," according to Karen Flores, head of the anticorruption agency at the time (cited in Luzzani 2001, 170). In one example, only fractions of the millions of dollars spent for disaster relief after serious flooding in 2001 reached the intended beneficiaries (Luzzani 2001, 170). Banzer's minister of health resigned in the face of corruption accusations, and, in 1998, for the first time a Bolivian judge was accused of corruption (F. Mayorga and Córdova 2008, 222–223). Defense Minister Fernando Kieffer faced charges of embezzling money intended to help earthquake victims. A short-lived investigation during the Quiroga administration claimed to have uncovered millions of dollars of funds stolen by Banzer, his son-in-law, and members of congress (Herrera, Urueña Cortés, and Rosen 2003, 106). The government minister during Sánchez de Lozada's second term, Yerko Kukoc, faced corruption charges in 2003 and became the first person in Bolivia to be convicted of misusing discretionary funds (González Roda 2005, 107).

Corruption thus was not a new phenomenon prior to the 2005 elections, but it was getting worse. During the 1993 presidential elections, the MNR sponsored a survey that indicated two main areas of public discontent: the prolonged impact of austerity measures and government corruption (Gamarra and Malloy 1995, 423). A decade later, in 2004, survey respondents rated corruption the most serious issue facing the country (Hodess and Wolkers 2004, 19).[14] A series of Encuestas y Estudios (2010, 4) surveys found that from 1995 through 1999, an average of 21.8 percent of respondents identified corruption as the country's most serious problem; the number then steadily rose, reaching 59 percent in June 2004. In 2005, a Transparency International survey asked how the level of corruption had changed in the past three years: 70 percent of Bolivians believed corruption had worsened leading up to the 2005 elections (Hutchinson, Lavers, and Wolkers 2005, 21). Another question from that survey revealed that Bolivians believed political parties to be extremely corrupt, with a score of 4.8 on a 5-point scale (with 5 as the most corrupt) (Hutchinson, Lavers, and Wolkers 2005, 19). Elites seemed to agree. The Instituto Interuniversitario de Iberoamérica (2010) surveys of congressional representatives showed corruption rising in importance as a problem: 66.3 percent of respondents agreed it was "very important" in 1997; 75.7 percent agreed in 2002.[15] Arguably, Bolivia's delegates would have had a better appreciation of corruption's fiscal implications: in 2005 corruption cost the country US$112 million, or the equivalent of half of the country's fiscal deficit and 25 percent of its public investment (*La Razón*, November 23, 2005).

With pervasive corruption as the backdrop, any deals, secretive or otherwise, with foreign corporations to sell the public's resources would naturally generate suspicion. When combined with rising frustration over neoliberalism's apparent failures to improve economic conditions, these moves would—and did—produce anger among the general population. Significant portions of the public considered these deals to be unfair not only in terms of their outcomes, since water prices would rise or foreigners, not locals, would benefit from the country's natural gas, but also in terms of the process, since so few had confidence that politicians were acting in the name of the citizens. These dual perceptions of disadvantage and corruption fueled anger and the desire to rectify the situation.

Morales the Populist: A Tale of Two Elections

In 2002, Sánchez de Lozada of the MNR narrowly defeated two political challengers, Evo Morales of the MAS and Manfred Reyes Villa of the NFR, by less than two percentage points each. The weakened party system and increased voter dissatisfaction contributed to the challengers' relative success. And, had it not been for the divided vote between Morales and Reyes Villa or the procedural quirk of a congressional runoff when no candidate receives a majority of the popular vote, the MNR might have lost. Still, the results are but a shadow of those three years later, when Morales almost tripled his number of votes (from 581,163 to 1,544,374) and took the election in the popular vote. The different results in 2005 owe to a combination of factors, including, as discussed above, the effective collapse of the party system, which left the vast majority of the voters up for grabs, and the heightened anger of the electorate. Another was the use of a populist strategy: the antiestablishment appeals and plebiscitarian linkages, as described in Chapter 2. None of the candidates in 2002 fully adopted such a strategy, despite the use of antiestablishment rhetoric and, more generally, the effort to position themselves as alternatives to the political status quo. That changed in 2005.

Political Challengers in the 2002 Election

Whether Morales and Reyes Villa were populists in 2002 is not a matter of consensus. Nevertheless, by the definition used in this study, neither qualifies. Reyes Villa, a former member of the ADN and mayor of Cochabamba from 1993 to 2001, tried to position himself as an antiparty candidate, actively criticizing the party establishment. He led the polls for a while, but attack ads and questions regarding the source of his personal fortune and relationship with Sun Myung Moon, controversial founder of the Unification Church, reduced his support (Singer and Morrison 2004, 176). More to the point, Reyes Villa was not an antiestablishment candidate. His ability to craft an appeal based in part on criticizing the establishment was undercut by not only his earlier membership in the party system and his long governance of Bolivia's third-largest city but also by his participation in Banzer's governing coalition in 1997. More importantly, despite his complaints of the government ceding control of natural resources to foreign interests, as mayor of Cochabamba he played a direct role in the Aguas del Tunari contract (Shultz 2003, 36). During the water wars, Olivera's Coordinadora called a town meeting, one result of which was the denunciation of Reyes Villa as a traitor for approving the deal (Assies 2003, 25). In 2002, his campaign's motto was "positive change," and he sought a middle position between that of the traditional political parties and the more radical stance of Evo Morales (Basset 2003, 165). Similarly, he did not attempt to make emotional connections based on messianic appeals; instead, he emphasized his reputation for effective management of Cochabamba (Basset 2003, 167). In short, his was at best a compromised antiestablishment position.

Morales's case may be more interesting. Some observers are adamant that Morales was not and is not a populist because he rose to prominence on the back of a grassroots social movement (e.g., Roberts 2007). This fact seems to go against the very top-down nature many associate with populism. Others argue the contrary (e.g., Hawkins 2009). Yet another group feels that Morales may not have started out as a populist but had become one by 2005 (e.g., Doyle 2011).[16] The present study agrees with the last group. Briefly, in 2002 Morales would be best understood as the leader of a coalition of grassroots movements. Changes made after that election, however, resulted in his development as a populist leader by 2005.

Morales's rise to national prominence is indeed inconsistent with populism. Writing of the phenomenon Morales represents, Roberts (2007) argues, "It is a logic not of populism but of autonomous, grass-roots social mobilization that is channeled into the electoral arena and translated into political power. It is, in fact, the very antithesis of populism" (14). To be sure, Morales's early relationship with the *cocaleros* movement and indigenous groups was not based on the plebiscitarian linkages associated with populism. Consider that he rose, along with other members, through the ranks of the *cocaleros*, becoming the president of one of the affiliated unions in 1988 and helping to create an umbrella organization, the Six Federations of Coca Growers of the Tropics of Cochabamba. Although not the organization's first president, he gained that role in 1994. Under his leadership, though, the *cocaleros* affiliated with the country's largest peasant organization, the CSUTCB, and quickly became an influential group within it. Through the CSUTCB, the mostly Quechua coca growers began emphasizing the cultural significance of coca, thus turning coca production into an indigenous issue (Yashar 2005, 185). Notably, however, Morales has not held the presidency of the CSUTCB. In fact, the membership divided between supporters of Alejo Véliz and Morales as they competed for organizational control in 1998. As a compromise, the body elected Felipe Quispe, a more radical indigenous leader. In short, Morales was not a personalistic leader of a top-down movement at this point.

The mass mobilizations of the early 2000s tell a similar story. Morales was not a singular leader of these demonstrations, nor were they reflective of support for Morales as an individual leader. In the water war of 2000, for instance, a number of uncoordinated groups under a variety of leaders took part (Barr 2005, 73). Indeed, if one organization was leading, it was Olivera's Coordinadora. Though Morales's *cocaleros* were important players, Felipe Quispe's CSUTCB blockaded roads in the La Paz department and

Dionisio Núñez led simultaneous protests in the Yungas. In addition, during this period the government considered Quispe, not Morales, to be the leading threat to stability: it arrested Quispe and sent him to the isolated department of Beni in a sort of internal exile. At least initially, the gas wars demonstrated a similar hydra-headed dynamic. According to MAS member and 2002 vice presidential candidate Antonio Pedrero, "we were not the organizers of those mobilizations. There wasn't an organizer, there were various" (cited in Madrid 2005, 175).[17]

Morales's first association with political parties, additionally, did not fit the top-down character one associates with populist organizations. Several indigenous leaders decided in the mid-1990s that the next logical step in promoting indigenous concerns would be the creation of a political party. Representatives at a 1995 meeting of the CSUTCB, Indigenous Confederation of Eastern Bolivia (CIDOB), and the Syndical Confederation of Bolivian Colonists decided to form a party, the Assembly for the Sovereignty of the Peoples (Asamblea por la Soberanía de los Pueblos [ASP]). It earned 3 percent in the municipal elections of that year. Morales's first campaign for office was with the ASP in 1997. He competed for (and won) a seat in the lower house of Congress. In the same elections, Véliz stood as the ASP's presidential candidate.

Following these contests, Morales began to lay the groundwork for his later success. He splintered away from the ASP and formed the Political Instrument for the Sovereignty of the Peoples (Instrumento Político por la Soberanía de los Pueblos [ISPS]). In order to compete in the 1999 municipal elections, the ISPS associated with the moribund but still legal MAS and won 3.27 percent of the vote. The MAS was Morales's personal instrument from the start (Eaton 2006, 6; Madrid 2012, 63), and over time he would use it to build plebiscitarian linkages to a significant portion—though not all—of his supporters. But this outcome was not a given, since the new MAS was still heavily dependent on relationships with multiple social movements (Domingo 2005; Madrid 2005; van Cott 2003, 2005). Morales, despite having control over the party, depended to a great extent on relationships with other groups. As an example, the CSUTCB was crucial in providing financial and logistical support to his campaign in 2002 (van Cott 2003). These relationships initially limited his room for maneuver. With the exception of his own *cocaleros*, which he still led in 2002, his connections to supporters were largely indirect, filtered through a variety of indigenous social movements. In addition, Morales was not the only indigenous candidate; he competed with Véliz, for the NFR, and Quispe, for the Pachakuti Indigenous Movement (Movimiento Indígena Pachakuti) to be the indigenous populations' primary representative (Stefanoni and do Alto 2006, 66).

Hence, Morales's rise to political prominence is not representative of a populist strategy. He capitalized on a grassroots phenomenon, much like

William Jennings Bryan in the United States in the late 1800s, but did not have his own movement based on top-down, plebiscitarian linkages. He did, though, use antiestablishment rhetoric in the 2002 campaign. As in the next election, he chastised the country's corrupt elite and the excessive influence of international actors (especially the United States and the IMF) and did so in Manichaean terms (Assies and Salman 2003, 55). He promised to reverse neoliberalism, end coca eradication, and rewrite the country's constitution. In these ways, he was directly challenging the status quo, and his status received a boost when Congress expelled him on charges of instigating violence. Though Morales did not adopt the exclusionary tone of Felipe Quispe, who condemned the country's white elite and denounced the Spanish language, he did emphasize indigenous themes. Roughly two-thirds of his party's candidates, for instance, were indigenous. They, including Morales, often dressed in traditional clothing, spoke using Aymara or Quechua, and participated in indigenous rituals (Madrid 2012). When he spoke of broader national themes, these still centered on indigenous concerns. Consider his view of coca, the "sacred leaf":

> There is a unanimous defense of coca because the coca leaf is becoming the banner for national unity, a symbol of national unity in defense of our dignity. Since coca is a victim of the United States, as coca growers we are also victims of the United States, but then we rise up to question these policies to eradicate coca. Now is the moment to see the defense of coca as the defense of all natural resources, just like hydrocarbon, oil, gas; and this consciousness is growing. That is why it is an issue of national unity. (Morales 2002)

Here, he prioritized a concern primarily of indigenous groups and related it to the concerns of a broader constituency. The emphasis on ethnic issues is not necessarily inconsistent with antiestablishment appeals, but it does limit them. It effectively restricts the definition of "the people." With fully articulated antiestablishment appeals, however, one expects an expansive and inclusive understanding. In 2005, Morales's relative emphasis would shift, reflecting one aspect of the development of his populism.

A Winning Strategy for 2005

Between the 2002 and 2005 contests, Morales's strategy changed. Not only did he tone down the ethnic character of his appeals in 2002 in an effort to be more inclusive (Madrid 2012), but he also sought to penetrate the country's urban areas and to develop top-down linkages across the country. These moves were crucial in forging the populist character of Morales's strategy since 2005. As discussed, the origins of the MAS tied it to a variety of social movements, which were primarily located in rural areas. To win national elections, however, Morales needed urban support, particularly from the large cities of La Paz and El Alto. Nevertheless, the bulk of the indigenous in these cities identify themselves as Aymara, and La Paz has a significant middle class, in contrast to the largely poor and Quechua *cocaleros*. As such, the residents initially resisted the MAS (Anria 2013, 32).

Morales's approach was first to create urban-based arms of MAS, which were under his personal control. However, these new urban structures lacked the participatory mechanisms of the earlier rural ones (Kohl and Farthing 2012, 232). In addition, he co-opted existing organizations, eliminated their autonomy, and converted them into top-down arms of his party (do Alto 2008, 32). Miguel Machaca, a MAS deputy representing El Alto, explained, "We can't deny we do that. We aim for our people to become leaders in these organizations. It is an effort to control the social organizations from the top" (cited in Anria 2013, 34). A member of the foreign diplomatic core agreed: "He'll gain control of a group and put his people in charge—if he can't, then he'll undercut it sometimes by creating a parallel group" (confidential interview with author, July 6, 2009).

Originally limited by his ties with the rural social movements, Morales wanted greater freedom moving forward, beginning with the urban areas. He penetrated groups like the Regional Labor Central (Central Obrera Regional [COR]) and the Federation of Neighborhood Boards (Federación de Juntas Vecinales [FEJUVE]) of El Alto, often taking advantage of a lack of strong leadership, according to Mario Quintanilla, director of a group that works with such organizations (interview with author, July 9, 2009). As Santiago Anria (2013) explains, the "MAS therefore was not an organic product of these cities; it inserted itself into La Paz and El Alto as something foreign. As such, it faced obstacles as it sought to organize a structure of its own on top of political configurations and existing social networks" (33), and the incorporation of these other groups was "accompanied by a transfer of top-down schemes of participation, as well as a set of co-optive practices that are now characteristic of the MAS" (33).

This strategy of building top-down relationships was not limited to urban areas, however. In some instances, according to Representative Armando de la Parra, where Morales could not gain direct control, he formed pacts as a way of exerting influence and as a stepping-stone toward greater control (interview with author, July 7, 2009). In other cases, the MAS formed parallel organizations (US Department of State 2008). The CSUTCB is one example: the creation of a Morales-backed and MAS-penetrated version was an open secret. Morales's first efforts to undermine the organization date to 2003, when the MAS attempted to undercut Felipe Quispe by creating a parallel CSUTCB led by Román Loayza (do Alto 2008, 33). Rufo Calle and Isaac Avalos later led the competing versions, and their respective supporters clashed. A telling cable from the US

Embassy in La Paz and published by Wikileaks refers to disputes between parallel groups as "clone wars," noting that "any group that does not conform with MAS goals risks being cloned" (US Embassy, La Paz 2007). The cable cites instances of the MAS forming parallel organizations not only in regard to the CSUTCB but also with organizations of campesina women, several FEJUVEs, and civic committees in various localities. These new organizations gained, and the original ones lost, the government's attention and access to resources. At times the media followed suit and began to ignore the original organizations (US Department of State 2008).

The development of these organizational relationships contributed to the development of top-down, plebiscitarian linkages. A former representative from La Paz and director of an influential nongovernmental organization argues that the social movements lost their autonomy, and their members became "almost employees" of Morales (confidential interview with author, July 9, 2009). In part this situation was the result of the MAS's structure, which was dominated by Morales himself. This structure helped him develop direct relations with the membership of social movements without concern for the groups' leadership (do Alto 2008, 32). Additionally, party members had directly dependent relationships with Morales, their lack of autonomy due in part to the "personal link established between the chief of the party and his 'guest'" (do Alto 2008, 31). Some spoke of an emerging Evismo, along the lines of Peronismo or Chavismo (*La Razón*, August 8, 2006; Madrid 2012, 64). As a result, observers began to label him a caudillo (e.g., Laserna 2007). The former representative from La Paz cited above explains, "He's a caudillo, unlike anything Bolivia has ever had." Despite the hyperbole, Morales developed into a top-down, personalistic leader.

Although Morales added plebiscitarianism to his linkage strategy, he also used vigorous antiestablishment appeals. In classical populist form, he framed politics as a Manichaean struggle between good and evil—the people versus the corrupt elite. The nature of the conflict, he argued, stemmed from a self-interested political and economic establishment that sold off the country's natural resources to foreign actors. Neoliberalism was the modern variant of a historic pattern of exploitation, one that had left most Bolivians trapped in poverty. Unlike his campaign of 2002, he crafted his message in a way that would appeal to an audience consisting not only of indigenous groups but also urban and middle-class voters (Madrid 2012). This us-versus-them battle had on the side of good a broadly defined people, namely, anyone who had complaints against those who wielded power. As one observer put it, Morales's appeals "captured all the frustrations of society" (Representative Armando de la Parra, interview with author, July 7, 2009). Such efforts involved a balancing act of sorts in that he had to pay attention the indigenous core of his constituency while simultaneously appealing to others. Morales's apparent turn toward the political center generated criticism from social movements, unions, and, especially, Quispe (Springer 2005, 9). Nevertheless, the use of these fully developed populist appeals was successful (Madrid 2012).

The target of this battle was the political and economic elite. He called them the "neoliberal parties," "political mafia," "oligarchy," and *mank'agastos*—those who eat without working (Assies and Salman 2005, 271). Morales established the divide between the virtuous people and the undeserving ruling elite, both domestic and international. "We all know that there are two Bolivias. One Bolivia of 'charlatans' who always make promises and sign agreements that they never fulfill; and the other Bolivia which is always tricked, subjugated, humiliated, and exploited" (Morales, cited in Postero 2004, 190). By casting these elites as corrupt, he tapped into a widespread public perception.

He further linked the self-serving behavior of the contemporary political establishment to centuries of subjugation. A common explanation of Bolivia's persistent poverty claims domestic and international groups have acted together in exploitative ways, putting self-interest over the needs of the citizens. By relating the policies and actions of recent leaders to historical patterns, Morales tied themes of racial domination with colonial-style exploitation and thus appealed to indigenous and nonindigenous voters alike. This inclusiveness—all ordinary Bolivians have a common foe—contrasted with his more radical counterpart, Felipe Quispe, in that Morales advocated neither separatism nor revolution:

> After 500 years of being subjugated, being slaves and servants, of extermination policies, we decided to go from resisting to taking over the territory. Territory means all the natural resources of this Mother Earth. But we chose to wage battle with her own tools, and are doing so *within the system.* Our hopes are based on the realization that we can regain power to seek a certain economic *balance.* (Morales, cited in Gutiérrez 2004; emphasis added)

This campaign, moreover, was a brawl. Observers describe Morales as a fighter using the confrontational "logic of unions" and as a "Jimmy Hoffa kind of guy" (Senator Tito Hoz de Vila, interview with author, July 8, 2009; confidential interview with author, July 17, 2007). Rather than offer opportunities for compromise—the "logic of parties"—Morales drew from his background with the *cocaleros* union and emphasized conflict. He used a method of *"provocacion permanente"* or permanent provocation (confidential interview with author, July 8, 2009). This style is consistent with other recent populists (e.g., Conaghan and de la Torre 2008). Morales framed this conflict over socioeconomic and political cleavages as one between good and evil, which Assies and Salman (2005) accurately characterize as "Manichean" (292). Hawkins (2010, 76) concurs: his content analysis of populist discourse, which emphasizes Manichaean rhetoric, rates Morales third among the twenty-five Latin American leaders in his study, behind only Hugo Chávez and José María Velasco Ibarra, and ahead of classical populists such as Juan Perón, Getúlio Vargas, and Lázaro Cárdenas.

Exploitation of the country's natural resources was the leading source of tension in this conflict and thus perhaps the primary theme of the 2005 campaign. Natural gas figured prominently, but so too did coca and water. This issue took a decidedly nationalistic tone; in other words, the Bolivian people, rather than international actors, should have say over the use of the country's resources. For instance, as Monte Reel reported in the *Washington Post* on October 31, 2008, Morales linked US antinarcotics policies to exploitation: "The pretext is going after the narco-traffickers, the narco-terrorists. But they really just want to take control of our resources." By continuing to argue against coca eradication and for legal uses of coca, Morales maintained a theme from 2002 that was of particular importance to indigenous groups. But by including natural gas, he tapped into the continued and widespread anger over Sánchez de Lozada's proposals. For instance, in analyzing the 2003 protests that forced Sánchez de Lozada from power, Morales said:

> The culprit responsible for so many deeds, and also responsible for the uprising of Bolivian people, has a name: it is called neoliberalism. Now, with the recent events in Bolivia, I have realized that what matters is the power of an entire people, of an entire nation. For those of us who are convinced that it is important to defend humanity, the best support we can offer is to create the power of the people. (cited in Postero 2004, 208)

Neoliberalism, in other words, was the economic model responsible for the recent loss of control to foreign interests.

In addition, he promised significant changes: correctives to a corrupt and exploitative system. He directed his permanent provocation toward a "second independence" and the "re-founding of the country." Morales thus framed a reformist agenda in very bold terms. For instance, he promised to "bury neoliberalism," promote the production of legal coca, nationalize hydrocarbons, and rewrite the constitution. "We want to live together in so-called diversity, changing the neo-liberal model and finishing off the colonial state" (Morales, cited in Goodman 2005). Elsewhere, Morales stated, "This is not just about a change of government. It is about starting a new history for the Bolivian people, a history free from corruption and discrimination" (cited in Kurtz-Phelan 2005).

His campaign, in short, effectively tapped into the concerns of many ordinary Bolivians. They were angry over the political establishment's willingness to sell off the national patrimony to international interests, as represented by the Cochabamba water privatization and the gas exportation plans. A corrupt elite used its influence and power not to bend the rules in order to help those in need but to benefit themselves and others, namely foreign interests. By offering significant reforms to the political and economic systems, he promised to end this situation. His antiestablishment appeals, in other words, capitalized on the public mood. Prior to the election, Morales expressed confidence since the Bolivian people "are betting on change because they are tired of the corruption, the neoliberal economic model, and the political mafia" (cited in Sosa 2005).

After President Mesa's resignation in June 2005, authorities decided to hold elections early, in December of the same year. In previous years, the parties best equipped to handle a quick electoral cycle would have been the MNR, ADN, and MIR. But by this point the party system had effectively collapsed. Nevertheless, some of the traditional parties attempted to present themselves in new lights. The MNR, for instance, fielded Michiaki Nagatani, a son of Japanese immigrants and a businessman with no political experience. He received 6.5 percent. The ADN attempted another strategy: keep the same candidate but change the name. Former president and head of the ADN, Jorge Quiroga, changed the party's name prior to the election so that the acronym was PODEMOS (the word means "we can" in Spanish). He received 28.6 percent of the vote. These hopeful attempts at making the most of the political context were no match for a populist alternative.

As mentioned earlier, Morales was the first candidate in modern times to receive enough votes in the general election to avoid a congressional runoff. Given the public mood, Morales's linkage strategies and appeals were quite effective. His support came from indigenous and nonindigenous voters alike. In 2006, a Latin American Public Opinion Project (LAPOP) survey revealed the country's ethnic composition as follows: 64.8 percent of the population identified as mestizo, 19.3 percent as indigenous, and 11 percent as white. Of those who voted for Morales, 61.3 percent self-identified as mestizo, 27.2 percent as indigenous, and 6.8 percent as white (Seligson et al. 2006, 86). Though his support was strongest among the indigenous and mestizo populations, a sizable share of whites also supported Morales. Raúl L. Madrid's (2012, 71) analysis shows that white Bolivian voters had a 42 percent probability of voting for him. Additionally, his voters were far more optimistic about the future economic situation—by ten percentage points over the national average (Seligson et al. 2006, 90). This fact suggests that Morales's promises of reform struck a cord. Madrid's (2012, 70) findings are consistent with this point: those on the ideological left, those supportive of gas nationalization, and those who participated in the demonstrations against Mesa were all likely to vote for Morales. In other words, those most dissatisfied with the current conditions were most likely to find Morales's platform appealing and were optimistic that his left-leaning policies would be effective.

Even more telling, Morales broadened his original, regional base of support to wide swaths of the country, including urban areas where he used plebiscitarian linkages. In 2002, his base was located firmly in the Chapare region within the Cochabamba department. He also performed relatively well in the other highland areas (the departments of La Paz, Oruro, and Potosí), but even there, "the farther from the city, the larger the MAS vote" (Oviedo Obarrio 2010, 94). Put differently, in 2002, his main support came from rural Bolivia. In 2005, by contrast, urban areas played a central role in his success. Whereas he captured less than 20 percent of the urban vote in 2002, three years later he received almost half (LAPOP, cited in Madrid 2008, 489). As Table 4.2 demonstrates, Morales did well in most of the departmental capitals, increasing his vote totals from 2002 by as much as 700 percent (Oviedo Obarrio 2010, 98). In the cities of La Paz and El Alto, for instance, only 16.1 percent of the vote went to Morales in 2002, but 55.7 percent in 2005 (Anria 2013, 30).

Results like these in the urban areas surprised many, in part because the cities were home to the most powerful economic sectors of society and the bases for the traditional parties. Even in the city of Santa Cruz, center of Morales's *media luna* opposition, he took nearly a third of the vote. The primary difference, in other words, between the two elections comes down to the rise in his share of the urban vote. As Fernando Oviedo Obarrio (2010) writes, "it was because of the figures generated in the cities that President Morales earned his 54 percent" (97). In short, his victory came from the very areas where his populism was fully expressed.

Table 4.2 Urban Support for the MAS

Department Capital	MAS 2002 (%)	MAS 2005 (%)
Sucre	16.8	50.8
La Paz	16.1	55.7
Cochabamba	23.4	53.0
Oruro	23.1	56.3
Potosí	14.5	49.3
Tarija	5.5	27.9
Santa Cruz	7.5	30.7
Trinidad	2.1	14.9
Cobija	4.3	26.6

Source: Oviedo Obarrio (2010).

Conclusion

Since his first electoral victory in 2005, Morales has gone on to take greater control of the country's natural resources, rewrite the constitution, and win two more presidential terms. He has, by and large, continued to pursue the populist strategy he began after 2002. His efforts have not been without hiccups, naturally, as his policies disappointed various groups, his tactics upset early supporters, and some promises remain unfulfilled. Polarization and demands from both indigenous groups and those pursuing regional autonomy presented significant governance problems early on (F. Mayorga 2006). Nevertheless, by generating electoral returns between 54 percent and 64 percent three times in a row, Morales has been a successful populist.

The developments leading up to his first victory illustrate the dynamics identified throughout this book. With a weakened party system and an angry electorate, the conditions in Bolivia were ripe for a populist to be chosen. Long-standing governance problems and programmatic decline gradually undermined the collective grip of the three traditional parties on the political system in the 1990s. In the early 2000s, failure to recognize and address the growing gap between the party system and society led to the system's collapse. At the same time, not only were indigenous issues becoming politicized in a majority indigenous country, but the general public was growing increasingly weary of persistent corruption and neoliberal policies. The latter had not positively affected the living standards for most citizens. The mood turned far worse after the turn of the century, when enough became enough. Secretive deals to privatize and exploit natural resources, in ways that appeared to benefit the few and harm the many, led to the explosive conditions from 2000 through 2005.

To be sure, interactive effects were at work; causality was not as straightforward as a linear sequence. Yet such a conclusion is to be expected, as social phenomena often illustrate causal complexity where individual factors can interact in meaningful ways. Some of the same kinds of factors that can lead to the weakening of a party system can also lead to public discontentment. However, changes to the party system are likely to stem from long-running issues. A system's collapse may seem sudden, but it will be based on persistent problems, in part because party systems are rather complex, multidimensional phenomena. By contrast, the public's mood can be—though is not necessarily—less complex and more volatile. Even where such nuances do not apply, nevertheless, any single factor can have multiple implications. In the Bolivian case, for instance, persistent corruption and neoliberal policies helped weaken the party system and set the stage for the public's anger. These factors then intersected in a dramatic way prior to the 2005 election. The established parties were in no position to defend themselves, which gave Morales a wide opening.

Citizens, furious at those parties for selling off Bolivia's resources for the apparent benefit of foreign actors and at the expense of its own citizens, wanted to both punish the perpetrators and foment real change. Morales's populism capitalized on this political opportunity and the public's mood.

Notes

1. Until 2009, if no presidential candidate received a majority in the general election, a runoff between the top contenders took place in congress.
2. See Bojanic (2009) for a discussion.
3. These figures include both those who indicated "a lot" of confidence in parties and those who had "some" confidence.
4. Evo Morales's MAS party was originally created years earlier but had been inactive until he resurrected it.
5. PODEMOS was a new party created by ADN member and former president, Jorge Quiroga.
6. The ILO data include only 1996 and 1999–2005.
7. They took with them their significant experience in labor organization from their days as the leading union within the country's labor confederation, the COB. The *cocaleros* would become one of the country's best organized movements.
8. The same government passed Law 1008 two years later. This law regulated coca cultivation for the first time, limiting legal cultivation to the Yungas area of the La Paz department and the Yungas area of the Cochabamba department. It also provided for the phased eradication of coca from the Chapare along with compensation for the *cocaleros* and established strict penalties for drug-trafficking activities (Thoumi 2003, 115).
9. Though both parties did well in the 1997 race, Fernández had died two years earlier in a plane crash and Palenque died of a heart attack three months before the elections. The parties' difficulties in finding replacements for these dominant personalities and their participation in governing coalitions (the UCS with the MNR and ADN, and CONDEPA with the ADN) weakened their positions. In 2002, for instance, the two parties together took less than 6 percent of the vote.
10. Percentages come from Latinobarómetro's surveys, summing the numbers of those who said they had either "a lot" of confidence or "some" confidence.
11. The results reflect the number of those who agree that democracy is preferable under any circumstances.
12. The public's satisfaction with democracy tells a similar story: averaging just 25 percent from 1996 until 2004, it increased dramatically beginning in 2005, rising almost 250 percent from 2004 to 2007.
13. This measure is based on expert opinions, but Canache and Allison (2005) have shown that the rankings correlate strongly with citizen perceptions of corruption, and thus the CPI scores are an effective indicator of citizens' views. They also show that citizens can and do connect their perceptions of corruption to judgments of political actors.
14. The exact phrasing of the survey's issue was "grand or political corruption." Poverty and unemployment were tied for second.
15. The only issue deemed to be more important was unemployment and underemployment.

16. Others still make the nuanced argument that to label Morales a populist is correct to an extent but oversimplifies matters (Panizza 2013, 112–113). Indeed, a populist strategy is but one aspect of a political actor's modus operandi. As discussed earlier, for instance, plebiscitarian linkages are frequently used in combination with others, like clientelism.

17. Nevertheless, the protests did begin to crystallize around key fundamental concerns. Morales, along with Óliver Olivera, Felipe Quispe, Jaime Solares, and Roberto de la Cruz stood out among the many participants. Writing about Morales and Quispe, Salman (2007) says, "Episodes such as the water war and the gas war confirmed their role as spokespeople for discontented and politically frustrated Bolivians and turned them into political parties that challenge not only specific policies but also the working of the system itself" (123). Morales's role in the gas war helps explain the MAS's dominance in the 2004 municipal elections (Anria 2013, 32).

5

A Regional View

IN THE PREVIOUS CHAPTER, I DEMONSTRATED THE LOGIC FOR POPULISM'S rise in modern Bolivia, but what of the rest of the region? President Morales has not been the only one to use this strategy in recent years. Obviously Hugo Chávez started the third era, and he was followed by a number of other populists. In 2006, Andrés Manuel López Obrador narrowly lost the Mexican elections. So close was the vote that he disputed the tally, refused to concede defeat, and encouraged his supporters to take to the streets. Using the "strategic mobilization of popular distrust" (Schedler 2007, 98), he rallied well over a million people in Mexico City in what may have been the country's largest protest ever. The same year Ollanta Humala made his first attempt at capturing Peru's presidency. Bragging about his antiestablishment credentials (Madrid 2012, 138), his nationalist and left-wing campaign had the explicit support of Hugo Chávez. In Ecuador, Rafael Correa outmaneuvered another populist, Álvaro Noboa, to take the 2006 elections. Correa succeeded despite Noboa's simultaneous use of clientelistic linkages and claims of being "God's hero" sent to save the country (Conaghan 2011, 270). Correa has since rewritten the country's constitution and won two more elections. Along with several others, these individuals constitute the third era.

Of the eleven countries considered here, six of them have had populist candidates between 1996 and 2010, leaving five that did not. In some cases, populists won convincingly; in others, they received relatively few votes. Thus, although the wave of populism has been a significant political development, it has not been a ubiquitous one. The variation among countries, as well as the variation from election to election within countries, presents an analytical opportunity. A study that includes the range of outcomes both within and across countries can provide substantial leverage in making causal inferences. In this chapter, I seek to take advantage of this opportunity. In so doing, I hope to offer support for the argument I presented earlier—bolstering the single-country study included in the prior chapter—and demonstrate the reasons why populism appears at some times and not at others.

This variation among countries also provides a good occasion to explore the range of alternative explanations found in the literature. Scholars have a strong tendency to explain populism's emergence with reference to multiple causal factors. Their accounts can be nuanced and complex, perhaps reflecting the difficulty of isolating independent effects of individual causes of populism, particularly across cases. For instance, those using statistical methods typically find support for one hypothesis but also note that other factors matter as well (e.g., Doyle 2011; Hawkins 2010). Weyland (2003) finds support for economic causes in explaining the election of Hugo Chávez but also warns against interpreting the results in "simple, materialistic fashion" (825), while arguing that additional factors must be included. Qualitative studies offer their own kinds of cautions. Crises frequently appear as contributing factors, though scholars are quick to note that populism can appear in times of noncrisis and may not even be exceptional (e.g., Knight 1998; Montúfar 2013). Arnson and de la Torre (2013) argue that Latin American populism is typically associated with problems of political, socioeconomic, or ethnic inclusion/exclusion, though these "can be intertwined, and reducing populism's emergence to one or another aspect can be artificial and even misleading" (354). This literature, in short, recognizes the inherent complexity of social phenomena.

By embracing causal complexity, one also may accept the possibility that multiple causal pathways can explain a given outcome. And given the literature's common use of causal configurations (combinations of factors) the potential complexity increases. Populism could be the result of one set of factors in the first case, and another, different set of factors in the second. Studying populism in contemporary Latin America, moreover, entails an intermediate number of observations, more than can be readily handled by conventional qualitative techniques and less than ideal for large-N statistical studies.

In light of these factors, in this chapter, I use QCA methodology, which previously has not been applied to the study of populism. QCA, including the fuzzy set type used here, brings together aspects of qualitative and quantitative analysis: in a replicable and transparent way it facilitates comparison of at least intermediate-N observations and does so while respecting the inherent diversity of cases and the heterogeneity of causal relevance (see Ragin 2000, 2008; Rihoux and Ragin 2009). QCA makes no assumption about causal uniformity, causal independence, or causal symmetry. As with traditional qualitative work, it accepts the possibility that causal factors can interact in meaningful ways as opposed to having only unique effects. Similarly, QCA allows for equifinality, where the results can show multiple causal pathways leading to the outcome across cases. The methodology accomplishes this in part by comparing the impact not only of individual causal factors but also all of their possible combinations, the results of which cast light on an important debate in the literature. In addition, this methodology facilitates a specific analysis of not only sufficient conditions but also necessary conditions. Though often implicit in the study of populism, necessity is rarely treated in an explicit manner, much less one based on a comparative analysis.

The results of the analysis, which uses a new index to measure party system institutionalization across time, support the argument presented earlier. They suggest, first, that a weak party system is the one necessary condition for populists to gain significant electoral support. Second, the results substantiate the logic of sufficiency, showing that the combination of party system weakness, corruption, and evidence of disadvantage account for all of the recent instances of populism in Latin America.

I proceed by discussing first the outcome to be examined (the electoral success of populist candidates) and its measurement, and then the six causal factors and their measurements. Given the different requirements of larger, multicase studies compared to single-case studies (i.e., to provide stable bases of comparison), I specify these factors in somewhat more formal ways than I did in the prior chapter. Next, I turn to the analysis itself, including the steps taken to reach the conclusions regarding both necessity and sufficiency. Following that, I explain the meaning of the results and use brief country studies to illustrate the points. In this section, I also provide evidence of the causal linkage in this argument—anger—and its connection to populism. To keep the text manageable, I have located a number of the technical details in the appendixes.

Populists, Nonpopulists, and the Vote

What qualifies as a case of populism, and what does not? In this section, I explain how I determine membership in the set of populist outcomes. At the study's core is the question of what causes populism, and this outcome is defined in terms of electoral support: When does a populist strategy result in sizable electoral support? As such, classification of instances of the outcome requires, first, the categorization of each presidential candidate as a populist or a nonpopulist and, second, the identification of each populist's share of the vote. A positive outcome means that, in a given presidential election, the candidates using a populist strategy collectively received significant electoral returns (more on this point below). Specifically, then, outcomes are framed in terms of electoral contests as opposed to individual candidates. The analysis includes all presidential elections in South America and Mexico from 1996 to 2010, with the caveats that they must be first-round contests, direct elections (which excludes the countries of Suriname and Guyana), and considered free and fair (which excludes the Peruvian election of 2000).[1] The choice of 1996 as a starting date stems from two factors. First, it is after the last elections of neopopulists and before the first election of a third-era populist (again, with the exception of Peru in 2000). Second, prior to this point, no systematic survey data existed.

Categorization of the candidates as populists or nonpopulists (those using a populist strategy and those not) is based on the definition offered in Chapter 2. Populism is a means of building and/or maintaining political power based on the mass mobilization of supporters using antiestablishment appeals and plebiscitarian linkages. This classical concept structure requires that instances must exhibit both attributes (antiestablishment appeals and plebiscitarianism) to be classified as populist. Of the 126 candidacies in the thirty-five elections under consideration, eighteen used a populist strategy (see Table 5.1). All other presidential candidates are nonpopulists. In Appendix 2, I discuss the operationalization of the concept in more detail.

Table 5.1 Populists in Contemporary Latin America

Country	Year	Candidate	Party	Vote (%)
Bolivia	1997	Kuljis	UCS	16.1
	2002	Fernández	UCS	5.5
	2005	Morales	MAS	53.7
	2009	Morales	MAS	64.2
Ecuador	1998	Noboa	PRE	26.6
	2002	Gutiérrez	PSP	20.6
		Noboa	PRIAN	17.4
		Bucaram	PRE	11.9
	2006	Noboa	PRIAN	26.8
		Correa	PAIS	22.8
	2009	Correa	PAIS	52.0
		Noboa	PRIAN	11.4
Mexico	2006	López Obrador	PRD	36.1
Paraguay	2008	Oviedo	UNACE	21.9
Peru	2006	Humala	PNP	30.6
Venezuela	1998	Chávez	MVR	56.2
	2000	Chávez	MVR	59.7
	2006	Chávez	MVR	62.9

Notes: See Appendix 2 for operationalization details.
See the List of Acronyms for the full names of these parties.

This list excludes a few individuals that some consider populists. Neither Néstor Kirchner nor Cristina Fernández de Kirchner of Argentina, for instance, makes the list because neither consistently used antiestablishment appeals as defined earlier in the book. By some accounts, Néstor Kirchner is considered a populist in part because he was an "outsider," coming from a remote province. However, and as is examined in depth in the next chapter, outsider status is not synonymous with populism, and, at least by the definition used in this work, Kirchner was not even a political outsider. Similarly, Álvaro Uribe of Colombia was something of a maverick in that he broke away from the Liberal Party and established a top-down electoral movement. Nevertheless, neither the Kirchners nor Uribe fulfill both necessary and sufficient conditions for the conceptualization of populism used here and thus fall outside of the classification.

Bolivia's Evo Morales, as discussed in the prior chapter, is a complicated example because his rise to national prominence came on the backs of the *cocaleros* movement. Given the role of this social movement, characterizing his 2002 campaign as involving top-down electoral mobilization is difficult; the campaign instead had a bottom-up quality. By 2005, however, Morales had changed his strategy (particularly in urban areas) enough to be considered a populist. Given his discourse and the use of the top-down mobilization, this analysis codes Morales negatively for 2002 but positively for the subsequent elections.[2]

The list also may include individuals whom others would exclude. Álvaro Noboa, for instance, made much of his economic wealth and used clientelistic linkages to build support, which at times took the basic form of handing out dollar bills (Conaghan 2011, 270). Yet he also attacked the political establishment (despite his status as the country's wealthiest person), consistently appealed to the people, and framed his campaign in messianic terms. He claimed he was on a religious mission to help the poor. His personal control over his party (the Institutional Renewal Party of National Action [PRIAN]), distaste for coalition building, and active efforts to undermine organizational intermediaries are consistent with plebiscitarian linkages, even if infused with patrimonial traits (see Freidenberg 2015). Others may emphasize Noboa's clientelistic linkages and thus categorize him differently; such disagreements are the nature of classification, after all. As discussed previously, nevertheless, multiple linkages may be used simultaneously, and thus his multiple campaigns are included here.

With the individual candidates thus categorized, the next step concerns the extent of their electoral support. Specifically, what share of the vote constitutes success? The most successful candidates, of course, are those who win the presidency, and so a possible threshold for membership in the set of positive outcomes could be victory versus defeat. However, in Latin America candidates have won elections on the basis of a wide range of electoral results, which means that considering only the instances where a populist takes office may be misleading. For instance, Ecuador's Rafael Correa received 22.84 percent of the first-round vote in 2006 and went on to become president. Ollanta Humala received 30.62 percent of all valid votes the same year in Peru but did not become president. If only the winning populists were included, the study would miss important contenders like Humala or Mexico's López Obrador. Additionally, the focus on individual candidates may mask the overall electoral support for populism. In the Ecuadorian example, Correa's results were not overwhelming, but when his share of the vote is combined with that of the other populist candidates, populists received 50 percent of the vote.

Putting aside a threshold defined by victory leaves two alternatives. One is to identify a cutoff point and thus establish a dichotomous classification: the given observation (election) would be positive if the vote total for all populist candidates met or exceeded some percentage threshold, or it would be negative. The other is to code in a way that takes into account the degrees of electoral support. This "fuzzy" coding is central to fuzzy set qualitative comparative analysis (fsQCA); outcomes and causal factors can be understood not just as positive/present and negative/absent but as partial instances. One election, for instance, could be "fully in" the set of positive outcomes or "more in than out," "mostly out," and so forth. This version allows for a more fine-grained analysis, and it presents a harder test for the analysis (Ragin 2009). In the analysis that follows, I try each version.

For the dichotomous option, I use 25 percent as the threshold. One might complain the number is too low, particularly in light of the stunning successes of some populists: Hugo Chávez, for instance, received 63 percent of the vote in 2006, and Evo Morales took 64 percent in 2009. Can we equate a 25 percent vote share with 64 percent? The response is, first, Latin American elections commonly have multiple candidates, which can divide the vote distribution. For this reason winning candidates frequently earn only a third or less of the vote in the first round. Second, a high cutoff of, say, 50 percent, would exclude a number of observations where populists were at least somewhat successful. López Obrador, for instance, earned over 36 percent of the vote in Mexico, which seems far too significant a percentage to classify negatively. By contrast, a share of, say, 20 percent seems too low to count as an electoral success.[3] Hence, this analysis settles on 25 percent for the cutoff in the dichotomous test.

Another response, however, is to accept the concerns and deal with them by using fuzzy coding. And so the analysis below includes two versions of fuzzy coding: one uses a five-value categorization and the other uses continuous coding. In the first, an election could be a "fully in" the set of instances of electoral success, "mostly in," "neither in nor out," "mostly out," and "fully out," and these would receive the codes of 1, 0.75, 0.5,

0.25, and 0, respectively. The second version is even more nuanced, with values ranging continuously between 1 and 0 reflecting the degrees of membership in the set.[4] (See Appendix 2 for coding details.) Put more plainly, in my analysis, I use three separate ways of measuring the success of populism.

Importantly, for each of these three ways of measurement, the analysis that follows includes positive outcomes alongside nonpositive outcomes. With the dichotomous version of success, outcomes are classified as either positive or negative, but none are partial or intermediate. In the fuzzy versions, partial cases are considered. The inclusion of nonpositive outcomes provides greater leverage for making causal inferences than the use of only positive outcomes. Concerns of selection bias, which happens when researchers study only positive outcomes, have been circulating for some time (e.g., Geddes 1990; King, Keohane, and Verba 1994). Barbara Geddes (1990) states the issue plainly: "Selecting cases on the dependent variable entails a high probability of getting the wrong answer" (149). One reason is that the causes associated with the positive cases may also be present in the negative ones. Though this view is contested, particularly regarding the use of process tracing within single-country studies (Collier, Mahoney, and Seawright 2004, 96; George and Bennett 2005, 22–25), the importance of including nonpositive cases holds true. Their presence provides a check for disconfirming observations as well as influencing the weight assigned to the various causal factors, a point that holds in multiple methods including, notably, Boolean analysis (Mahoney and Goertz 2004, 668). Additionally, negative cases not only help determine causal sufficiency but also are required to determine whether or not necessary causes, which are important to the present study, are trivial (more on this below) (Braumoeller and Goertz 2002). Having nonpositive cases in the study, in short, can result in much greater confidence in the findings.

That said, the inclusion of nonpositive but irrelevant cases or outcomes can be problematic. Doing so can introduce new forms of bias regarding the results. Hence one must take care in selecting the instances to be studied alongside the positive ones. James Mahoney and Gary Goertz (2004) suggest the "possibility principle" as a means of choosing appropriate negative cases. The central idea is that the outcome should be possible in the instances under observation. To evaluate possibility, Mahoney and Goertz (2004) suggest the rule of inclusion: "Cases are relevant if their value on at least one independent variable is positively related to the outcome of interest" (657). In the terms of QCA analysis, this rule suggests that a particular case should be included as long as it exhibits at least one of the causal factors. Those factors are discussed in detail below, but note here that the rule of inclusion holds for each of the countries considered. Mahoney and Goertz's (2004) second rule is that of exclusion, under which a case is considered irrelevant if it holds a value on a causal factor known to make the outcome impossible. The rule of exclusion does not apply to any of the countries under review. In sum, the analysis includes positive and nonpositive outcomes to maximize its analytical leverage, and none of the nonpositive instances takes place in a country that could be considered irrelevant for this study. Populism is abbreviated in the tables and equations below, where the use of uppercase letters (*POP*) represents its presence and the use of lowercase letters (*pop*) represents its absence, following standard symbolism of Boolean algebra. Upper- and lowercase lettering holds the same meanings, presence and absence, respectively, for all of the causal factors.

Causal Factors

The discussion of the literature in Chapter 3 highlights the six leading causal factors most commonly used to explain populism.[5] These factors include three that are more political in nature (the level of institutionalization of the party system, citizens' confidence in political institutions, and their perception of corruption) and three that are of an economic nature (the level of economic misery, exposure to globalization, and social spending).[6] Part of the debate in the literature is which combination of these factors can best account for populism's emergence. The analysis includes them all, testing both extant explanations and the one offered in this book.

Perhaps the most prominent causal factor concerns the level of party system institutionalization or quality of representation. A number of scholars cite this factor, arguing for instance that an inchoate party system increases the likelihood of populism or the likelihood that populist candidates will gain support. Although researchers do not always explicitly state whether the causal linkage is on the demand or the supply side, or whether party system weakness is a necessary factor, the relationship is the same. As Roberts (2013) explains, populism "is a permanent possibility where representative institutions are weak, fragile, or ineffective at articulating or responding to social concerns" (38).

To measure the level of party system institutionalization in this analysis, I use an index that captures changes to the party system over time (represented by the acronym PSI). The concept itself is rooted in Mainwaring and Scully's (1995) notion of institutionalized versus inchoate party systems and includes four dimensions: the stability of interparty competition, the extent of party roots in society, the legitimacy of elections and parties, and the level of party organization. The PSI, meanwhile, builds on Mark P. Jones's (2005) multifaceted version in which he attempts to capture each of these dimensions. His version, in turn, relies on multiple quantitative indicators to measure each dimension. As thorough as Jones's index is, it and other efforts to measure party system institutionalization are static, allowing comparisons among countries but not within countries over time. To overcome this problem, many use electoral volatility as an indicator that can demonstrate readily changes from one period to the next. However, volatility touches on just one of the four dimensions of the broader concept and it can vary independently of levels of institutionalization, thus leaving its appropriateness as an indicator in question (Luna and Altman 2011; Mainwaring and Torcal 2006).

In my PSI, I attempt to capture both the full range of the concept and changes over time. I do so by making slight modifications to Jones's index, finding indicators that have better time series coverage. Two to four such indicators measure each dimension of the concept. (See Appendix 1 for details.) The overall level of institutionalization can be demonstrated on a 100-point scale, with higher numbers reflecting greater levels of institutionalization. Given the logic of this factor, one expects to see low scores associated with instances of populism. The data here range from a low of 27.1 to a high of 75.3. For the high points of each country, the scores vary from 40.1 to 75.3, and, for the low points of each country, they vary from 27.1 to 67.9. Variation can be found within countries and across countries. Argentina's scores, for example, vary from a low of 35.5 to a high of 59.4. For all the countries, the year 2010 showed scores from 27.6 (Peru) to 74.7 (Uruguay). Put simply, this range (with an average standard deviation of 10 points each year) should provide ample variation on this factor. Table 5.2 provides the full range of data for all of the countries in the study from 1996 to 2010.

To assess the relationship of this factor and all others on populism, only scores associated with elections are used. In addition, the analysis uses a one-year lag for all indicators in an attempt to capture factors leading up to the elections but independent of the electoral cycle itself. The emergence of a populist candidate, for instance, could cause a party system to weaken rather than represent the result thereof. By using data from the year prior to the election, this concern can be mitigated. From the 165 data points in Table 5.2, then, thirty-five are applicable to the elections under investigation. As an example, Chile's very stable (by regional terms) party system prior to its 2005 election had a PSI score of 57.29. Bolivia, on the other hand, had a score of 45.37 prior to its 2002 elections, when the traditional parties were clearly under threat and the winning candidate won a meager 22 percent of the vote. Relatively few points separate these examples, but many agree in characterizing Chile as having a stable and strong party system and Bolivia as having the opposite (e.g., Mainwaring, Bejarano, and Leongómez 2006; Stein et al. 2006).

Unlike all of the other causal factors, which use fuzzy codings, this one has a dichotomous coding: the party system is either inchoate or it is

Table 5.2 Party System Institutionalization Index

	ARG	BOL	BRA	CHILE	COL	ECU	MEX	PARA	PERU	URU	VEN
1996	59.4	51.4	50.3	60.0	49.7	54.7	59.4	59.3	33.5	70.5	41.6
1997	57.4	50.4	51.4	62.3	52.1	47.7	61.7	54.5	32.2	74.0	42.7
1998	55.9	50.9	52.8	61.2	52.3	45.5	57.8	55.4	32.4	73.7	44.7
1999	57.5	50.6	52.6	60.1	51.7	44.3	52.5	55.0	39.1	73.7	48.3
2000	56.5	47.2	51.9	57.4	48.3	43.8	51.1	54.6	39.6	72.6	51.9
2001	49.6	45.4	51.6	56.0	44.7	43.2	48.7	52.0	40.1	71.2	51.5
2002	47.4	45.3	51.3	55.6	44.7	42.9	44.2	51.5	39.1	68.1	53.4
2003	48.6	45.1	51.4	55.8	44.5	42.8	43.2	51.7	38.7	67.9	42.3
2004	41.3	40.8	52.6	57.3	46.0	46.1	42.3	51.3	39.9	69.2	43.8
2005	35.5	42.7	53.7	57.1	45.0	49.0	50.3	51.8	38.0	71.0	45.1
2006	42.6	42.0	55.6	56.8	44.9	47.0	52.7	58.2	39.8	69.6	45.5
2007	48.9	45.2	55.0	57.2	45.1	47.4	50.8	59.1	38.9	74.2	46.0
2008	46.3	48.1	57.0	57.9	44.1	38.1	47.9	62.8	37.9	74.6	46.3
2009	45.6	48.9	59.1	58.3	42.5	38.1	48.5	63.7	27.1	75.3	43.8
2010	47.1	48.7	59.2	58.5	42.9	38.3	48.4	62.6	27.6	74.7	41.4

Sources: Adam Carr's Election Archive; Economic Commission for Latin America and the Caribbean (Comisión Económica para América Latina y el Caribe [CEPAL]); Iberoamerican Institute of the University of Salamanca's Parliamentary Elites in Latin America (PELA); LAPOP; Latinobarómetro; Payne, Zovatto G., and Díaz (2007); Political Database of the Americas; Wikipedia; and the World Bank.

institutionalized. The reason for this exception stems from the literature. Mainwaring and Scully's (1995) original conceptualization understood party system institutionalization to be dichotomous, and subsequent uses (e.g., Jones 2005) reinforce this understanding.[7] A positive coding follows from the logic of this causal factor: low levels of institutionalization should relate to the electoral success of populist candidates; hence, those party systems coded positively (indicated by the value of 1 in the tables) are those with low scores on the index. This causal factor is represented by *INCHOATE*.

The second causal factor is the perception of corruption (represented by *CORRUPT*), which could affect the demand for a populist political alternative. This factor plays a key role in the argument presented in Chapter 3. To measure corruption, I use Transparency International's CPI, which captures citizens' subjective assessment thereof. The data are arranged on a 10-point scale and range from 1.5 (Paraguay prior to its 1998 election) to 7.4 (Chile prior to its 2005 election), with a mean of 3.53 and median of 3.4. According to Transparency International, any country with a score below the midpoint (5) has a "serious" corruption problem. Sadly, of the thirty-five observations here, only five have scores above the midpoint; the norm for much of Latin America is a high level of perceived corruption. Nevertheless, a qualitative difference may be found between persistent levels of corruption to which citizens have become accustomed and instances of critical or crisis levels.

The observation closest to the midpoint came from Uruguay prior to the 2004 elections (with a CPI score of 5.5). Arguably the most politically stable country in Latin America, it and Chile are the only two countries in this study to have positive ratings from the World Bank on its control of corruption score (which is not a matter of citizen perception). Compare their situations to, say, Venezuela prior to Chávez's first election in 1998, when its control of corruption score was deeply negative and its CPI score was 2.7. As Moisés Naím (2001) points out, corruption at that time had become a national obsession for Venezuelan citizens. In other words, this relatively narrow range of data captures a substantial array of experiences. The fuzzy coding schema attempts to represent these differences. Observations with coded CPI scores approaching a value of 1 therefore represent corruption crises and thus may give citizens reason to be dissatisfied with the political status quo and in turn offer their support to a populist candidate.

The third causal factor is the lack of trust in political institutions (represented by *DISTRUST*). As with corruption, the general idea is that citizens may demand a populist alternative when they have lost their confidence in or withdrawn their belief in the legitimacy of the country's political institutions. Though a few cite institutional distrust, only Doyle (2011) studies it directly by using an index based on three separate Latinobarómetro questions. The measure used here is the same. It consists of the average aggregate score for those who say they have "a lot of confidence" and "some confidence" with respect to each of three institutions: political parties, congress, and the judiciary.[8] The data range from 7.47 (prior to the Argentine elections of 2003) to 46.13 (prior to Uruguay's 2009 elections) and have a mean of 25.58 and median of 27.43. The regional norm, then, is for citizens to have little confidence in institutions. As with the perception of corruption, however, a qualitative difference may be identified between a score of, say, 32.2 (such as Brazil leading up to the 2010 elections when President Luiz Inácio "Lula" da Silva enjoyed very high approval ratings) and 15.4 (such as Bolivia prior to its 2005 elections and in the aftermath of two successive presidential resignations). Those observations showing a value close to 1 are those that had not just low levels of confidence but a crisis of confidence.

The next set of factors addresses versions of the socioeconomic argument, according to which some sort of economic dislocation or disadvantage may lead voters to demand populism. The literature on populism includes a debate regarding the specifics of this point: Does economic suffering mean high levels of inflation, low levels of growth, high levels of unemployment, or something else? To accommodate these differences, I use an index that captures economic misery over a five-year period to measure the fourth causal factor (represented by *ECONMIS*).[9] Arthur Okun (1962) developed an early such index by simply combining the current levels of inflation and unemployment. Robert J. Barro (1996) offered an alternative that incorporated the level of per capita GDP growth along with inflation and unemployment and took into account changes in the levels from year to year.

The index for economic misery employed here is a combination of sorts of the two models and one that deals with longer-term economic conditions. Using World Bank data, I take the five-year average level of inflation, add it to the five-year average level of unemployment, and then subtract the five-year average level of per capita GDP growth.[10] The index technically has no limit: Brazil's extremely high inflation rates in the 1990s give it a score of 822.43 leading up to its 1998 elections. On the lower end of the scale is Mexico prior to the 2006 election with a score of 7.48. The mean for this measure is 44.58 and the median is 414.96. Though these data are obviously skewed by Brazil's score for 1998 (without it, for instance, the mean would be 21.70), nevertheless, a very wide range of index scores represents a similarly wide range of experiences. Those observations that have coded scores at or approaching 1 are those in a state of economic misery, and thus the citizens may be receptive to a populist's antiestablishment appeals and efforts at mobilization.

The fifth causal factor deals with neoliberal economic reforms and the resultant exposure to the international market economy (represented by

GLOBAL). Many explanations of populism over time have pointed to one or another kind of disruptive economic change, such as the collapse of the export-led model of development or the debt crisis of the 1980s. Contemporary versions of this kind of explanation involve neoliberalism and globalization (e.g., Stokes 2009): their dislocating impact may lead citizens to support candidates who promise some relief. Economic globalization or the wrenching economic reforms that allowed it may have led citizens to the conclusion that government is more concerned with foreign economic interests than the plight of ordinary citizens. The mere presence of more imported goods on retail shelves is unlikely to stir much angst; more likely to agitate the populations may be high-profile actions such as privatization of utilities, decisions to open up areas to foreign companies for petroleum exploitation, or weakening labor standards as a result of international pressure. Steps like these are part of the terrain of an international market orientation. Where the global economic presence is high compared to the value of domestic production, these kinds of measures may appear more prominent and politically salient.

Hence, a standard measure of globalization serves as the proxy here: imports of goods and services as a percentage of GDP plus exports of goods and services as a percentage of GDP.[11] The data come from the World Bank and cover a wide range, from 103.25 for Paraguay leading up to the 2003 elections down to 15.84 in Brazil prior to its 1998 contests.[12] The mean is 51.16; the median is 49.86. Coded scores for *GLOBAL* at or approaching the value of 1 represent instances where the country has a very high level of exposure to the global markets. Citizens in these countries may conclude their governments favor foreign interests, and thus they may be attracted to a populist candidate.

The final causal factor taps into the issue of unmet social needs. A variety of studies highlight socioeconomic exclusion or unmet social needs, signifying a state's failure to provide for the basic needs of its citizens (e.g., Navia and Walker 2010; Panizza and Miorelli 2009). This concept is not about employment or economic conditions, nor does this factor necessarily reflect the quality of democratic governance (see Mainwaring, Scully, and Cullell 2010). Instead, this factor is a matter of governmental or state attention to citizens: To what extent does the state attempt to meet citizens' social needs, including education, housing, and health care? Where such needs go unmet, citizens may turn their backs on incumbents and seek out a populist alternative.

The World Bank governance indicators do not quite capture a state's abilities to take care of its citizens (see Kaufman, Kraay, and Mastruzzi 2010). Hence, to measure this factor (designated as *SOCIAL*), I use data compiled by the Economic Commission for Latin America and the

Caribbean (Comisión Económica para América Latina [CEPAL]) on social expenditures as a percentage of GDP.[13] Through this indicator, I attempt to capture the overall allocation of societal resources. The data range from 3.49 in Ecuador prior to the 1998 elections to 27.06 in Brazil prior to the 2010 elections. The mean and median are 13.96 and 13.48, respectively. As a point of comparison, the Organisation for Economic Co-operation and Development (OECD) reports an average social spending of 22.1 percent of GDP in 2009 for its thirty-four countries, and of them, only four spent less than 15 percent of GDP (two of which were Mexico and Chile). As a region, then, Latin America spends relatively little on social needs. Still, a real-world gap does indeed exist between, say, Brazil under Lula da Silva, when that country had the region's highest level of social spending due to his generous social policies, and even midrange countries like Bolivia in 1997, which spent 13.9 percent of its GDP on social needs. Hence, an observation with a coded score for *SOCIAL* at or approaching a value of 1 is not meeting the social needs of its citizens, and thus they may have a reason to be dissatisfied with the political status quo and willing to support populist candidates.

As described previously, most of the arguments in the literature and the one here rely on some combination of factors. For instance, Walker (2008) includes three factors covering both political institutional and socioeconomic conditions. Roberts (2006) considers institutional and economic factors. Even those that prioritize an individual variable often round out their explanations with reference to one or more other conditions. Doyle (2011) argues that citizens' confidence is key, but other political factors are also significant. The largest source of divergence among those who have analyzed populism is not which single factor they conclude causes populism, but which two or three they include in the causal combination. The six described above cover the leading possibilities in the literature. (Table 5.3 provides the raw data for each factor.) A key advantage of the QCA methodology is the ability to simultaneously test every possible combination of factors. In this way, the following analysis includes the many different combinations used in the literature. It also includes the argument put forth in this book, that electoral support for populism results from the combination of a weakly institutionalized party system, the perception of prevalent corruption, and evidence of disadvantage.

Necessity Results

The analysis covers both the necessary conditions for populism and the sufficient conditions. For each, I discuss the results of all versions of coding

Table 5.3 Raw Data for Causal Conditions

Election	INCHOATE	CORRUPT	DISTRUST	ECONMIS	GLOBAL	SOCIAL
ARG1999	55.91	3.0	18.60	14.16	23.35	20.12
ARG2003	47.44	2.8	7.47	24.49	41.75	19.67
ARG2007	42.63	2.9	23.63	22.33	43.99	20.81
BOL1997	51.37	3.4	21.37	13.34	49.86	13.91
BOL2002	45.37	2.0	16.70	8.22	45.23	17.74
BOL2005	40.79	2.2	15.40	8.10	57.46	18.11
BOL2009	48.07	3.0	19.43	8.97	82.87	18.42
BRA1998	51.37	3.6	30.50	822.43	15.84	19.29
BRA2002	51.61	4.0	28.53	13.93	25.68	21.27
BRA2006	53.73	3.7	28.63	16.47	26.65	22.51
BRA2010	59.06	3.7	32.20	10.71	22.12	27.06
CHI1999	61.23	6.8	34.33	8.43	55.87	13.65
CHI2005	57.29	7.4	27.67	8.84	68.26	13.48
CHI2009	57.89	6.9	26.73	8.17	81.04	14.11
COL1998	52.14	2.2	31.63	29.10	35.60	12.63
COL2002	44.67	3.8	18.23	29.18	33.90	11.47
COL2006	44.98	4.0	31.77	17.36	35.63	12.83
COL2010	42.45	3.7	33.23	13.86	34.28	14.45
ECU1998	47.68	2.8	22.80	37.73	45.02	3.49
ECU2002	43.20	2.3	12.03	61.86	50.75	4.46
ECU2006	49.03	2.5	13.17	19.25	56.10	4.68
ECU2009	38.06	2.0	24.30	7.81	68.06	7.30
MEX2000	52.45	3.4	35.60	27.89	63.09	8.63
MEX2006	50.33	3.5	27.43	7.48	55.65	9.42
PAR1998	54.51	1.5	33.17	16.89	95.74	8.66
PAR2003	51.49	1.7	10.30	19.51	89.28	10.27
PAR2008	59.09	2.4	12.57	13.10	103.25	9.17
PER2001	39.64	4.4	23.30	13.74	34.16	8.62
PER2006	37.96	3.5	17.50	9.19	44.26	9.55
URU1999	73.69	4.3	42.33	35.57	35.64	19.68
URU2004	67.93	5.5	27.47	27.53	51.76	20.78
URU2009	74.58	6.9	46.13	11.88	65.21	21.65
VEN1998	42.72	2.8	29.70	71.99	51.25	9.81
VEN2000	48.34	2.6	28.80	66.72	42.07	9.45
VEN2006	45.08	2.3	42.63	33.96	60.13	11.52

Note: Lower values signify worse/crisis conditions for *INCHOATE, CORRUPT, DISTRUST,* and *SOCIAL,* whereas higher values indicate worse/crisis conditions for *ECONMIS* and *GLOBAL.*

populists' electoral success (dichotomous and the two kinds of fuzzy) in the following sections. Beginning with the necessity analysis, the results show that among the causal factors only a weakly institutionalized party system is necessary for populists to have electoral success.

QCA analyses for necessity require setting thresholds for consistency and coverage, which are akin to goodness-of-fit tests. Specifically, consistency refers to the percentage of the set of positive outcomes that exhibit the causal condition under investigation. Charles C. Ragin (2000) recommends threshold standards of "usually" or "almost always" necessary, rather than a deterministic perfect necessity (which would be reflected with the value of 1 on a scale from 0 to 1). The claim that a condition is necessary even if it is *not always* necessary may seem odd at first glance, but it is in keeping with the reality of imperfect social phenomena. Though the category "almost always" is inherently flexible, it provides the general standard used here. Still, to help provide clarity regarding necessity, a fairly stringent threshold is used. Hence, only those factors meeting or exceeding a consistency threshold of 0.85 are necessary to account for populists' electoral success.

Coverage concerns the empirical relevance of the causal condition, thus offering an important nuance. Thinking of coverage in terms of the issue of trivialness may be helpful (Goertz 2006a; Ragin 2006). A "trivial" necessary condition is one that may be present in all of the observations with positive outcomes but is also present in many of those with negative outcomes. Consider, for instance, the causes of admission to an elite university with an acceptance rate of, say, 15 percent. To have a chance at acceptance, one must first apply. Hence, applying for admission to the university is a necessary condition for acceptance. At the same time, applying is also present in all of the cases of rejection. The set of applicants is far larger than the set of admissions, since only 15 percent win admission. As such, applying is a trivial necessary condition and not helpful in understanding the admission criteria of the elite university. Coverage scores illuminate trivialness by showing the relationship of the two sets (causal factor and outcome).[14] If fewer than half of the instances with the causal factor also show positive outcomes, then the condition is considered trivial even if it is technically necessary. A coverage threshold of 0.50 therefore could be used, but setting it slightly higher helps rule out the truly borderline observations. The coverage threshold used here, then, is 0.55. Of those instances exhibiting the causal factor, then, at least 55 percent of them must be positive for the outcome in order to be considered nontrivial.

With these thresholds, the analysis produces the one necessary condition, a weakly institutionalized party system. When populists' electoral success is scored with a dichotomous coding, *INCHOATE* has a perfect consistency (1.00), far surpassing the threshold of being "almost always" necessary and meaning party system institutionalization is present in every single positive case of populism in this data set. With the more demanding fuzzy versions, the results demonstrate a similarly strong set relationship, with *INCHOATE* consistency scores of 0.91 (for the five-value version) and 0.90 (for the continuous version). *INCHOATE* also has a reasonably high coverage, ranging from 0.61 (for the dichotomous version) to 0.58 (for both fuzzy versions). In other words, the results show that party system institutionalization is a nontrivial necessary condition, regardless of how it is measured. Figure 5.1 has a Venn diagram illustrating the set relations between weakly institutionalized party systems and populism.

Interestingly, two other causal conditions come close to but do not meet the thresholds for necessity. The level of social spending, for one, has a consistency score ranging from 0.79 to 0.81 and a coverage score ranging from 0.50 to 0.53. These results suggest that it is on the borderline, but still under the threshold, of having a nontrivial necessity. The results for corruption are even more interesting. *CORRUPT* has a very high consistency level, ranging from 0.93 to 0.98, making it present in more positive instances of populism than even *INCHOATE* for some versions of the coding. However, its coverage scores never rise above 0.49, which keep it below the threshold for trivialness. These numbers do not suggest that corruption is unimportant or not problematic, only that it is not explanatory with respect to necessity. This point, in turn, has implications for the understanding of populism. For instance, Hawkins (2010) argues that corruption is a necessary condition: "Populist leaders are found only in countries with high levels of corruption" (233). Although Hawkins's conclusion may be largely accurate, the coverage scores for corruption should give one pause. Corruption is a common problem in all of the countries under review and is not specific to instances of populism. For those observations showing a crisis of corruption, most were elections in which populists did not receive much electoral support. Consider Paraguay: of all of the countries, the very worst corruption scores were here prior to its 1998 and 2003 elections. However, the very old Colorado Party faced no populist opponents and won each contest. In sum, a weakly institutionalized party system is the sole necessary condition for populists to achieve electoral success.

Figure 5.1 Venn Diagram of Necessity

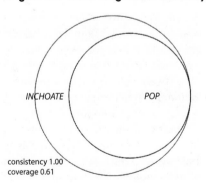

Note: Results shown are those for the dichotomous coding of *POP*.

Sufficiency Results

Turning to sufficiency, the results for all three versions of coding populists' electoral success are very similar. Each of them shows the same two combinations of factors, which together include weakly institutionalized party systems, the perception of prevalent corruption, inadequate social spending, and globalization. The initial results allow for ruling out the level of confidence in political institutions and economic misery as possible contributing factors. In turn, this step leads to results showing that party system weakness with corruption and *either* inadequate social spending *or* globalization can account for populism in contemporary Latin America.

As with the necessity analysis, certain criteria must be established (excluding coverage thresholds, which are not required). The results show the score, but their function is to help one assess the utility of causal combinations that meet the consistency threshold. For the sufficiency analyses, this consistency threshold is 0.80. This standard is slightly less stringent than that used to determine necessity, but it allows for more causal expressions to pass the sufficiency test than higher thresholds might. Hence, although still indicating "almost always sufficient," the 0.80 level is slightly more generous for the literature, making confirmation of competing hypothesis somewhat more likely.

One must also consider the number of simplification procedures—"minimization"—to conduct. Minimization involves first the elimination of irrelevant factors and then the use of simplifying assumptions to reduce long and complex causal combinations into more parsimonious ones (for a concise explanation, see Rihoux and de Meur 2009, particularly pages 34–39). For instance, using the consistency threshold of 0.80 and revealing only the primitive expressions, the results of the sufficiency analysis include eight causal combinations, each of which contains all six causal factors and explains either one or two, but no more, of the positive instances for populism (for the dichotomous coding of populists' electoral success). In other words, without any minimization at all, the fsQCA analysis returns almost unique explanations for each instance. These are no more than descriptions, not generalizable explanations. Using a higher minimization standard, the QCA software can produce more parsimonious results by, in effect, conducting automatic counterfactual analysis. Though some raise objections to this step, it is in fact an important part of the scientific enterprise. As Gary King, Robert O. Kohane, and Sidney Verba explain (1994), "the key distinguishing mark of scientific research is the goal of making inferences that go beyond the particular observations collected" (8). Although acknowledging the potential pitfall, in this study, I prioritize parsimony and seek the simplest explanation that can account for populism in this set of countries.

In this case, using the highest minimization setting (to produce the parsimonious results) gives a very different result:[15] two causal combinations can account for all instances of populism. Following the symbolism of Boolean algebra, upon which QCA is based, uppercase letters indicate the presence of a factor, and lowercase letters indicate its absence. Additionally, the symbol * indicates the logical AND, whereas + indicates the logical OR. The results, then, can be displayed in this manner: (*INCHOATE*GLOBAL*) + (*INCHOATE*CORRUPT*SOCIAL*). Table 5.4 presents the results for the dichotomous coding of populism. Regardless of the coding, nevertheless, the analysis returns the same formulas and they have similar scores for collective consistency (from 0.87 to 0.88) and coverage (from 0.83 to 0.89). This result is quite interesting given the range of coding schema used.

Translated, the results show that a weakly institutionalized party system *and* the prevalence of corruption *and* inadequate social spending can account for most of the instances of populism. This combination, the second formula in Table 5.4, explains all of the positive instances of populist electoral support except for Bolivia in 2005 and 2009. It has high consistency and coverage scores. The other formula suggests that a weakly institutionalized party system *and* globalization can account for the Bolivian instances as well as four other positive instances. In other words, several cases can be explained by both formulas (and thus might be considered overdetermined). That corruption does not figure into this solution for Bolivia is interesting (and possibly misleading) because the country had trouble with the perception of corruption: the CPI score for each election was within the "crisis" range as identified for the study, and Bolivia's score for the 2005 election was the fifth worst of all the observations. Additionally, the necessity analysis revealed that, although trivial in accounting for necessity, a crisis of corruption was present in virtually all of the positive instances of populism.

Nevertheless, one could stop here. The solution that explains most of the positive outcomes directly supports the argument presented earlier: weak party systems along with corruption and evidence of disadvantage

Table 5.4 Six-Factor Model Sufficiency Results, Parsimonious Solution

Combination	Consistency	Raw Coverage	Unique Coverage
*INCHOATE*GLOBAL* +	0.94	0.48	0.14
*INCHOATE*CORRUPT*SOCIAL*	0.88	0.75	0.41
Total Solution	0.88	0.89	N/A

Notes: Results shown are those for the dichotomous coding of *POP*, using KIRQ's simplification setting 3.
See Appendix 3 for the results of the fuzzy codings of *POP*.

(inadequate social spending) lead to populists' electoral support. The other solution is necessary for just Bolivia, and, with good reason, one could consider this case an outlier. However, additional steps may contribute to the identification of the core causal factors or at least shore up confidence in these results.

Six causal factors produce sixty-four possible combinations, which far exceeds the number of observations in this study ($N = 35$). A number of the outcomes can be explained by the same set of causal conditions, leaving forty logical remainders—combinations for which there are no empirical referents. By itself, limited diversity is not a problem but instead a fact of social phenomena. Nevertheless, the "limited diversity problem" can complicate analysis. For this reason, some advocate the use of relatively few causal factors in QCA analyses: with fewer causal factors come fewer possible combinations and, therefore, less limited diversity: "The fewer the number of 'causes' we need to explain a phenomenon of interest, the closer we come to the 'core' elements of causal mechanisms. Moreover, the better we are able to identify fundamental causes, the easier it will be to produce results that may be tested on other cases" (Berg-Schlosser and de Meur 2009, 27).

The principal way to deal with limited diversity and the resulting logical remainders is to rely upon fewer assumptions. Rather than use either no minimization at all or the highest level of minimization, one could use the "intermediate" solution. The cost of doing so, however, is usually a less parsimonious set of causal combinations. In this case, the results return four combinations that together include all six causal factors, and none of the combinations can explain more than half of the positive outcomes. (Perhaps tellingly, however, *INCHOATE* and *CORRUPT* are included in every combination.) Another possible response is to simplify the causal "recipe" (see Ragin 2008, especially Chap. 6). Reducing the number of factors from six to four, for instance, lowers the number of combinations from sixty-four to only sixteen. One can compare the competing recipes using consistency and coverage scores as a guide. Ragin (2008) suggests if "a simpler version has comparable consistency but greater coverage than a more complex version, then it might be preferred" (119). A plausible extension of this logic is that where the consistency and coverage scores are comparable but one version substantially reduces the extent of limited diversity, that solution might be preferred.

Toward this end, the analysis takes the step of eliminating two factors, economic misery and distrust of political institutions. Neither of these appeared in the parsimonious sufficiency results reported above, nor was either a necessary factor (or even a "close" necessary factor like *CORRUPT* and *SOCIAL*). These results are not particularly surprising. A simple linear regression, for instance, shows these two factors having the weakest correlations with populists' electoral results.[16] Consider the economic factor. Even though some scholars associate the likelihood of populism with economic crisis, many highlight the fact that populism can and does appear in noncrisis situations. The literature, in other words, provides a reason for excluding this factor. With respect to the other, in all but five of the elections under consideration, less than a third of citizens expressed confidence in their political institutions. This fact suggests a certain level of trivialness. Also, this index might be at best an indicator of some deeper cause; citizens are unlikely to withdraw their trust in institutions if their quality of representation is high, the economy is booming, and so on. For these reasons, *DISTRUST* and *ECONMIS* can be excluded in an effort to reduce the number of logical remainders that must be explained and thus close in on the core causal factors.

Excluding these two factors, the analysis (again using the highest simplification setting to achieve parsimonious results) provides three combinations. Two combinations are the same as above; the third is *CORRUPT*GLOBAL*social*, which means that the perception of prevalent corruption, excessive exposure to globalization, and *adequate* social spending can account for populism. However, this solution has a consistency of 0.72 and a unique coverage of 0.00. Because its consistency is below the threshold and because it offers no added explanatory power, this combination is suspect.

Interestingly, choosing not to rely on any simplifying assumptions provides a very similar set of solutions and retains a similar level of parsimony. In this case, again only two solutions provide a reasonably parsimonious explanation (see Table 5.5).[17] The only difference in the solutions compared to the six-factor model is the addition of *CORRUPT* to the first solution (*INCHOATE*CORRUPT*GLOBAL*). Importantly, the consistency and coverage scores for the two solutions combined are exactly the same as the parsimonious results of the six-factor model, regardless of the coding used for *POP* (see Figure 5.2).[18] On these grounds alone, there is no loss or gain from one recipe (the six-factor or the four-factor) to the other. Using just four factors, however, leaves but five logical remainders, representing a much more circumscribed limitation of diversity. By using the lower simplification setting, moreover, no assumptions are required.[19] In other words, the findings do not rely on counterfactual analysis or going beyond what is empirically observable.

The results are indeed compelling: together, the two solutions far exceed the "almost always" threshold for sufficiency, do not suffer from a serious limited diversity problem, are empirically grounded, are reasonably parsimonious, and explain every positive instance of populism. Furthermore, among the observations where either no populists competed or they received very little electoral support, none are full members of the set exhibiting these causal combinations (see the truth table in Appendix 3).[20]

The first solution (*INCHOATE*CORRUPT*GLOBAL*) suggests that a combination of a weakly institutionalized party system, crisis of corruption,

Table 5.5 Four-Factor Model, Complex Solution

Combination	Consistency	Raw Coverage	Unique Coverage
INCHOATE*CORRUPT*GLOBAL +	0.94	0.48	0.14
INCHOATE*CORRUPT*SOCIAL	0.88	0.75	0.41
Total Solution	0.88	0.89	N/A

Note: Results shown are those for the dichotomous coding of *POP* using KIRQ's simplification setting 2.

Figure 5.2 Venn Diagram of Sufficiency

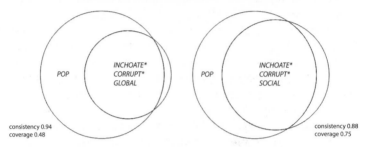

Note: Results shown are those for the dichotomous coding of *POP*.

and excessive exposure to globalization can explain 46 percent to 48 percent of the positive outcomes, depending on the coding used for populists' electoral success. The second solution (*INCHOATE*CORRUPT*SOCIAL*) suggests that the combination of a weakly institutionalized party system, crisis of corruption, and inadequate social spending can explain 69 percent to 75 percent of the positive outcomes, depending on the coding used for populists' electoral success. (Tables for each coding schema appear in Appendix 2.)

Together, the two solutions account for every empirical instance when a populist candidate received significant electoral support. The second solution is only necessary to explain the Bolivian elections of 2005 and 2009. The first solution can account for all of the other outcomes. Put differently, the outcome in four of the cases (Ecuador 2006 and 2009, Mexico 2006, and Venezuela 2006) was overdetermined. Some (e.g., Doyle 2011) exclude the case of Venezuela in 2006, arguing that Chávez had become by this point the establishment himself and thus the definition of populism would not apply. Running the same tests while excluding Venezuela 2006 produces the same results and at similar consistency and coverage scores, for both the dichotomous and continuous fuzzy codings of populists' electoral success (0.87 and 0.89 for the dichotomous coding; 0.85 and 0.82 for the continuous fuzzy coding).[21] Figure 5.3 illustrates the results graphically, showing the particular combination and the outcomes each can explain.

Figure 5.3 Graphical Representation of Sufficient Conditions

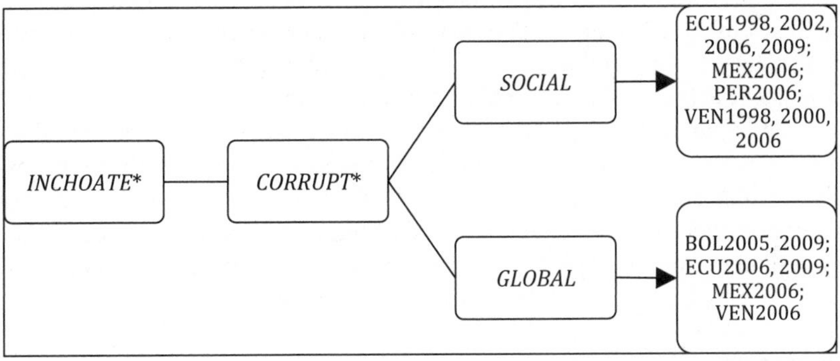

Best practices suggest testing for the negation of the outcome, even if it is not part of the hypotheses under consideration (Schneider and Wagemann 2010, 408). Because causal asymmetry is assumed in qualitative comparative analysis (Berg-Schlosser et al. 2009, 9), one should not expect a mirror image of the solutions for the positive outcome to explain the negation of that outcome. Testing for the negation, therefore, may help validate the findings for the positive outcome. That is, "if a certain combination of conditions leads consistently towards the outcome, but also leads towards the non-outcome then that raises serious doubts about the explanatory strength of the conditions employed" (Mello 2012, 10).

When including the six original factors, the sufficiency analysis for the absence of populism (*pop*) produces five causal combinations when the outcome has a dichotomous coding and six causal combinations when using a continuous fuzzy coding (see Table 5.6).[22] Together they have a consistency score of 0.99 or 0.96, depending on the coding, and coverage scores of 0.86. None is the inverse of the solutions that explain the presence of populism. When using a dichotomous coding, interestingly, the solution with the highest consistency and coverage scores (1.00 and 0.71, respectively) includes only a single factor, *inchoate*, meaning the absence of a weakly

Table 5.6 Sufficiency for Negation of Populism, Parsimonious Results

Combination	Consistency	Raw Coverage	Unique Coverage
inchoate +	1.00	0.71	0.32
corrupt*ECONMIS +	0.99	0.15	0.02
distrust*social +	0.99	0.43	0.01
ECONMIS*social +	0.98	0.24	0.06
corrupt*social	0.99	0.35	0.00
Total Solution	0.99	0.86	N/A

Note: Results shown are those for the dichotomous coding of *pop*.

institutionalized party system. However, it is not a solution when using a continuous fuzzy coding of the outcome. Also, the results from the necessity analyses of the absence of populism, which include sixty-one to seventy-four solutions (depending on the coding schema) that meet or exceed the consistency threshold of 0.50 and coverage threshold of 0.55, do not include *inchoate* by itself. It appears in a variety of combinations, but does not meet the established thresholds.[23] These tests for sufficiency and necessity of *pop* confirm the assumption of causal asymmetry and point to a number of possible explanations for the absence of populism. The absence of populism, in other words, has more explanations than its presence.

Discussion

The results of the necessity and sufficiency analyses support the argument presented in Chapter 3. With respect to the former, the argument suggests that a weakly institutionalized party system would be necessary to provide a supply of populist candidates. Where party systems are well institutionalized, disincentives and obstacles discourage the use of the populist strategy; the opposite is true when they are weakly institutionalized. The analysis supports this logic by finding a single causal factor that surpasses thresholds of consistency and coverage: a weakly institutionalized party system. As discussed previously, a number of scholars note the importance of party systems and their connections with citizens. However, most assign this factor at best the role of permissive condition, but such an assignation understates the importance of this factor and underspecifies its role. As this study demonstrates, a weakly institutionalized party system is a necessary condition and helps explain the supply side of the equation.

The case of Hugo Chávez may be instructive here. Venezuela's deteriorating party system provided a variety of political opportunities through the 1990s. Chávez's emergence may have been the death knell of the party system, but it had been weakening since the end of the 1980s. Prior to his first election, the country's PSI score was 42.27, ranking in the bottom fifth among the observations. A number of factors contributed to the party system's weakening, among them declining living standards, unpopular neoliberal economic reforms, and the handling of the 1989 riots (the *Caracazo*). All the while, the parties became increasingly removed from society and became vehicles for controlling patronage (Crisp 2000). This deterioration began to alter the calculations of politicians. In 1993, for instance, rather than run as a candidate with the party he founded, the Independent Political Electoral Organization Committee (Comité de Organización Política Electoral Independiente [COPEI]), Rafael Caldera split from it and ran on a new label, National Convergence (Convergencia Nacional). Prior to the 1998 elections, moreover, the leading candidate for a time was Irene Sáez, a former Miss Universe and political independent. Though her campaign faltered, the two top runners were populist Chávez and Henrique Salas Römer, who happened to be leading a newly formed party. The two traditional parties were effectively out of the picture. One has difficulty imagining two challengers receiving over 96 percent of the vote in Venezuela in, say, 1980, when the party system was still well institutionalized. As it weakened, however, the political dynamics changed, creating opportunities for a range of political alternatives and, by 1998, incentives to use a populist strategy.

The argument receives additional support from the sufficiency analyses. These show two similar paths leading to populists' electoral success. Each path contains a weakly institutionalized party system (as would be expected given the necessity results), a crisis of corruption, and an additional factor that can be interpreted as evidence of disadvantage. Recall the logic of the argument pertaining to the demand side: the perception of corruption is insufficient by itself to lead voters to select a riskier option, but when combined with evidence of disadvantage, it will have that effect. The analyses show that either globalization or inadequate social spending can serve in this role. In other words, corruption combined with signs of governmental neglect of citizens' needs or selling out to foreign economic interests produced feelings of frustration and anger, which in turn affected the electoral fortunes of populists. Before discussing each of the causal combinations that can account for the demand side, the linkage deserves some attention.

Can one in fact identify an increase in anger in those countries where populists gained electoral support? A family of emotions, including dissatisfaction, frustration, discontent, and anger, has been associated closely with Latin American politics in recent years. The turn to the left, for instance, may result from dissatisfaction with democratic representation (Mainwaring 2006a; Roberts 2007), frustration at political marginalization (Blanco and Grier 2013), or displeasure with market-oriented reforms and economic performance (Cameron 2009; Luna and Filgueira 2009; Stokes 2009; Wiesehomeier and Doyle 2013). Similarly, anxiety over economic conditions (Corrales 2008) or discontent with representation as political parties declined (Carreras 2012; R. A. Mayorga 2006) may contribute to the rise of political outsiders and newcomers. Others make similar cases about voter discontent (Dietz and Myers 2007), moral outrage (Coppedge 2005), or anger (Seawright 2012) leading to the collapse of party systems. Widespread agreement can be found among scholars regarding the presence and importance of these moods (see also Arce 2008; Bellinger and Arce 2011; Kohl and Farthing 2006; Silva 2009.)

That said, no one would suggest that all Latin Americans are angry; obviously there has been wide variation on this point. The level of anger, its distribution among groups and across societies, and the frequency and types of its manifestations fluctuate widely not only among countries but within them, too. To say there is a lot of anger, then, may be accurate but not very telling. Nevertheless, the effort to understand the emotional state of the region is hindered by limited data. Though no systematic regional surveys ask about anger per se, one might find indirect confirmation through other sorts of questions, such as those about confidence levels. The Latinobarómetro surveys, for instance, demonstrate a dramatic decline in citizens' confidence in their political parties, dropping from a high point of 29.3 percent in 1997 to just 10.8 percent in 2003. Citizens' opinions of their national legislative bodies were similar, falling from 37 percent confident to 17 percent in those same years.[24] However, these data are highly indirect and could reflect attitudes other than anger. Hence researchers rely on a variety of means to illustrate citizens' emotions.

Seawright (2012, 146–149), for one, gives examples of small incidents of anger, whether such an incident involves two men shouting in a bookstore or negative reactions to an activist's comments.[25] Others cite as evidence occurrences like the massive demonstrations in Argentina in 2001, Bolivia's "wars" over water and gas policy (as discussed in Chapter 4), and the rise of indigenous mobilization in Ecuador, not to mention the rise of political challengers and the ousters or resignations of presidents facing insurmountable opposition in several countries. Indeed, a number of observers highlight the resurgence of contentious politics across the region in the 1990s and early 2000s (Almeida 2007; Roberts 2008; Silva 2009). Duncan Green (2003) describes the phenomenon as a "continent-wide tide of protests" (187).

Along these same general lines, one may consider antigovernment protests as an indicator. The Cross-National Time-Series Data Archive shows the number of such protests in each country (Banks and Wilson 2015), using newspaper and online reports to identify demonstrations of at least 100 individuals that voiced explicit opposition to government policies or authority. A simple analysis shows a statistically significant relationship between the number of such demonstrations and the level of electoral support for populist candidates ($r = 0.395$ with a p-value of 0.0378).[26] Higher levels of anger are positively correlated with greater vote shares of populists. Ecuador, for instance, had a relatively high number of demonstrations prior to all of its recent elections: five in 1997 and another in 1998, when one populist candidate received 26.6 percent of the vote, and three in 2001 and two more in 2002, when populists won almost 50 percent of the vote. By contrast, Uruguay had none in the years of or the years prior to its elections in 1999, 2004, and 2009, and it had no populist candidates. Bolivia had seven such protests in 2004 and 2005, leading to

Morales's election. Chile had one protest in the same years, and no populist candidates.

Because of the limited number of observations, this correlation should be treated cautiously. Nevertheless, the data offer some validation to the causal linkage of this argument (i.e., that anger is related to electoral choices). Additionally, this conclusion is in line with other literature. Arce (2010), for instance, writes it is "perhaps no coincidence that the Latin American countries that have experienced a significant number of street protests are also some of the same countries where political party systems have been imploding" (682). Perhaps more directly, Eduardo Silva (2009) investigates the "outbursts of rage" in Argentina, Bolivia, Ecuador, and Venezuela, three of which elected populists (1).

Returning to the causal combinations that produce the emotional state, the first of them is particularly powerful: the solution *INCHOATE*COR-RUPT*SOCIAL* can explain all examples of populism but that in Bolivia.[27] Perhaps governmental neglect, as measured in this way, is a potent indicator of disadvantage. Indeed, it fits well with the literature on corruption that shows tolerance or acceptance of corruption as long as citizens benefit from it (i.e., through clientelism). However, where social spending is so low, corruption can be seen as happening at the direct expense of the people.

Consider again the case of Venezuela. In addition to the deterioration of the party system through the 1990s, the country also experienced an increase in the saliency of corruption. Complaining about it had become something of a national pastime in the 1990s: "The mantra—tirelessly repeated, seldom scrutinized, and deeply ingrained—is that corruption is the main, if not the only, roadblock to prosperity. Once corruption is eliminated, the popular expectation goes, the wealth that is already there will spread almost instantaneously and effortlessly throughout society" (Naím 2001, 22). The highly visible examples of the abuse of political power for personal gain (the Venezuelan Congress impeached President Carlos Andrés Pérez in 1993 for embezzlement) contrasted starkly with the apparent neglect of public needs. The party system deterioration opened the door for political challengers like Hugo Chávez, Henrique Salas Römer, and Irene Sáez, but the combination of corruption with declining social spending provided the advantage for populism.[28]

Despite the massive petroleum reserves, which fueled steadily rising standards of living until the end of the 1970s, politicians asked citizens to sacrifice in the name of neoliberalism beginning in the late 1980s. In the three years leading up to the 1998 elections, the average rate of social expenditures was a mere 8.31 percent of GDP. A 1998 survey asked voters what they thought was the most important thing the next government should do. The top four responses included fight corruption, improve education, and improve hospitals (the other was reduce unemployment) (Red Universitaria, cited in Hawkins 2010). Meanwhile, the number and intensity of protests saw an uptick around 1997. This round of contention "expressed popular sector and middle-class feelings of abuse, indignation, anger and frustration over their economic and political exclusion" (Silva 2009, 223). Chávez capitalized on this context in his campaign against corrupt and inept politicians. Keeping in mind the weakness of the party system as discussed earlier, one should see that citizens here had good reason to support the candidate promising not only the replacement of those in power but real change in the nature of government.

As another example, consider Mexico, where the combination of factors may not be as self-evident as in, say, Venezuela, but here too they were at work. The party system was suffering from a number of deficiencies so that, by 2001, it could be categorized as weakly institutionalized. It hit a high point in 1997, when its score on the PSI was 61.68, and its average score for the four years prior to the 2000 election was 57.83. By contrast and despite the continued relevance of the traditional parties, in the four years prior to the 2006 election, the average fell to 45; for the ten years after 2001, the average was 47.70.[29] Leading up to the 2006 contest, when Andrés Manuel López Obrador narrowly lost, party roots in society were weak, citizens had very little confidence in the parties, and they had very little faith that elections were clean (only 23 percent in 2005 believed elections were run honestly). In the aftermath when López Obrador claimed the elections were fraudulent, his audience was ready to believe it. The legacy of prior vote rigging by the PRI was strong enough to overcome the many institutional safeguards in shaping public perception (Schedler 2007).

Similarly, the legacy of authoritarian rule affected the perception of corruption, and, when combined with the increased scrutiny that accompanied the transition to democracy, it became one of the most important problems in the minds of citizens (Baily and Paras 2006; Morris 2009). The CPI score prior to the 2006 election was 3.5, which puts Mexico in the middle of the pack. Nevertheless, this score is well into the category of "serious" corruption problems according to Transparency International. An Americas Barometer survey in 2006, meanwhile, reported that 13.7 percent of Mexicans had been solicited by a public official to pay a bribe in the last year—the third-highest percentage, behind Ecuador and Bolivia, in the Americas (Seligson and Zéphyr 2008). The same survey shows that the percentage of the population "victimized" by corruption at least once in the last year was 37.1 percent, behind only Haiti.

This concern about corruption coincides with the steady retrenchment of social protection programs since the 1980s. The state now provides "less income security for, and imposes new means-tests and conditions on, beneficiaries" (Dion 2008, 446). As a percentage of GDP, social spending increased slightly after the transition, but it remained under 10 percent until 2009. Prior to the 2006 elections, Mexico spent 9.42 percent of GDP on social programs; the regional average was 13.96 percent. Congressional candidates that year from both the PRD and the National Action Party (Partido Acción Nacional [PAN]) agreed the country's key problems were jobs or employment followed by education, health, and social spending (Bruhn and Greene 2007). These issues were also front and center in the presidential campaigns, though the proposals to deal with them varied significantly (Greene 2009). In this context, populist López Obrador's campaign slogan, "For the good of all, the poor first," was fitting. He pledged to provide a broad social safety net and redistribute income to the poor. This acute attention to the plight of the lower classes tapped into a perception that the state was not doing enough on their behalf (Schedler 2007, 98). Although the populist did not win the election, he did receive over 35 percent of the vote. As in the Venezuelan case, the combination of weak party system institutionalization, corruption, and inadequate social spending accounted for populism's support in Mexico.

The same general logic applies to globalization and the second causal combination uncovered by the analysis. Given the time frame of this study (1996–2010) when public dissatisfaction with neoliberal economic policies grew throughout the region, no one should be surprised that the level of foreign economic influence would help produce public interest in a political alternative. Indeed, this view is common with respect to the surge of the left in recent years (e.g., Baker and Greene 2011; Castañeda 2006). The argument here, however, is that globalization when combined with the perception of corruption and a weakly institutionalized party system can account for *some* of the region's support for populist politicians. The Bolivian elections of 2005 and 2009 are the only ones that can be explained solely by this combination. That several outcomes are overdetermined may not be surprising: the implementation of neoliberal economic reforms has gone hand in hand with declining social spending (e.g., Kaufman and Segura-Ubiergo 2001; Stokes 2009; Wibbels 2006). Increasing openness to the global markets puts significant pressure on governments to downsize, thus reducing expenditures for social spending. Thus, in at least a few instances, citizens may have been reacting to both factors alongside corruption.

The concern for globalization or neoliberalism has not been about trade per se but instead the view that politicians have been selling out to foreign economic interests at the expense of ordinary citizens. In several countries protesters have staged a number of massive demonstrations relating to globalization or neoliberalism in some way, from the *Caracazo* in

Venezuela to the ouster of Ecuador's president, Jamil Mahuad (see Silva 2009). When combined with the perception that those same politicians are corrupt, these economic positions can help explain the demand for a populist candidate.

The Bolivian case, which is discussed in detail in Chapter 4, clearly demonstrates this logic. In the years prior to Morales's first electoral victory, although support for the traditional parties steadily declined, several important flashpoints can be identified in which public protest erupted over foreign economic influence, among other issues (Barr 2005). The water war of 2000, which elevated Morales's visibility, concerned the sale of a public water utility to a foreign consortium and caused massive countrywide demonstrations. Three years later came the gas war, sparked by a plan to sell natural gas abroad. Importantly, Bolivians questioned why foreign corporations should benefit from the country's enormous natural gas reserves at the expense of ordinary citizens who, by and large, lacked access to natural gas at all. The resulting conflicts led to the resignation of the president and the vice president who succeeded him. In his 2005 campaign, Morales's appeal included a vigorous opposition to neoliberalism, specifically expressed as the objection to losing control over the national patrimony to foreign economic interests (see Madrid 2008 for details on his appeals). With a weakly institutionalized party system providing an opportunity for populist challengers, the concern about globalization and domestic corruption in the political class helped turn voters in overwhelming numbers to the candidacy of Evo Morales.

In Ecuador, a similar dynamic took place that contributed not only to the country's instability but to support for a series of populist candidates. In 1997, for example, hundreds of thousands of demonstrators paralyzed the country when they protested President Abdalá Bucaram's free-market economic plan (Gerlach 2003). Around this time, moreover, "public indignation over corruption allegations reached fever pitch" (Conaghan 2011, 262). Following Bucaram's impeachment, the 1998 general elections resulted in 26.6 percent of the vote for populist Álvaro Noboa in the first round's five-way contest, and 48.8 percent in the second round. Nevertheless, the victor, Jamil Mahuad, implemented a series of reforms that included plans to adopt the US dollar. Citizens vehemently opposed his economic policies and viewed him as corrupt and as selling out to banking interests. "Feelings of rage, desperation, and frustration against policies that deepened people's misery" motivated massive protests (Silva 2009, 179). In 2000, a round of protests culminated in the storming of the presidential palace and Mahuad's ouster. The leaders of the ouster, including Lucio Gutiérrez, demanded a total change from neoliberal economics and an end of the government's "appalling corruption" (Silva 2009, 187).

Gutiérrez continued with that theme in the subsequent elections and used a populist strategy, and he won the presidency in 2002. However, upon taking office he changed economic course by embracing neoliberalism and, like his predecessors, was seen to be corrupt. These factors contributed to his resignation in 2005. The following year Rafael Correa won the presidency. Tapping into the concerns about corruption and globalization, his campaign had two primary themes: "(1) the degeneration of state institutions and the moral bankruptcy of the political class and (2) the disintegration of the nation/homeland (patria) as a result of elite-imposed economic policies that sacrificed the public interest in favor of private gain" (Conaghan 2011, 265). The demand-side aspects accompanied the country's very weak party system. Of all the countries in the study, only Peru had a weaker party system during this period. Ecuador's average PSI score for 1996 to 2010 was 44.59. As a result of these factors, politicians had persistent incentives to use a populist strategy, and citizens had ample reasons to lend them support.

Conclusion

In this chapter, I use fsQCA to test my argument about support for populism alongside the leading explanations in the literature. Given the tendency among scholars to explain the rise of populism with reference to multiple causal factors, though in different combinations, this methodology seems particularly well suited for this subject. It considers all possible combinations of the individual factors under consideration and it allows for equifinality. Thus, the analysis permits a variety of causal combinations across multiple countries. The results here, nevertheless, are reasonably parsimonious and provide support for the argument that weakly institutionalized party systems, perception of prevalent corruption, and evidence of disadvantage are collectively sufficient to lead to the electoral support for populist candidates. Additionally, either inadequate social spending or a neoliberal, globalized economic orientation can serve as evidence of disadvantage.

In each case, citizens may perceive that the corrupt political class is acting not on behalf of or for the benefit of ordinary people. Instead, they may deem corrupt behavior to take place at the expense of those in need or in favor of foreign economic interests. As discussed in Chapter 3, such a combination leads to perceptions of unfairness on both distributive and procedural grounds, which causes anger and a desire to rectify the situation. The two solutions, which differ only with regard to evidence of disadvantage, can explain the support for populists in every election under consideration. Also, among the contests where either no populists competed or they received very little electoral support, none exhibits these causal combinations. These demand-side factors combine with a weakly institutionalized party system on the supply side, providing incentives to use a populist strategy. The analysis, moreover, not only confirms the logic for sufficiency but for necessity as well. Very few explicitly consider, let alone test for, the necessary conditions for populism. In this chapter, by contrast, I demonstrate that weak party system institutionalization is the sole nontrivial necessary condition.

To put to rest any doubts that these same factors might account for any sort of political alternative or political challenger, not just populists, I continue with the QCA analysis in Chapter 6. Touching on themes raised earlier in the book, I use the same data set of causal factors to analyze support for outsiders, newcomers, and mavericks. The results help confirm the distinctiveness of populism and its causes.

Notes

1. The smaller countries of the Caribbean basin that had a somewhat different historical trajectory and different sets of contemporary challenges, including gang-based crime and less immunity to international pressures, are excluded.

2. Doyle (2011) treats Morales the same way.

3. However, some use this cutoff to measure populists' electoral success (e.g., Doyle 2011).

4. The same range of coding options applies for the causal factors as well. However, because continuous fuzzy coding is the most precise and thus most demanding among them, all causal factors use only this version, save for party system institutionalization that has a dichotomous conceptualization.

5. Some factors have been tested previously using statistical analyses (e.g., Doyle 2011; Hawkins 2010; Weyland 2003); despite their treatment in probabilistic terms, they remain applicable in set-theoretic, complex causation analyses. That is, although a factor like corruption could have an independent impact on the decision of voters to support populist candidates, it could also work in conjunction with other factors, as the theory presented in Chapter 3 explains.

6. See Chapter 3 for explanations of the causal logic of these factors.

7. Shortcomings in the data support the choice of dichotomization rather than fuzzy set calibration. Specifically, some indicators are available only episodically rather than annually.

8. The respective questions from the Latinobarómetro survey are those with codes A60201D, A60201B, and A60201C.

9. A preferable indicator might show citizens' perception of economic misery. However, suitable polling data on this point that cover each country for each year do not exist. The study used perception-based data where possible: the CPI and PSI incorporate survey data, and confidence in political institutions relies entirely on survey data. The others are necessarily more indirect in nature.

10. All World Bank data in this study came from its data bank website: http://databank.worldbank.org.

11. Increasingly the literature uses complex indices to capture the multifaceted nature of globalization. However, the interest here is only the economic aspect of globalization, not its cultural, social, or other dimensions. The use of a trade openness indicator, moreover, is typical in economic and political research. On the latter, see for example Bussmann and Schneider (2007), Giavazzi and Tabellini (2005), Grofman and Gray (2000), Li and Reuveny (2003), Rigobon and Rodrik (2005), and Rudra and Haggard (2005).

12. That a country's globalization score can be over 100 simply means that the country imports and exports more than it produces, thus acting as a trade hub, a not uncommon situation for some small countries.

13. CEPAL data for this and other indicators come from its CEPALSTAT database: http://estadisticas.cepal.org/cepalstat. These data include spending on education, health and nutrition, social security, employment, social welfare, housing, water, and sewerage systems.

14. This follows Ragin's (2006) calculation of trivialness rather than Goertz's (2006a).

15. This is the KIRQ software's simplification setting of 3.

16. The relevant values are as follows: $r2 = 0.1980$ for *INCHOATE*, 0.1929 for *SOCIAL*, 0.1883 for *CORRUPT*, 0.0691 for *GLOBAL*, 0.0342 for *DISTRUST*, and 0.0058 for *ECONMIS*.

17. The intermediate solution (as determined using fsQCA) is exactly the same as the complex solution.

18. The necessity scores remain the same as well.

19. The results are exactly the same using KIRQ's simplification settings of 1 and 2, the latter of which is the equivalent of the fsQCA software's complex solution.

20. That the consistency scores are not perfect reflects the existence of degrees of membership, which fuzzy coding permits.

21. When using the five-value fuzzy coding, the six-factor model produces similar results whether including or excluding Venezuela 2006 (with consistency and coverage scores of 0.87 and 0.84 when including the case versus 0.85 and 0.84 when excluding it), but the four-factor model returns just a single solution: *INCHOATE*CORRUPT*GLOBAL* (at 0.95 and 0.44).

22. The use of a five-value fuzzy coding of the outcome produces contradictory results for the six-factor model. For the four-factor model, contradictory results appear when using either fuzzy coding schema. Three solutions result when using the dichotomous coding of the outcome (0.97, 0.79).

23. The necessity analysis reports a consistency score of 0.71 for *inchoate*.

24. Figures represent the mean of the seventeen countries consistently surveyed, showing the sum of those who express "a lot" and "some" confidence in the institutions.

25. He backs up his points about anger with experimental techniques.

26. This analysis uses the sum of the number of antigovernment demonstrations in the year of a presidential election and the year preceding it, and it excludes elections involving the reelection of sitting presidents ($N = 28$).

27. Some do not consider Evo Morales to be a populist. These results could be supportive of that interpretation: in other words, one might argue that this causal combination produced not populism but some other political phenomenon, whereas the other combination did result in populism. Nevertheless, in this book, I consider Morales in 2005 and 2009 to be a populist.

28. Though Sáez was an early frontrunner in the 1998 campaign and used antiestablishment appeals, she lost credibility by accepting COPEI's endorsement (the

party later endorsed Salas Römer) and eventually finished with just 2.8 percent of the vote.

29. Interestingly, the one year during this period when Mexico's score rose above the threshold was 2006, the year of the election. The analysis, nevertheless, lagged all data one year to avoid conflating the impact of the election cycle itself with underlying factors.

6

Outsiders and Others

THE RECENT POPULISTS IN LATIN AMERICA HAVE HAD A VARIETY OF LABELS attached to them. Observers have described these politicians not only as populists but also as "outsiders" and "populist outsiders" and as "running as outsiders." Describing them as outsiders can get tricky, though, since some have had military experience or high levels of public exposure, and a few have had actual political experience as legislators or ministers. Nevertheless, the ideas underlying these terms are sometimes linked, apparently inextricably, at the conceptual level (e.g., Doyle 2011, 1449; Roberts 2013). Linz (1994), for instance, defines outsiders in reference to populism. These terms also often merge with another category of verbiage: the anti-*something*s. For instance, one finds the "antiparty political outsiders" (Mainwaring and Scully 2008) and "anti-party populists" (Montes, Mainwaring, and Ortega 2000, 799). These phrases seem to belong to slightly broader categories including "antipartyism" and "antiparty politics" (Ignazi 1996; Kenney 1998; Scarrow 1996), "antipolitics" (R. A. Mayorga 1995; Panfichi 1997; Schedler 1996a, 1996b), and "antisystem" politics (Keren 2000). Of course significant variation exists among the definitions of these terms, whether referring to rhetoric, partisan independence, and so on, but frequently the phrases link together distinct things. For example, Henry A. Dietz and David J. Myers (2007) write of "antiestablishment personalist leadership" that combines charisma and independence of party organizations. As an indicator of how these ideas are often intertwined, a few have tried to untangle them (e.g., Barr 2009; Carreras 2012; Kenney 1998).

The ideas contained in this assortment of terms undoubtedly go hand in hand at times. Venezuela's Hugo Chávez, to give an obvious example, campaigned against the political establishment (his warning to the "oligarchs" that he would make them squeal certainly counts in this regard), and he had neither prior political experience nor connections with an established political

147

party. Arguably, then, he was more than just an outsider or an antiparty politician, and perhaps he deserves more than one adjective. However, these ideas do not necessarily or always go together. Was Evo Morales a newcomer to politics if he had served in the Bolivian Congress and led what had become the country's second-largest party prior to his election?

Obviously, partisan independence is technically distinct from both political inexperience and antiparty or antiestablishment campaign tactics, but this fact has not stopped analysts from using these ideas together and linking them with populism. By associating these ideas with one another, researchers seem to suggest that these are distinctions without a difference. Perhaps populism is no different in real terms from these other ideas. Perhaps it is a reaction to the status quo just like any other sort of political alternative. Perhaps people support populist candidates for the same reasons that they support outsiders and newcomers. Perhaps populism as a concept, then, adds little empirical leverage, or even none at all. By the same token, perhaps populism as defined here is no more useful or less useful than other conceptualizations. It is one thing to define a concept and even find data that support its use, but it may be another to demonstrate that the concept is useful compared to conceptual alternatives.

Those who want to shelve the concept of populism may complain either of its vagueness or its lack of utility. The response to the first complaint is to gain precision through careful concept construction, as I attempt to do in this book. Precision helps illuminate the positive and negative ends of the spectrum: what cases are included and what cases are excluded. To demonstrate that the concept is useful, one should not only use it in an empirical analysis, as in the previous chapters, but also show that it adds something to the understanding of social phenomena compared to rival concepts, which is the goal of the present chapter. Is there, in short, anything distinctive about the political understanding of populism as presented in this book?

Specifically, this chapter fulfills multiple, interrelated goals. The first, returning to themes articulated earlier, is to explore the boundaries of populism by examining these closely related notions: other concepts that seem similar in nature or are treated as conjoined with populism. In examining them, can one determine logical or empirical reasons to disassociate populism from other sorts of non–status quo politics? Or should one just understand populism as a subset of some broader category or even as a redundant concept? The second goal is to illustrate the importance of concepts with respect to defining or constituting populations. How one crafts a concept can have profound consequences for case inclusion and exclusion, a point which highlights the need to treat concepts carefully (Hewitt and Goertz 2005). Similarly, the third goal is to illustrate how conceptual alternatives impact the understanding of causality. Using different concepts causes a variance in those outcomes considered positive, and thus a reasonable expectation is that the causes will vary. Given the recognition of complex causality and the heterogeneity of causal effects, however, the same causal combination could possibly account for different versions of the outcome. Either way, these similarities or differences can be illustrated plainly through an analysis of causality. The final goal is to assess these results as a way of evaluating the distinctiveness of populism. On the whole, this chapter serves as an additional test of the concept and the causal argument. It therefore complements the other empirical chapters.

To achieve these ends, I first unpack the variety of ideas often associated with populism, attempting to distinguish clearly each idea in ways that permit operationalization. I then argue that partisan independence, political inexperience, and antiestablishment appeals can be understood as various kinds of alternatives to the status quo, what I call "challenge politics": political dynamics in which some actors are challenging the dominance of entrenched parties, and portions of the citizenry are seeking some significant change. Additionally, I provide an accounting of the empirical instances of each of these, including those candidates who use the sort of rhetoric associated with the ideational definition of populism. From this explanation, one can readily grasp the variation among populations included under each conceptualization. In the next sections, I explore the conceptual alternatives to populism, both challenge politics and the ideational understanding of populism. Specifically, I compare the conditions under which citizens support challenge politicians, "ideational populists," or populists as defined by this book.

There are many conceptual rivals to my understanding of populism, but assessing them all in this way is far beyond the scope of this research. Nevertheless, challenge politics and the ideational understanding of populism deserve special attention. The focus on challenge politics helps highlight the importance of careful concept structure and the reasons to treat ideas like outsider status as distinct from populism. The focus on the ideational definition of populism, meanwhile, permits a direct comparison of the leading alternative understanding of this concept. The results highlight a special role for party system institutionalization with respect to my political understanding of populism, which in turn lends weight to the idea that populism as a concept continues to offer some empirical leverage.

Challenge Politics

The literature dealing with "challenge politics"—a term used simply to disassociate it from the multitude of concepts named anti-something and thus clean the slate—typically mentions one or more of the following: a politician's relationship with the established party system, prior political experience, and nature of their appeals.[1] These components may and some-times do go hand in hand but not always. Alberto Fujimori, for one, is a classic example of the combination. He had no prior political experience when first running for the Peruvian presidency in 1990, held no associa-tion with the country's traditionally competitive political parties, and used a kind of appeal that blasted the political establishment. His case is atypi-cal, however. More common are individuals who may challenge the status quo in one or two of these ways but not all three. Argentina's Elisa Carrió said during her antiestablishment campaign that the political class was spent, but she had served multiple terms in Congress with the old Radical Civic Union (Unión Cívica Radical [UCR]) before creating her own party.

What, then, are the individual components? In keeping with a few other works (e.g., Kenney 1998; Barr 2009), I consider "outsider" or "insider" to be in reference to the party system. In Chapter 2, I discussed this idea briefly, but it serves to reiterate the points here. An outsider is someone who gains political prominence not through or in association with an established, competitive party but as a political independent or in asso-ciation with new or newly competitive parties. Insiders, by contrast, are those politicians who rise through or within the established, competitive parties of the nation's party system. By this reckoning, one can be an out-sider and have a great deal of political experience. Colombia's Antanas Mockus was twice the mayor of Bogotá, but his independence and then backing by the Green Party—a new party—for his 2010 presidential bid qualifies him as an outsider.

The notion of a political challenge is obvious enough in examples like these. When a political actor campaigns and gains traction without the sup-port of a major political party, those parties must consider the person a threat to at least some degree. As the candidate's fortunes grow (as a per-centage of the vote), theirs shrink. From the perspective of voters, the choice of supporting such a candidate must reflect, at least in part, some dissatisfaction with the established parties and a willingness to take a risk on something new. By contrast, supporting an insider candidate, all else being equal, represents a less risky option. And, although one insider's electoral gains may be a threat to other traditional parties, they are not a threat to the party system itself.

Between insiders and outsiders is room for an intermediate category: the maverick. Mavericks are the politicians who rise to prominence within established, competitive parties but then either abandon their affiliations to compete as independents or in association with new or newly competitive parties, or they radically reshape their own parties (Barr 2009).[2] Examples such as Argentina's Carlos Menem or Mexico's Carlos Salinas, who under-mined the power structure within their own parties, or Venezuela's Rafael

Caldera or Mexico's Cuauhtémoc Cárdenas, who broke from their parties to compete with new ones, fit this last category.[3] Though the circumstances are slightly different, mavericks too could be considered a kind of challenge politics. Abandoning an established party can, though it does not always, suggest a desire or demand for change from the status quo.

The second component to consider is that of political experience, specifically experience with governing. Experience can take many forms, from elected positions at the local level to appointments at the national level and on to activism outside of halls of government. Though the latter often involves interaction with and knowledge of government processes, it stands apart in that the activist remains independent of government and can claim to be fighting against it. Hence, for the purposes here, experience consists of holding significant elected positions (as mayor of a large city, governor of a province, representative in the national legislature, or, naturally, the presidency) or cabinet-level appointments. Lacking any such experience, that candidate should be considered a newcomer.

In some ways newcomer status is akin to being outside the party system: the lack of experience shows voters that association with government has not tainted the candidate. Newcomers can signify change through their inexperience. Voters' support for such politicians may indicate a willingness to take a risk on something new. However, not all newcomers are political outsiders; some are associated with old, established parties. In such instances, the traditional party itself is willing to take a risk, or, to put it differently, the party sees a strategic advantage in offering a candidate who can signify something new. The party may be under significant pressure to offer up an alternative to the status quo. Consider Bolivia's Michiaki Nagatani, who was a political neophyte but also the presidential candidate for the historic MNR party. Nagatani was nominated in 2005, three years after the MNR won the presidency with just 22.46 percent of the vote and two years after the victor, Gonzalo Sánchez de Lozada, resigned his post and fled the country. The party was in no position to wheel out more of the same. Hence, the status of newcomer, whether or not associated with political outsider status, represents a kind of challenge politics.

The third component concerns a candidate's appeals for support. The relevant ones here are those described in detail earlier: antiestablishment appeals. Briefly, these are efforts at building popular support based on a challenge to those that hold power—the political or economic elite. This challenge goes beyond opposition to a policy or an incumbent or even a party. Instead, the message is directed against "them" or "their system," which can be and is defined in multiple ways. And, as such, it pits some collective "we" (i.e., "the people") against this target. Whereas the status of outsider or newcomer symbolizes a political challenge, antiestablishment appeals tend to be more explicit. The rhetorical aspect is an important and obvious component in these appeals, which contain the colorful language that the media likes to report. That said, these appeals are not limited to words alone but can include behavioral aspects, dress, manner of speaking, and the like. For example, Felipe Quispe's use of the Aymara language in his campaign (in addition to the content of his speeches) signified a challenge to Bolivia's Spanish-speaking elite. Abdalá Bucaram's campaign spectacles, in which he cultivated the image of El Loco and behaved unlike Ecuador's typical politicians, represent a form of this appeal as well (see de la Torre 2010). As discussed previously, these appeals are necessary components of populism but by themselves do not constitute populism. Instead, the combination of antiestablishment appeals and plebiscitarianism defines populism. Many candidates use these appeals without also using plebiscitarian linkages and thus are not considered populists.

As specified, the categories of outsiders, newcomers, and those who use antiestablishment appeals are not only distinct from one another but also from populism as defined here. At times they can overlap, but each of these notions has its own empirical referents. As a result, one should make no a priori assumptions that they necessarily correlate empirically, and each could be studied independently of the others. In other words, the casual or automatic linking of populism with outsider status, for instance, is neither logically nor empirically valid.

Constituting Populations

In this section, I address the implications of these conceptual alternatives by first discussing the means of classification and then presenting the results in table form. The identification of an outsider or maverick depends on the association of the person in question with insider or outsider parties, something that can be determined by using data for the number of effective (competitive) parties. Put simply, those parties that constitute important members of the party system are insiders. (See Appendix 4 for details.) Note that the party's age is not the determining factor: new parties can quickly become the most important actors in a government. Rafael Correa's party, to use the term loosely, fielded no congressional candidates in 2006 but dominated the elections for the Constituent Assembly the following year. Similarly, old parties can remain marginal for some time. For instance, Brazil's Green Party (Partido Verde) emerged in 1986 but has yet to become one of the country's effective parties. Rather than age, then, the distinction is one of importance or weight vis-à-vis the party system.

Table 6.1 Challenge Candidates

Country	Year	Candidate	Party	Vote (%)	A	O	N	M
Argentina	1999	Cavallo	APR	10.1				M
	2003	López Murphy	RECREAR	16.4				M
		Carrió	ARI	14.1	A			M
	2007	Carrió	CC-ARI	22.9	A			
		Lavagna	UNA	16.9				M
		Rodriguez Saá	JUL	7.6				M
Bolivia	1997	*Kuljis*	UCS	16.1	A	O	N	
	2002	Morales	MAS	20.9	A	O		
		Reyes Villa	NFR	20.9	A	O		
		Quispe	MIP	6.1	A	O	N	
		Fernández	UCS	5.5	A			
	2005	*Morales*	MAS	53.7	A			
		Doria Medina	UN	7.8				M
		Nagatani	MNR	6.5			N	
	2009	*Morales*	MAS	64.2	A			
		Reyes Villa	NFR	26.5	A			
		Doria Medina	UN	5.7				M
Brazil	1998	Gomes	PPS	11.0	A			M
	2002	Garotinho	PSB	17.9				M
		Gomes	PPS	12.0	A			M
	2006	Helena	PSOL	6.9	A			M
	2010	Silva	PV	19.3				M
Chile	2005	Hirsch	PH	5.4			N	
	2009	Enríquez-Ominami	Independent	20.1				M
Colombia	1998	Sanín	Sí Colombia	27.1	A			M
	2002	Uribe	Primero Col.	54.0				M
		Garzón	PDI	6.3	A	O	N	
		Sanín	Sí Colombia	5.9				M
	2006	Gaviria	PDA	22.5		O		
	2010	Mockus	PV	21.5	A	O		
		Petro	PDA	9.2	A			
Ecuador	1998	*Noboa*	PRE	26.6	A			
		Ehlers	MCNP	14.8	A	O	N	
		Arteaga	MIRA	5.1				M
	2002	*Gutiérrez*	PSP	20.6	A	O	N	
		Noboa	PRIAN	17.4	A			M
		Roldós	Independent	15.4				M
		Bucaram	PRE	11.9	A			
	2006	*Noboa*	PRIAN	26.8	A			
		Correa	PAIS	22.8	A	O		
	2009	*Correa*	PAIS	52.0	A			
		Noboa	PRIAN	11.4	A			

(continues)

Table 6.1 continued

Country	Year	Candidate	Party	Vote (%)	A	O	N	M
Mexico	2000	Cárdenas	PRD	17.0				M
	2006	*López Obrador*	PRD	36.1	A			
Paraguay	2003	Fadul	MPQ	21.9		O	N	
		Sánchez	UNACE	13.9				M
	2008	Lugo	APC	40.9		O	N	
		Oviedo	UNACE	21.9	A	O	N	
Peru	2001	Toledo	PP	36.5		O	N	
		Olivera	FIM	9.9	A	O		
	2006	*Humala*	PNP	30.6	A	O	N	
Uruguay	N/A							
Venezuela	1998	*Chávez*	MVR	56.2	A	O	N	
		Salas Römer	Proyecto Ven.	40.0	A	O		
	2000	*Chávez*	MVR	59.7	A			
		Arias	La Causa R	37.5		O		
	2006	*Chávez*	MVR	62.9	A			
		Rosales	UNT	36.9				M

Notes: A = antiestablishment politician; O = outsider; N = newcomer; M = maverick. Candidates' names in italics represent cases of populism.
See the List of Acronyms for the full names of these parties.

Determining candidates' political experience requires the use of a variety of sources, including published biographies, news reports, and the secondary literature. Though some include failed political campaigns as experience (e.g., Corrales 2008), in this chapter, I do not. The challenge aspect of inexperience comes from association with governance. If citizens are upset with government and seeking an alternative, a previously failed presidential candidate would seem to represent a challenge to the status quo as much as another newcomer who has not yet run. By this reckoning, Alejandro Toledo counts as a newcomer in Peru's 2001 election despite his campaign in the fraudulent elections the previous year. Meanwhile, someone like Andrés Manuel López Obrador was not a newcomer in 2006: despite an absence of national-level political experience, he was mayor of Mexico City, an unambiguously important elected position. Finally, those who used antiestablishment appeals, whom I will refer to as "antiestablishment politicians," are determined as indicated in Appendix 2. The classification requires an interpretation of each candidate's campaign behavior, as indicated primarily from media reports and the secondary literature. Table 6.1 lists the candidates in the South American and Mexican elections from 1996 to 2010 categorized as outsiders, mavericks, newcomers, and/or antiestablishment politicians.

Some observers might disagree with a few of these classifications, for example, with Mexico's Vicente Fox. He was a "change" candidate and railed against the PRI, calling the election a choice between the PRI and democracy (see Shirk 2005). Despite its special role, however, the PRI was not the only party to define national politics in the year 2000. In short, because his appeals were more narrowly framed against the one party, as opposed to, say, the political class, he does not fall into the category of challenge politics here.

The classification of Argentina's Néstor Kirchner is another subject for disagreement. A number of observers have called his candidacy and presidency ambiguous cases, not fitting neatly into any classification schema (e.g., Etchemendy and Garay 2011, 283; Madrid, Hunter, and Weyland 2010, 172). He was an "outsider" candidate according to those who emphasize his lack of national name recognition, but he had also been a governor and had the support of the PJ's bona fide insider, Eduardo Duhalde. He had an anti-something discourse, campaigning against neoliberalism in classic Peronist caudillo style, yet his rhetoric lacked the Manichaean, us-versus-them tone one might expect of a populist (see Hawkins 2010). His candidacy does not easily fit any classification schemes. By the criteria used here, nevertheless, he is excluded from any of the challenge politics categories. His exclusion becomes problematic for the analysis, however, a subject that is discussed further below.

Each of these classifications (outsider, newcomer, maverick, and antiestablishment politician) is distinct from the other and can be operationalized independently. Yet one can easily understand why they are sometimes considered together. Some of the politicians using antiestablishment appeals are populists, many outsiders use these same appeals, some outsiders, too, are populists, and so on. Additionally, it seems obvious why one or more of these, in whatever combination, might be used to indicate a form of anti-something. With the partial exception of mavericks, who straddle the line of being part of the establishment and yet signifying at least a change, each of these notions can be associated with a confrontation with the political status quo, assuming some level of political stability. Frequently, too, a given election cycle might produce multiple examples of challenge politics. For instance, in Ecuador's 2002 election, three candidates used antiestablishment appeals, one of whom was a maverick and another of whom was an outsider and a newcomer, and a fourth candidate was a maverick who did not use antiestablishment appeals. In Paraguay in 2008, two candidates were both outsiders and newcomers, one of whom also used antiestablishment appeals.

Hence, each in its own way represents a form of challenge to the political status quo. And perhaps this fact helps account for the tendency in the literature to lump these forms together and to associate them with the concept of populism. Likewise, this point suggests that the reasons citizens might support an outsider, newcomer, or antiestablishment politician may be quite similar if not the same. In fact, a reasonable assumption might be that their causes are equivalent. Although each could and should be studied independently, in other words, they can be grouped together. If one wants to compare populism to conceptual alternatives, then one option is to take seriously the literature's common treatment and categorize them collectively. The concept of challenge politics, then, can encompass outsiders, newcomers, and antiestablishment politicians jointly. Mavericks represent a special case, however, which is discussed below.

To accomplish this goal, a family resemblance concept structure may be the most useful. With this structure, the concept can include distinct ideas that nevertheless reflect something in common. Chess, solitaire, and darts have very little in common, but one can associate them as diversions or forms of recreation, and so they fall under the category of games. Here, each type of politician constitutes some manifestation of opposition to the status quo. With this concept type, each—outsider, newcomer, and antiestablishment politician—is a full member of the concept: one kind of challenge politics rather than a subtype or diminished subtype. If one were to use a classical concept structure in this case, then the only instances of challenge politics would be those that exhibit all of the characteristics, not just one or two.

Should the concept of populism itself be included alongside outsider, newcomer, and antiestablishment politician, since it, too, represents a challenge to the establishment? The answer is no, and the reason for its exclusion stems from its two defining characteristics: antiestablishment appeals and plebiscitarianism. The latter is a manner or means of connecting leaders to their followers, and linkage techniques are independent of political challenges. The appeals, on the other hand, are part of challenge politics. All populists use antiestablishment appeals, but not everyone who uses those appeals is a populist. By incorporating antiestablishment appeals as part of this family resemblance concept structure, all instances of populism are therefore already included. Listing populism as a fourth member of challenge politics would therefore be repetitive on the one hand (because the cases are already covered by the appeals) and somewhat misleading on the other (because of the role of linkages).

What about mavericks? Should they be included as full members of this category? The presence of a maverick who receives substantial electoral support should indicate some dissatisfaction with the status quo. However, that a former insider could represent a challenge to the establishment as much as, say, an outsider or newcomer defies logic. Perhaps, then, mavericks can be considered partial members of the category. Of course, the maverick who employs antiestablishment rhetoric would be considered a full member.

Table 6.1 reveals the implications on case inclusion of using this conceptualization. Putting aside for the moment standards of "significant" electoral support, twenty-seven of the thirty-five elections in the data set have outsiders, newcomers, and/or antiestablishment politicians.[4] An additional four elections included only mavericks. One interpretation of the literature's casual treatment, in other words, shows that the vast majority of Latin American elections contain political challengers. One might defend this very broad extension by noting this period (since 1996) is the same that has generated the literatures on the crisis of representation and the return of populism, witnessed the Argentine debacle and cries of *"Que se vayan todos!"* ("All of them must go!"), the collapse of successive governments in Bolivia, coups in Ecuador, party system collapses, and so forth. Hence, perhaps one could reasonably expect a large number of empirical referents. The counterargument, however, is that such a broad extension undermines the concept's ability to capture a political phenomenon that warrants distinction. Consider, by contrast, the number of elections in which populists competed (again, shelving the issue of level of support): fourteen. Now applying to 40 percent of the elections, the concept's extension is much more moderate.

The candidates classified above as using antiestablishment appeals serve here as the proxy for ideational populism, which is the leading alternative understanding of this concept. Scholars who use ideational definitions have their own nuances, and some certainly would highlight distinctions between the present definition of antiestablishment appeals and their definitions of populism. Nevertheless, the use of antiestablishment appeals stands as a reasonable approximation since it contains the key notions of antagonistic language and symbols along with the division of politics into an us-versus-them contest. By studying these appeals on their own, then, one can illustrate the implications of choice of definitions of populism— the ideational versus the definition presented in this book. As seen in Table 6.1, some twenty-three elections, including thirty-four individual candidates, can be classified in this way. In terms of the number of contests, some 65 percent therefore contain ideational populists. The extension here is not as broad as with the concept of challenge politics, but it remains wide nonetheless.

Explaining Challenge Candidates' Support

What are the possible factors that might account for the electoral support received by challenge candidates? The analysis relies on the same causal factors discussed and used in Chapter 5. Not only does relying on the same factors facilitate comparison with the causes of populism, but the same logic applied to each causal factor in the case of populism can be applied here as well. Under adverse economic conditions (*ECONMIS*), for instance, substantial portions of the electorate might be upset with those in charge—not only the ruling party—and thus find challenger candidates, of whatever kind, attractive. When citizens have lost confidence in the governing institutions (*DISTRUST*), they might support a candidate representing more than just a change of personnel in government, but something more fundamental.

Crises of corruption (*CORRUPT*), similarly, could have the same effect. When citizens feel that the political class, not just a single individual, is corrupt, then they may turn in numbers to those challenging the establishment. Exposure to globalization (*GLOBAL*) in the contemporary context could anger citizens, causing them to feel as though the political class has sold out to international capital and abandoned ordinary citizens. Inadequate government attention to the social and welfare needs of its citizens (*SOCIAL*) could also create a level of dissatisfaction great enough for citizens to want a real change from the political status quo. And, turning to the supply side, weaknesses in the party system (*INCHOATE*) might provide the environment in which challengers have an opportunity to present themselves to the electorate.

Importantly, there are reasons to expect that a single factor by itself would be insufficient to produce challenge politics and that a combination of multiple factors presents a more likely scenario. Corrales (2008), for instance, argues that a combination of party crises and economic anxiety explains the rise of newcomers (and ex-presidents). R. A. Mayorga (2006) explains challengers in reference to governance problems, including ineffective economic and social policies, and party system crises. Contained in these works is the idea of interactive effects: that conditions do not act independently of one another but together can impact politics in ways greater than the sum of their parts. Dissatisfaction with the level of social spending, for instance, may be insufficient by itself if the voters still have confidence in their governing institutions. In a context of eroding legitimacy, however, that level of social spending can take on a new significance: no longer would voters have some faith that a change from one party to another might alleviate their conditions. Instead, under these circumstances the voters may reach for change of a more fundamental sort. One can hypothesize, then, that for citizens to engage in risky electoral choices, multiple factors must come into play. Which combination of factors can account for challenge politics is the real question. Using fuzzy set QCA is appropriate for the present exploratory analysis in that it takes into account all possible combinations of factors under review. For details on the data and sources for these causal conditions, see the discussion and relevant tables in Chapter 5 and the appendixes. As with all the causal conditions save *INCHOATE*, the outcome (*CHALLENGE*) is coded according to fuzzy logic.

Turning to the results of the analysis, the sufficiency tests for *CHALLENGE* show contradictions. Contradictions occur when two or more instances sharing the same values on certain combinations of causal conditions—which should lead to the same outcome—have different outcomes. One case causes these contradictions: Argentina in 2003, the year Néstor Kirchner ran for president. In terms of the causal conditions, the context in Argentina that year was very similar to that of 2007 and yet the scores for challenge politics (based on the share of the vote for those using antiestablishment appeals, those with maverick status, etc.) are quite different. However, if one acknowledges the previously discussed ambiguity of the Kirchner example, and thus the difficulties of "correct" coding, and then reclassifies his example, the results are quite different and show no more contradictions.[5] In the remainder of this chapter, including the discussion of the test for antiestablishment appeals, I consider this electoral cycle as one that featured significant support for challenge politics.

With that change, the fsQCA sufficiency tests produce reasonably clean results.[6] With the standard thresholds of 0.80 for both consistency and coverage, including all six causal conditions, and using the highest simplification setting, the results are as follows: *INCHOATE + (DISTRUST*SOCIAL) + (DISTRUST*GLOBAL)* (see Table 6.2).[7] These results mean that either a weakly institutionalized party system (*INCHOATE*), or the combination of a crisis of confidence in governing institutions (*DISTRUST*) along with inadequate social spending (*SOCIAL*), or the combination of a crisis of confidence in governing institutions along with high exposure to globalization (*GLOBAL*) is *sufficient* to cause challenge politics. To put it slightly differently, any of these three combinations can lead to significant electoral support for challenge candidates. Unlike standard statistical analysis, QCA allows for equifinality, where multiple pathways may lead to the same outcome, which appears to be the case here.

The first solution contains but a single factor: a weakly institutionalized party system. It has a high level of consistency (0.91) and can account

Table 6.2　Sufficiency Results for *CHALLENGE*, Parsimonious Solution

Combination	Consistency	Raw Coverage	Unique Coverage
INCHOATE +	0.91	0.86	0.43
DISTRUST*SOCIAL +	0.85	0.43	0.00
DISTRUST*GLOBAL	0.82	0.31	0.00
Total Solution	0.85	0.96	N/A

Note: Results based on KIRQ's simplification setting 3.

for most of the outcomes, though Colombia 2006 is inconsistent, meaning the results suggest it should be an example of challenge politics but it is not. Given the consistency score, nevertheless, the one inconsistent case does not undermine the results.

In countries with weakly institutionalized party systems, this solution suggests, political actors can gain an advantage by presenting themselves as challengers to the status quo (by using antiestablishment appeals), and those lacking party ties or experience have opportunities to step into the fray. Citizens, meanwhile, lack close connections with the established parties or have little faith in them—characteristics of weak party systems—and thus have greater latitude in shifting their votes.

Consider, for example, the case of Argentina in 2007. In a sense, this election was another victory for the establishment because Cristina Fernández de Kirchner of the PJ and wife of the president at the time took the presidency. On the other hand, however, her victory was a continuation of the party system's deterioration that had begun some years earlier. Though by some accounts (e.g., Levitsky and Murillo 2008) the prevalence and victory of Peronist candidates in 2003 and 2007 demonstrate the resiliency of Argentina's party system, it was clearly not a healthy one. Survival of a party system is not equivalent to party system strength. Whereas the country had a party system institutionalization score of over 59 in 1996, it plummeted to its nadir of 35 in 2005, the same year that the PJ effectively split as a result of the feud between President Néstor Kirchner and Eduardo Duhalde. In 2007, Duhalde's dissident Peronists competed against Fernández de Kirchner's Front for Victory (Frente para la Victoria) under the Justice, Unity, and Liberty (Justicia, Unión y Libertad [JUL]) label with Alberto Rodríguez Sáa as their candidate. Similarly, internal tensions led to the ouster of Roberto Lavagna as minister of the economy in 2005, and he then formed a new party to compete against his former boss's wife. Meanwhile, the UCR imploded. Because of its perceived role in the economic crisis of 2001, its members were fleeing for safer ground: both Ricardo López Murphy and Elisa Carrió abandoned the UCR and formed new parties in 2002. Hence, even prior to the elections of 2007, the country's party system was in bad shape. When citizens cast their vote, they could choose among the multiple mavericks competing for office and the antiestablishment candidacy of Carrió.

On the other end of the spectrum stands Uruguay. It has the highest level of party system institutionalization among these countries, which is true not only on average (the mean for 1996–2010) but also for every single year. Uruguay is the only country to have no examples of outsiders, newcomers, mavericks, or candidates using antiestablishment appeals.

The other two combinations of factors that can account for challenge politics, however, suggest that weak party systems are not always part of the equation. The first of these indicates that a lack of confidence in governing institutions (*DISTRUST*) combined with inadequate levels of social spending (*SOCIAL*) can lead citizens to support challenge candidates. Paraguay's 2008 election serves as a good example. Despite various indicators of political instability (e.g., the assassination of Vice President Luis María Argaña in 1999, the exile of Lino Oviedo, and the rising insurgency) and even the rise of new parties (e.g., Oviedo's National Union of Ethical Citizens or, in Spanish, Unión Nacional de Ciudadanos Éticos [UNACE]) in 2002 and Fernando Lugo's Patriotic Alliance for Change [Alianza Patriótica para el Cambio] in 2008), the party system remained strong according to the PSI. Its scores for party roots in society and party organization are exceeded by only one country in each case: Uruguay. In no small part these scores owe to the longevity and strength of the Colorado Party, which lost the 2008 election, ending sixty-one years of continuous power, but regained it in 2013. At the same time, however, the credibility of governing institutions was low. Prior to Paraguay's 2008 elections, its citizens had less confidence in their governing institutions (at a mere 12.57 percent) than in any other observation save three: Ecuador prior to its 2002 election, Paraguay prior to 2003, and Argentina prior to 2003.[8] Paraguay also had one of the lowest levels of social spending at just over 9 percent of GDP (by contrast, Brazil spent more than 27 percent of its GDP on social programs in 2010). These data show the limited relationship, at least at any given point in time, between the strength of a party system and factors like institutional credibility or social spending. In short, prior to the 2008 campaign, citizens had very little confidence in the institutions of governance and received very little support from their government in the form of social spending. This context, then, was the one in which Fernando Lugo campaigned. The so-called Bishop of the Poor, who promised to deal with Paraguay's economic inequality, straddled the line in his appeals, presenting himself as a symbol of change but not targeting the establishment (Brugnoni 2009, 580). Yet he was an outsider and a newcomer, and 41 percent of voters supported him in the election.

This outcome along with three others (Ecuador in 2006 and 2009, and Paraguay in 2003) can also be explained with the third causal configuration, the combination of low confidence in governing institutions and high exposure to globalization. One interpretation is that these four instances were overdetermined to produce support for challenge politics. For instance, Paraguay in 2008 had the highest exposure to globalization of any observation in the data set. Again, in combination with the lack of confidence in governing institutions, globalization was sufficient to produce challenge politics as represented in the figure of Lugo.

The sufficiency results, in short, indicate that the concept of challenge politics can be understood in empirical and causal terms and, as such, may have some utility. On the other hand, interpreting the results requires the reclassification of one instance and bypassing another. The results from Chapter 5 seem neater by comparison. In any case, this test makes plain the point that populism emerges under different circumstances than challenge politics. As such, it offers additional support for the point that populism should not be conflated with these other concepts.

Turning to necessity, party system weakness does not appear to play the same role for challenge politics as it does for populism, and the fsQCA necessity analysis bears this out. Using the same thresholds as in Chapter 5 (0.85 for consistency and 0.55 for coverage), the analysis returns ten configurations, a highly complex array. *INCHOATE* appears individually as one configuration, as does *CORRUPT*, but one cannot isolate either of these as a necessary condition by itself. In other words, necessity involves party system weakness *and* a crisis of corruption *and* either low confidence in institutions or inadequate social spending *and* so on. (See Appendix 4 for the results.) With these results, pinpointing the necessary conditions for challenge politics becomes difficult; one cannot readily generalize. In short, no primary lesson can be drawn regarding what conditions must be in place for challenge politics to gain electoral support.

That said, what if one used more restrictive thresholds to eliminate the less necessary configurations? Raising the thresholds to the highest possible level that still produces results (0.96, 0.78) returns one configuration: *INCHOATE + DISTRUST*. This solution is quite parsimonious: challenge politics requires either a weakly institutionalized party system *or* low confidence in institutions. However, one should treat these results carefully, given the artificially high thresholds used. Still, the results reveal an important comparative point: weakly institutionalized party systems have a slightly different relationship with challenge politics than they do with populism. Populism requires weakly institutionalized party systems and nothing more; challenge politics, by contrast, can result from low confidence regardless of the quality of the party system. I return to this point later.

Explaining Support for Antiestablishment Politicians

In this section, I consider one component of challenge politics, that of anti-establishment appeals, as an indicator of populism if one were to use the ideational definition. In terms of conceptual structure, there is but one defining characteristic and each instance is a full example of the concept. Regarding causal factors, here again they are exactly the same as above and as in Chapter 5: same data set, same coding schemes, same one-year lag. The outcome (*ANTI*) uses a continuous fuzzy coding. Testing all six causal conditions and using the same sufficiency thresholds of 0.80 for both consistency and coverage returns these results: *INCHOATE*CORRUPT* (see Table 6.3). That is, the combination of a weakly institutionalized party system and a crisis of corruption is sufficient to lead to significant electoral support for candidates using antiestablishment appeals. These results are rather interesting and very parsimonious.[9] This solution can explain most of the examples that are fully in the category of *ANTI* (with scores of at least 0.75), though it fails to account for Colombia in 2010.

This combination of corruption and party system weakness in explaining support for antiestablishment politicians presents an interesting point of comparison with Hawkins's (2010) argument. Using an ideational definition of populism, he highlights the importance of corruption in its emergence in Latin America. However, his statistical analysis shows that it is insufficient by itself and in combination with the other factors he considers. To round out the understanding of causes, he posits the need to incorporate supply-side explanations, specifically the supply of extraordinary leadership (see Hawkins 2010, 160–165). The solution for *ANTI* (the combination of a crisis of corruption and weakly institutionalized party system) is to some extent consistent with his argument. In other words, a crisis of corruption is clearly important but not by itself sufficient, but, together with a supply-side factor, it can account for the support for candidates using antiestablishment appeals (again, serving here as a proxy for an ideational definition of populism).

Party system institutionalization is of course not the same as extraordinary leadership, but it should be interpreted as a supply-side factor. Party system weakness may provide an opportunity for clever political actors: a skilled politician could carve out an opening for himself when established parties have lost their connections with society, particularly in a context like the one suggested here, where citizens are upset at the appearance of widespread corruption. Although in this book I agree that the literature needs to pay more attention to leadership skills and capacity, these are extremely difficult to test. Nevertheless, addressing the role of party system institutionalization helps to at least broach the supply side of the equation. If one were to use an ideational definition of populism, then, this combination could account for its sufficient conditions in a way that incorporated both supply- and demand-side factors.

Table 6.3 Sufficiency Results for *ANTI*, Parsimonious Solution

Combination	Consistency	Raw Coverage	Unique Coverage
INCHOATE*CORRUPT	0.91	0.83	0.83
Total Solution	0.91	0.83	N/A

Note: Results based on KIRQ's simplification setting 3.

That said, reasons remain to question the parsimonious result of *INCHOATE*CORRUPT*. From the discussion in Chapter 3, corruption by itself is clearly insufficient to cause people to change their vote. The perception of corruption leads people to withdraw from participation but not necessarily to seek some resolution by supporting alternative candidates. Whereas weakly institutionalized party systems may be adequate to account for the supply side, the perception of corruption should be inadequate in explaining the demand side.

To flesh out these results, one might turn to more complex, less minimized solutions (see Table 6.4).[10] In this case, using the second simplification setting on the KIRQ software, one finds four combinations of factors, each of which includes more than only *INCHOATE* and *CORRUPT*. As such, the perception of corruption has additional support that may help explain the demand side, such as poor economic circumstances, lack of confidence in institutions, or excessive foreign economic influence. Two, nevertheless, also include surprising factors: low levels of foreign economic influence and relatively good economic conditions. Accounting for these factors would require further investigation, though doing so is beyond the scope of this chapter. Additionally, compared to the results for populism as described in the previous chapter, these are less parsimonious (with four combinations involving all six causal factors, none of which explains more than 38 percent of the outcomes) and have a total coverage of only 0.77, thus leaving a number of instances unexplained. The results for *ANTI*, in short, are complex and incomplete and require additional exploration. As such, they also underscore the utility of populism as defined in this book compared to an ideational definition.

With respect to the necessary conditions, the story is similarly complicated. Using the standard necessity thresholds of 0.85 and 0.55 for consistency and coverage, respectively, the results in this case include four combi-

Table 6.4 Sufficiency Results for *ANTI*, Complex Solution

Combination	Consistency	Raw Coverage	Unique Coverage
INCHOATE*CORRUPT* DISTRUST*global +	0.91	0.38	0.09
INCHOATE*CORRUPT* ECONMIS*SOCIAL +	0.89	0.35	0.14
INCHOATE*CORRUPT* DISTRUST*econmis +	0.97	0.31	0.11
INCHOATE*CORRUPT* GLOBAL*SOCIAL	0.99	0.24	0.04
Total Solution	0.93	0.77	N/A

Note: Results based on KIRQ's simplification setting 2.

nations. Collectively, these combinations include five of the six causal factors. As with the analysis for *CHALLENGE*, both *INCHOATE* and *CORRUPT* appear by themselves as individual solutions. However, one cannot isolate specific combinations in order to understand necessity. Though not as difficult to comprehend as necessity for challenge politics, generalization remains problematic here, too. The results indicate that a weakly institutionalized party system *and* a crisis of corruption *and* either low confidence in institutions *or* inadequate social spending *and* either low confidence in institutions *or* subpar economic performance are necessary for candidates using antiestablishment appeals to generate significant electoral support. At these standard thresholds, then, necessity results are not as helpful as those from the sufficiency test. Using an understanding of populism as advocated in this study, however, provides a clear and simple necessary condition: party system weakness. This parsimony illustrates an advantage of the political definition.

If one attempts to eliminate the less necessary configurations by raising the thresholds to the highest possible levels (0.95 and 0.65), the solution is a parsimonious *INCHOATE + DISTRUST*. This is the same necessary configuration as in the case of challenge politics when using artificially high thresholds, and the same general point may be extracted: weakly institutionalized party systems have a slightly different relationship with antiestablishment appeals than they do with populism, as defined in this study. For this kind of appeal to gain traction, either weak party systems or low confidence in institutions is required. Membership, to put it one way, is not as restrictive for the ideational approach as it is for the political.

Discussion: What Is It About Parties?

Compared to the causes of support for both challenge politics and antiestablishment appeals, the causes of populism differ in that party system institutionalization has a distinct role. A number of scholars identify a causal role for party system weakness in the success of outsiders or antisystem actors (e.g., Mainwaring and Scully 2008; Mainwaring and Torcal 2006; R. A. Mayorga 2006), but these findings suggest a slight modification to that view. Weakly institutionalized systems can lead to challenge politics, but they are not necessary. Based on the results using the standard necessity thresholds, no single factor has a close necessity relationship with challenge politics. In the case of populism, by contrast, a weakly institutionalized party system is not sufficient, but it is necessary. This begs the question of why populism, compared to these other concepts, is so closely linked to the sole necessary factor of party system institutionalization.

Weakly institutionalized party systems have higher levels of volatility, fewer or weaker connections with civil society, lower levels of credibility among the electorate, and lower levels of organization when compared to well-institutionalized party systems. Each of these components can have a bearing on challenge politics and antiestablishment appeals. First, higher volatility is likely to inhibit party identification by voters (Mainwaring and Zoco 2007). As the power and influence of given parties change dramatically from election to election, voters have more difficulty establishing a firm understanding of the various parties' positions and platforms. This effect may be exacerbated when the volatility is "extrasystemic" rather than "intrasystemic" (see Sanchez 2009). High volatility also creates greater uncertainty with respect to electoral outcomes, which in turn affects strategic voting (Moser 2001). The conditions under which voters "waste" their votes are far less clear in this context than in well-institutionalized party systems with competitive stability. High volatility, then, should facilitate the entry of those not associated with the established, effective parties: outsiders or newcomers may be no more unfamiliar than candidates from any other party, and voters may not feel that casting a vote for them is wasting that vote.

Second, where parties have few or weak roots in society, little sense of allegiance is likely to exist among voters. Loyalty should be more prevalent and thus influential in determining voters' choices in well-institutionalized systems. As such, where roots are shallow, voters are more open to the appeals of those challenging the system (Mainwaring and Torcal 2006). Third, where the legitimacy of parties and elections is low, citizens are not likely to be loyal voters. Instead, they may actively seek out alternatives to the discredited parties. In institutionalized systems, voters consider parties a necessary component of democracy regardless of whether they disagree with or are skeptical of parties or their platforms (Torcal, Gunther, and Montero 2002).

Fourth, poorly organized parties are subject to the whims of individual party leaders, are less able to contain party switching among legislators, have less of a presence nationally or at local levels, and have fewer resources with which to communicate and link to citizens (Mainwaring and Scully 1995). Although these factors, or at least some of them, might contribute to ideological flexibility and thus allow parties to shift positions when necessary (see Seawright 2012), they also likely lead to worse programmatic representation. The gap between parties and citizens, in other words, should be greater than in well-institutionalized systems. As such, those not associated with or campaigning against the effective parties have room to step in and claim to be better representatives of the wishes of the people.

These explanations help account for connections between party systems and challenge politics in general. And clearly challenge politics has a more welcoming environment when party system institutionalization is low, thus accounting for the sufficiency relationship. Outsiders, newcomers, mavericks, and those using antiestablishment appeals may be more likely to gain electoral traction when the party systems are weakly institutionalized, but they can do so under other circumstances as well. Consider the relative success of maverick Marco Enriquez-Ominami in Chile's strong party system, the victory of outsider/newcomer Fernando Lugo in Paraguay, or the modest but still significant support for Ciro Gomes's antiestablishment appeals in Brazil. In other words, party system weakness is not a necessary condition for challenge politics. The reverse is true for populism: a weakly institutionalized party system is a necessary condition but not by itself sufficient. The literature, by and large, does not differentiate the impact of party system institutionalization on populism from its impact on other kinds of challenge politics. Herein lies the distinction of the present analysis.

To account for the necessary relationship between weakly institutionalized party systems and populism, one must consider the combination of antiestablishment appeals *and* plebiscitarian linkages. Specifically, party system weakness has a bearing on both of these attributes, which has the effect of raising the threshold for membership. Or, to put it differently, the impact of the level of party system institutionalization is increased. That citizens support nontraditional candidates (because of their either symbolic or explicit challenge to the political status quo) when party systems are poorly institutionalized is clear. And, where party systems are well institutionalized, the connections voters have with established parties presents a dilemma for political challengers: using an antiestablishment appeal might alienate the voters from whom support is needed.

Consider again the case of Paraguay, with its outsiders, newcomers, and mavericks in the elections of both 2003 and 2008. Despite the presence of these challengers, the country had a relatively well-institutionalized party system. The Colorado Party had for decades controlled the national government and used it effectively for patronage distribution, whereas the Liberal Party since 1991 controlled patronage from many local-level governments (Abente-Brun 2009). Patronage-based though these roots were, they provided strong incentives for partisan loyalty despite the public's concerns about corruption (of the thirty-five observations in the data set, the two with the worst corruption perception scores were Paraguay prior to the 1998 elections and prior to the 2003 elections). As such, the maverick and the outsider/newcomer in Paraguay's 2003 election (Guillermo Sánchez and Pedro Fadul, respectively) faced a predicament: how to represent change without threatening the system from which so many citizens benefited. Even in 2008 when Fernando Lugo defeated the Colorado Party, he walked the line between change and threat, specifically avoiding antiestablishment appeals (Brugnoni 2009). His victory, moreover, did not represent a transformation of the party system but simply rearranged it by redistributing, slightly, the votes for the Colorado and its splinter party (UNACE) and a united opposition (Abente-Brun 2009, 150). On the other hand, one of Lugo's competitors, Lino Oviedo, did try antiestablishment appeals. Oviedo received less than 22 percent of the vote, coming in last among the three candidates, revealing the relatively limited success of such a strategy in a context where citizens had strong ties to established parties.

Where party systems are weakly institutionalized, not only are politicians more apt to use antiestablishment appeals, but also citizens are more likely to accept plebiscitarian linkages. Research shows that in well-institutionalized party systems, parties tend to compete on programmatic grounds (Jones 2005), the case of Paraguay notwithstanding. By contrast, in weakly institutionalized party systems, competition tends to center on personalism (Mainwaring and Torcal 2006). As an obvious conclusion, the level of party system institutionalization has a bearing on the ways in which candidates are likely to have electoral success. Where institutionalization is high, not only is less room available for an outsider candidate to make inroads given the ties between parties and citizens, but also greater obstacles are present to plebiscitarian linkages operating effectively. In a context of stable parties with high levels of organization that compete on programmatic grounds, to use personalistic, top-down means of linking with potential supporters would be akin to using the wrong tactics, as though playing a different game. Well-institutionalized party systems have stable interparty competition, which suggests voters are not dissatisfied with their electoral choices. A candidate who emphasizes plebiscitarian linkages in this context is unlikely to either find sufficient numbers of voters who find nonprogrammatic linkages attractive or be able to compete against the resource-rich and organizationally strong traditional parties. Potential challenge candidates might be better off developing a level of party organization capable of competing against the establishment according to the rules of the game.

By contrast, in weakly institutionalized party systems much more room is available for alternative candidates to make inroads, given the lower level of partisan identity among voters. Additionally, well-organized parties become less important in this climate. Instead, candidates are better positioned to generate support by using plebiscitarianism. The rules of the game, so to speak, are not about stable organizations connecting with voters in a sustained way and offering programmatic linkages. Instead, the rules are less well defined, which provides space for a variety of tactics.

This logic is consistent with the literature. Consider an extended explanation from Scott Mainwaring and Mariano Torcal (2006, 226):

> Personalistic linkages between voters and candidates tend to be stronger where party roots in society are weaker. They also tend to be stronger with weak party organizations and weakly institutionalized parties. In most semi-

democracies and democracies in less developed countries, parties have precarious resources and are weakly professionalized. Many parties are personalistic vehicles (Conaghan, 2000). In more institutionalized systems, voters are more likely to identify with a party, and parties are more likely to dominate patterns of political recruitment and political deliberation. In less institutionalized party systems, many voters choose according to personality or clientelism more than party; anti-party politicians are more able to win office. Populism and anti-politics are more common. Personalities more than party organizations dominate the political scene.

Compared to the use of just a certain kind of appeal (i.e., the ideational definition of populism), the political conceptualization of populism that includes not only appeals but also linkages raises the threshold for membership. It requires the conditions favorable not only for the use of antiestablishment appeals but also for the use of plebiscitarian linkages. Weakly institutionalized party systems work on both counts. In their absence—where party systems are strong—prospective populists are not only unlikely to find an audience for their antiestablishment appeals but also unlikely to compete against the establishment's programmatic linkages with plebiscitarianism.

Conclusion

In this chapter, I make several points. First, I argue that populism should be disassociated with similar but distinct notions like outsider or newcomer status. In the first place, such categories have distinct meanings. By delineating the variety of challenge politics, including the relationship to the established party system, political experience, and electoral appeals, one can see that these classifications at times go hand in hand and at other times do not. Studies that treat these categories as synonymous with one another or with populism therefore conflate various ideas and may complicate the search for cases and causes. Another point of the chapter is to highlight the implications of concept design in terms of constituting populations and determining causality. The empirical referents of challenge politics and of ideational definitions of populism overlap only partially with referents of this book's political definition of populism. As one might expect, the causes of each concept vary significantly as well. These results should highlight once again the importance of careful concept development: one's choices will influence not only the definition of what the thing is but also what cases it includes and excludes, and what conclusions are reached about its causes.

In addition, in the chapter, I make the case that the present understanding of populism has some advantages over alternatives. In particular, it has a balanced extension and its causes—necessity and sufficiency—can be articulated clearly. Compared to the others, the necessity results are of particular interest and in turn underscore the distinctive nature of this concept because of its relationship with party system weakness. The literature suggests that weakly institutionalized party systems increase the likelihood of challenge politics, and the findings here are consistent with that conclusion. The results also suggest, however, that challenge politics can gain significant electoral traction in other circumstances, whereas populism cannot. And if observers were to use an ideational definition of populism, they might see examples in both strong and weak systems. Perhaps the latter point explains a general tendency for those studying populism in the European context, with its higher frequency of well-institutionalized party systems, to emphasize discourse, rhetoric, or ideology, whereas those studying it in the Latin American context emphasize the political behavioral component that includes mobilization and linkages.

These results, of course, should not be applied in deterministic fashion. Agency is certain to play an important role, where, for instance, skilled politicians may be able to successfully use a populist strategy in stable party systems. Nevertheless, in the absence of further theorizing on political agency and from the results of the prior analyses, a reasonable conclusion is that party system weakness plays a more important role for populists than other kinds of anti–status quo politicians.

Notes

1. To this list, one might add "name recognition." A candidate could be well-known but have no prior political experience (e.g., Mario Vargas Llosa of Peru) or come through the ranks of established parties but have little public recognition (e.g., Mishiaki Nagatani of Bolivia). Then there are cases like Néstor Kirchner of Argentina: many considered him to be a political unknown, but he was elected as governor three consecutive times. Certainly some knew him very well indeed. Difficulties like these, along with the limited data availability and the fact that virtually all politicians are unknown at some point, render the operationalization of name recognition too cumbersome.

2. Bunker and Navia (2013) note that distinguishing insiders from mavericks may require an ex post evaluation in that a maverick may not reshape the party until after an election. Their conclusion may be true, but an important consideration is that one's status can change: a former outsider becomes an insider with successful electoral experience. Similarly, an insider may, after being elected, reorganize the power structure within the party and, as a result, thus become a maverick. Hence, an appropriate analysis of, say, elections of these candidates should consider their status at the time of the election, not what they subsequently become.

3. Carreras (2012) adds another category, that of "amateur": politicians who compete with established parties but are new to politics. However, the category of "newcomer" captures these instances.

4. Not all elections are equivalent, however. In some, the challenge candidates received little more than 5 percent; in others they received the vast majority of the vote. The fsQCA analysis uses a set of thresholds to evaluate support; these are discussed in Appendix 4.

5. This discussion could indicate a weakness in the concept of challenge politics as defined here. The contrary position would note concepts are imperfect and political reality is messy, meaning one often encounters cases that are hard to classify. Further research would be necessary to evaluate these claims.

6. In order to facilitate discussion, I focus primarily on the parsimonious results. The complex results appear in Appendix 4.

7. Recall that the symbol + refers to the logical OR and * to the logical AND.

8. Recall that the data used in the analysis include a one-year lag. Hence the confidence scores for, say, Paraguay's 2008 election are taken from the 2007 Latinobarómetro survey.

9. The lower simplification setting (KIRQ's setting of 2) returns four formulas, each with four causal factors, which is not at all parsimonious.

10. Unlike the exploration of populism's causes, this analysis cannot exclude two of the causal factors (*ECONMIS* and *DISTRUST*) because each appears in the necessity results. As such, one has reason to believe that they may have a bearing on the sufficiency results. Hence, the complex results are based on the use of all six causal factors.

7

The Implications of Populism

TO SUPPORT HIS RUN FOR ECUADOR'S PRESIDENCY IN 2006—HIS VERY first campaign—Rafael Correa created a new political party, the Alianza PAIS (PAIS Alliance).[1] It had no prior history or roots in society, no established party structure, and no other candidates save Correa himself. His campaign lacked the support of the country's business community, he had no ties to the military, and the indigenous movement rejected his appeals. But he campaigned effectively against the corrupt political elite and neoliberal economics and in favor of wiping the slate clean by writing a new constitution. He won 57 percent of the vote in the second round. Upon taking office, he immediately pushed for a constituent assembly, though he did so not by maneuvering through the halls of government but by circumventing them. The referendum put before the people returned overwhelming results: 82 percent supported drafting a new constitution. In the elections for the assembly that followed, his still-new party won eighty of the 130 seats. The assembly proposed a constitution that would grant Correa enhanced powers, including the ability to dissolve congress, and allow him to run for two new consecutive terms. The people approved it by 64 percent. They then elected Correa to his new term as president in 2009: he won 52 percent in the first round. His supporters took fifty-nine of the 124 seats in the National Assembly. One can fairly say that Correa's first few years in electoral politics have been exceptional.

An essential element to his story has been the use of populism, not only in his race for office but also afterwards. Catherine Conaghan and de la Torre (2008) call Correa's approach a permanent campaign, forged of necessity given the importance of public approval in his efforts to transform the political landscape. Facing a hostile congress upon first taking office, Correa needed to maintain the momentum of his electoral campaign and build his personal, mass base of support. A sophisticated communications strategy fostered seemingly direct linkages, while his rhetoric blasted the establishment. In so doing, he amassed a great deal of political power, which in turn helped him overcome congressional resistance, rewrite the constitution, and continue with his reformist agenda. As in so many other Latin American examples, in short, the impact of Correa's populism did not end with his electoral victory.

According to Conaghan and de la Torre (2008), the combination of the permanent campaign with plebiscitarianism reconfigures power relations and erodes democratic quality. Populism's emphasis on top-down, personalistic relations and the framing of politics as a battle can undermine checks and balances as well as polarize society (Conaghan and de la Torre 2008, 282). Where institutions are strong, the risk is slight; where they are weak, however, the risk is high. This dynamic involves a vicious cycle of sorts: weak institutions, at least party systems, are necessary for populism to emerge, and the emergence of populism is likely to weaken institutions. On the other hand, however, populism can mobilize and include previously marginalized segments of society. The classical populists in particular made great strides at political incorporation and in improving the standards of living for many. Consider Juan Perón's labor reforms in Argentina or Lázaro Cárdenas's land redistribution in Mexico. Consider even the phenomenal impact that Victor Raúl Haya de la Torre had on Peruvian politics, despite never holding the presidency. Whether the cumulative effects are positive or negative, the point remains: populism tends to be consequential for a polity.

This potential is exactly why populism matters. The use of plebiscitarianism and antiestablishment appeals in the right circumstances can be, and often is, powerful. A populist strategy is designed to build a mass base of support behind a single individual. When successful, that individual will have enormous political power and may use it in transformative ways. At least in the Latin American context, the names of populists are so well known for this reason. Certainly populists do not hold the exclusive rights to influential politics; still, a robust understanding of populism reveals that such consequences are the logical result of this strategy. Thus to call populism a style of politics is to discount this capacity; to leave populism in the realm of ideas is to belittle the manifest consequences of political action.

Therefore, how one conceptualizes populism is important, a point that constitutes a central theme of this book. In the previous chapters, I have attempted to demonstrate the costs and benefits of alternative conceptual strategies, develop an appropriate and useful definition of populism, demonstrate its causes by using multiple methodologies, and identify its extensional boundaries and its distinctiveness. By way of concluding, I continue in this final chapter to make this broad case about concept importance, but I turn away from causes and instead consider effects. Specifically, I discuss the logical consequences of using a populist strategy. Where does populism take us and why? The conceptualization presented here helps one make sense of the powerful nature of populist presidents.

Logical Consequences

Recall populism is defined as a means of building and/or maintaining political power based on the mass mobilization of supporters using antiestablishment appeals and plebiscitarian linkages. As discussed in the previous chapter, this conceptualization helps account for the special role that party system weakness has with respect to populism's causes. This concept, however, does more than facilitate an understanding of causes; it also facilitates an understanding of consequences. These real-world effects include the tendencies of populists to have a strong reformist program (often framed as revolutionary, not just reformist) and to concentrate power when in office. A closer consideration of linkages, specifically a comparison of participatory and plebiscitary linkages, helps illustrate why.

Participatory linkages include mechanisms by which citizens themselves have some role in government or policymaking (see Lawson 1980, 1988). Choosing a party's leaders or candidates from its support groups would be an example of such a linkage, as would citizen influence over ballot access and party platforms and other mechanisms of internal party democracy. The exchange in this form of linkage is inclusion in the process: citizens gain a stake in policymaking through the capacity to influence the outcome. Some antiestablishment politicians, though they are not populists, offer these linkages. The notion in such cases is "we can do it for ourselves." As such, efforts to implement such linkages are sometimes characterized as the promotion of "direct democracy."

Plebiscitarianism is of a very different sort. As discussed previously, it concerns the public affirmation of a leader's authority. The opportunities for affirmation may be episodic and irregular, but they all have a central logic based on accountability. Rather than offering citizens the chance to make their own decisions, as with participatory linkages, plebiscitarianism allows citizens to judge whether the leader is doing a good job. This linkage vests a single individual with the task of representing "the people," replacing political parties in that role (Mainwaring 2006a). The notion inherent in plebiscitarianism is "I can do it *for* you." As Weber (1978) notes, "regardless of how its real value as an expression of the popular will may be regarded, the plebiscite has been the specific means of deriving the legitimacy of authority from the confidence of the ruled, even though the voluntary nature of such confidence is only formal or fictitious" (267). Whereas initiatives (and participatory linkages more generally) grant citizens substantial control over the process, plebiscites offer them a "take it or leave it" choice. Leaders use the demonstrations not only to convey their appeals but also to demonstrate their responsibility to the people. De la Torre (2010) explains that, although citizens feel like direct participants, they "are reduced to follow the lines of a drama that has assigned them a central though subordinate role. They are expected to delegate power to a politician who claims to be the embodiment of their redemption" (19). One should note, however, that these mechanisms do not necessarily affirm a leader's authority—they can backfire—but such is the intention.

These linkages also are associated with a form of direct democracy, albeit in a different way than participatory linkages. The plebiscitarian form is a highly majoritarian, Rousseauian version in which any intermediation or distribution of the responsibility of representation leads to inefficiency and ineffectiveness.[2] These linkages are the source of the common populist claim of promoting direct democracy; such connections serve as a detour around vested interests (Laycock 2002, 95). The underlying logic is that by concentrating power, and thus accountability, in fewer hands, fewer opportunities exist for the wishes of citizens to be manipulated, distorted, or ignored in a maze of government agencies. The more diffuse responsibility and accountability are, the worse the government functions. Indeed, plebiscitarianism reflects a claim for not more representative government but for better governance (Taggart 2002, 67). As Weber (1978) argues, those rulers dependent on plebiscites attempt to create "an organization of officials which functions promptly and efficiently" (269). Since this kind of linkage emphasizes accountability for effective governance, the fewer the representatives, the better. It is an extremely vertical form. Empirical examples of these linkages are characterized by the lack of autonomous intermediaries between leaders and their followers.

With these traits in mind, and bringing antiestablishment appeals back into the discussion, one can explain the reformist tendency of populism. Specifically, the interaction of these two defining characteristics of populism sets the stage for a certain kind of reformism. This result comes about because these appeals inherently criticize the establishment for failing to govern well, and the use of plebiscitarian linkages implies that the solution to that failure involves increased accountability (in addition to throwing out the political class). All antiestablishment appeals criticize the political class as having failed to tend to the needs and interests of ordinary citizens and, as a result, changes are necessary. As Susan E. Scarrow (1996) notes, "antiparty rhetoric helps set the agenda for political action because it mobilizes diffuse disaffection, and transforms it into support for specific reforms" (298).

Aside from merely replacing the political class—*que se vayan todos*—there are two possible lines of reform suggested by this challenge:

enhanced citizen participation or improved accountability and government effectiveness. Changes in specific policies may be included as well but are not essential parts of antiestablishment politics.[3] Both offer ways of improving (but not replacing) the political system to ensure that it can effectively attend to the needs and interests of the governed. The first suggests that citizens should represent themselves. Perhaps obviously, this option offers participatory linkages as the solution: these are the means by which citizens can represent or govern themselves. This bottom-up sort of linkage allows citizens to hold a degree of political power in their own hands. The other option suggests that the system of representation must be streamlined to increase accountability and thus encourage greater effectiveness: plebiscitarianism. Although allowing for little in the way of citizen participation except at the polls and in demonstrations, this version offers the clearest line of accountability, resting it with a single individual. As a result, everyone knows whom to hold responsible for success or failure.

An observer might accurately conclude that both forms favor unmediated decisionmaking (direct democracy) over representation, but that conclusion is not sufficient. The two reform options offer different kinds of direct democracy. The implication is that not all antiestablishment appeals or visions of direct democracy are equal: some offer diffuse influence and participation whereas others entail singular leadership and control. The particular form, in turn, carries significant implications with respect to governing dynamics and the level of citizen control or influence. The combination of antiestablishment appeals and plebiscitarian linkages, the latter version, is the hallmark of populism. Even when populists adopt certain participatory mechanisms, their influence is circumscribed and eclipsed by plebiscitarianism. For instance, Chávez created new means of participation, such as the Bolivarian circles and *misiones* (social programs involving popular participation), yet these were within relatively top-down structures and the overall effect of his reforms was the centralization of power (McCoy 2010), and thus the pinpointing of accountability.

As should be obvious, this combination of appeals and plebiscitarianism leads not only to reformism but also to the concentration of executive power. Those populist leaders successful enough to gain political office and to build a substantial basis of power characteristically enact constitutional reforms or take other steps that enhance the power of the presidency. Typical among these steps are measures that reduce the power and influence of other branches of government, thus diminishing horizontal accountability (O'Donnell 1998). The reasons for this follow from the reformist character of populism. Given the kinds of changes implicit, if not explicit, in the populist strategy, institutional changes are virtually a requirement. Reducing the influence and oversight of other branches of government, including representative bodies, and concentrating power in the hands of the executive fit with the populist logic of fixing the system. However, not all efforts at concentrating power come at the hands of populist leaders, and not all populist leaders are able to concentrate power. Nevertheless, populism has an inherent logic, as revealed by the definition presented in this book, that provides substantial incentives to do so.

This logic also helps explain the strong tendency of populists to rewrite their national constitutions and to do so in ways that enhance executive power. Chávez, Correa, and Morales all followed this pattern. Writing about the process in Ecuador, Conaghan (2008, 47) describes Correa's plebiscitarian approach:

> True to the literal meaning of the word, the president tied his administration, his very continuance in office, to winning two elections in a row: first to approve the idea of a new constituent assembly, and then to fill the seats in this body with supporters of his views. He framed both votes as referenda on his presidency, warning that a defeat would mean "I'll go home."

His strategy was effective: voters overwhelmingly agreed with his idea to rewrite the constitution and his party dominated the elections for the constituent assembly. In 2008, voters (63 percent) approved the new constitution. The new charter rested on three pillars: (1) a raft of constitutional rights emphasizing collective over individual rights; (2) "a hyperpresidential political system; and (3) a plebiscitary model of democracy operating via elections and a variety of direct participatory mechanisms" (Montúfar 2013, 312). As a result of this process, the executive gained powers over other branches of government, for instance, by limiting the oversight capacity of the legislature and gaining further discretion over funds for subnational government units. The constitution also allows for consecutive reelection of the president, gives him greater control over the economy, particularly strategic sectors like oil and mining, and allows him to abolish the legislature once each term. Correa described the vote in this way: "Today Ecuador has decided on a new nation. The old structures are defeated. This confirms the citizens' revolution" (Joshua Partlow and Stephan Küffner in the *Washington Post*, September 29, 2008). This new structure, however, enhanced his powers at the expense of others, both inside and outside of government, making him "the only point of reference" (Montúfar 2013, 315).

Correa's constitutional changes are similar in many ways to those enacted by not only his third-era contemporaries but also populists of earlier periods, like Juan Perón and Alberto Fujimori. The concentration of presidential power, however, is not limited to articles of the constitution. Fujimori famously enacted his *autogolpe* (self-coup), closing the Peruvian Congress. He also took aim at other government branches, for instance by closing regional governments and replacing their elected officials with presidential appointees. He reduced the amount of the national sales tax dedicated to municipalities, eliminated local governments' capacity to issue business licenses, and restricted their decisionmaking authority over areas like urban planning and public transportation. Decree 776 shrank municipal budgets by almost 80 percent (O'Neill 1999, 261) and established FONCO-MUN, a fund for municipal governments that was directly linked to the president. By undercutting several autonomous sources of funding and replacing them with presidentially controlled funds, Fujimori made municipal governments dependent on his goodwill. As Bruce H. Kay (1996) notes, Fujimori populism, which circumvented existing intermediary institutions and created new ones that forged direct and personalistic connections with supporters, depended on a kind of "executive philanthropy backed by a liberal state" (56).

Well before Fujimori, classical populists enacted similar changes that enhanced their personal power. Perón, for instance, rewrote the Argentine constitution in 1949 in ways that granted unlimited presidential terms and gave the president new powers over provincial government, he undermined independent labor unions by sacking uncooperative leaders, and he impeached supreme court justices. Over the years, populist presidents have exhibited a pattern of concentrating power. Even those who never took office exhibited similar patterns. Haya de la Torre of Peru, for instance, created a highly organized party, the APRA, but he controlled it in a way that echoes others' control over their state apparatuses. Haya de la Torre was a "God figure" in the party who "enjoyed charismatic-like authority within APRA and was largely unconstrained by internal norms of accountability to party organs" (Burgess and Levitsky 2003, 903).

More recently, Andrés Manuel López Obrador failed to take Mexico's presidency, but he did serve as mayor of Mexico City. His record there demonstrated his "contempt for the nation's judiciary and legislative bodies" (Grayson 2007, 207), and he defined democracy "as 'government of the people' rather than statutes enacted by legislators or decisions rendered by judges" (Grayson 2007, 208). As with others, however, the will of the people is a matter of interpretation—from above. Whether or not populism leads a candidate to the highest office, it provides strong incentives to monopolize power to the extent possible. Populism takes many organizational forms (Roberts 2006), but the common factor is the dominance of the singular leader. Fujimori explained it well: "In Peru parties don't exist. . . . I am the power. But it is a power that was given to me be the people. I represent them" (cited in Crabtree 1998, 19).

This strong tendency toward the concentration of power leads to the troubled relationship between populism and democracy, at least with respect to modern, representative understandings of democracy. Populism itself, to be clear, is no more than a political strategy. Yet when this strategy is used successfully in launching a candidate to a country's highest office and when its inherent incentive structures are followed to their logical conclusions, populist politicians are apt to undermine democracy. The concentration of power in the hands of the president and the weakening of other government branches run counter to the principles of representative democracy by eroding the means of horizontal accountability. In addition, given the importance of mass mobilization, which is the goal of this strategy, populists often seek greater influence over the media to control their messages—hence the seizure of media outlets by Correa and Chávez. Similarly, when opposition politicians begin to erode the support base, they present a direct, possibly existential threat to the foundations of the populists' power. The same applies to social movements that resist control from above. And so curtailing those hazards takes on critical importance, even if such action comes at the expense of legal means. As a result, many apply the term *authoritarianism* (or its "soft," "electoral," and "competitive" variants) to examples of populism.

Additionally, this strategy can be socially polarizing. Antiestablishment appeals frame politics as a battle; the very notion of us-versus-them undercuts prospects for cooperation and compromise. Such appeals instead set the stage for confrontation and conflict. The divisions created by Perón and Haya de la Torre in their respective countries, for instance, lasted for decades. The legacy of the third-era populists may be similar. Moreover, these appeals rhetorically divide society between the people and the elite, and the latter are by definition powerful. Even if the elites' political influence wanes, their economic clout provides a certain potential for disrupting a populist's reform agenda. In turn, populists have even greater incentives to control the institutions of government in order to undercut this sector. And as populist leaders attempt to concentrate executive power, the response can be greater opposition. The crippling protests against Chávez in 2002 and the *media luna* revolt against Morales illustrate the point. This dynamic, in short, can undermine the basic democratic practice of compromise, increase social volatility, and enhance incentives for further concentration of power.

Populists themselves, however, understand democracy in a different way. They contend that theirs is not a kind of representative democracy but instead a participatory one. They claim to be giving power to the people and representing the general will. Their often explicit argument blasts the entrenched elite for subverting the essence of democracy, which, in their view, is not first about the rule of law but instead about the rule of the majority. As a consequence of their appeals they seek out those groups upset with the status quo, which typically are the subaltern and political marginalized. Perón incorporated workers, as Fujimori did with informal sectors and Morales with indigenous groups. By this interpretation, the result might be an improved democracy in the form of broader inclusion. Indeed, many populists are credited with improving the lives of many, whether through improved working conditions, distribution of land, or higher wages. Chávez, Correa, and Morales, for instance, have substantially reduced the percentage of their countries' populations living in poverty, in part by gaining higher rents from the extraction of petroleum and the like (de la Torre 2013). Whether these efforts produce positive long-term effects is a separate question (see Weyland 2013); in the short term, during populists' administrations, many groups have experienced symbolic and material inclusion.

Herein lies the often discussed paradox: that populism can simultaneously erode and expand democracy by both concentrating power in the hands of a single person and extending political and economic incorporation. If one prioritizes a representative understanding of democracy, the negative consequences are clear. But what if one instead emphasizes a Rousseauian, majoritarian version? Even here, a tension remains, specifically because of the populist leader's claim to speak for the people. Panizza and Miorelli (2009, 45–46) offer a compelling analysis of this tension:

> But the voice of the people can never be equated with the voice of the leader, and the populist rupture with the status quo should not signify a rupture with the basic principles of democracy. In this regard the concentration of power in the executive and the lack of consideration for checks and balances—as in Chávez's Venezuela—cannot be justified by a leader's claim to speak for the people. If democracy is about the enactment of popular will, its survival depends on acknowledging that the will of the people can never be fully enacted.

Despite the plebiscitary mechanisms populists implement, allowing citizens to vote on constitutions, recalls, and so on, and all the claims of returning power to the people, leaders following populist strategies do not enhance direct democracy of a participatory kind; the result is quite the opposite.

Populism is simply a strategy to build and maintain political power— no more, no less. Nevertheless, its effects—not populism itself—can produce complicated results. That it can shine a light on excluded groups is likely a positive for those affected, but the incorporation of these groups should be understood as a means toward an end. Public attention and the provision of economic benefits are not the same as actual political inclusion. The concentration of power in the single individual is not the manifestation of the general will; it is its denial. Plebiscitarian linkages tend to pinpoint accountability in the sense of identifying the appropriate actor to credit or blame. They are not, however, a means of holding someone accountable. They do not provide a way for the people to make certain their voices are heard. And so when conditions deteriorate and the people again desire change, they now may lack the ability to get it. Regardless of whether one understands democracy in institutional or majoritarian terms, populism's logical effects, in short, are a challenge to democracy.

Summing Up

A central theme of this book is that populism matters. If for no other reasons, its effects should justify continued research into the phenomenon. But also of interest to many observers are, among much else, its individual characteristics, relationship with party systems and voters, and use by ambitious politicians. Despite those occasional calls to retire the concept, its real-world importance and intellectual salience entice us, leading us to discuss its essential character and the best way to capture its distinctiveness. In this book, I offer one perspective, a conceptualization of populism as a political phenomenon, specifically as a strategy of building support. It is a tool, a means toward an end. Understanding populism in this way, one can easily see that such a strategy would be useful in certain circumstances but less so in others. Not everyone knows how to use each and every tool, and at times tools are misapplied. But, when circumstances warrant, skillful use of the right instrument can be effective in producing the desired result. The strategy of populism can be and has been quite effective at mobilizing mass support, thus generating enormous political power and producing the consequences discussed above.

People of course have competing visions of populism, and many disagree about its essential nature. Debates along these lines are healthy as they force us to further refine our understanding of political realities. Progress, though, requires more than competing claims on the truth. Instead, the utility of alternative definitions should be evaluated. In this book, I attempt to present one conceptualization of populism that not only captures the essence of what many observers recognize to be populism but in a way that permits empirical study. For instance, the idea of populism presented here sets clear boundaries and aids in the classification of cases, it can apply across countries and over time, it can be studied directly, and its effects can be understood as logical consequences.

Conceiving of populism as a means of generating political support with two key characteristics—antiestablishment appeals and plebiscitarianism—helps elucidate not only what populism is but also what it is not. The use of a classical concept structure contributes as well: an empirical instance must exhibit both attributes to be classified as populist; just one is not sufficient. Additionally, by calling explicit attention to incidental characteristics commonly associated with populism, I tackle the negative end of the spectrum (see Goertz 2006b). So the charismatic politician who promises continuity with prior policies and makes alliances with parties across the political spectrum would be excluded. Lula da Silva's victory in 2002, for instance, cannot be attributed to a populist strategy (Bethell 2013, 196). The personalistic leader who buys support from important groups also would be excluded. Hence, and despite his beginnings, Alberto Fujimori ended his career as a neopatrimonial leader, not a populist.

Some of populism's alternative conceptualizations present empirical challenges. For instance, multidomain understandings and certain concept designs result in grouping together dramatically different phenomena. Other alternatives can be observed and researched only indirectly or through subtypes. Granted, appropriate conceptualization depends in part on the aims and parameters of the research agenda. For goals like those found in this book (to understand and empirically evaluate the nature and causes of populism in Latin America), a classic concept structure with a limited number of definitional attributes works well.

The country study and the comparative analyses illustrate this definition's utility, and they reveal the distinct causes of third-era populism in Latin America. Though the region has had a number of political newcomers, partisan outsiders, and other challengers, its instances of populism still stand apart, both conceptually and empirically. The theory offered here articulates the necessary and sufficient conditions to make populism a successful electoral strategy (i.e., when voters would support populist candidates). But populism's rise is not only about the voters. Politicians must choose to use this strategy; otherwise, citizens have no populist option. As such, the theory deals with both supply and demand. Incentives or an opening for a political actor to use this strategy as opposed to some other must be present, and large numbers of voters must have a compelling rationale to reject the status quo and throw their support behind a plebiscitarian leader. Party system weakness provides the opportunity. Where party systems are strong, which entails positive relationships between party organizations and citizens, a winning electoral strategy is unlikely to involve antiestablishment appeals. The opposite, though, is true when party systems are weak. A variety of factors may affect the strength of party systems, and these may or may not correlate with those that affect voter attitudes. This level of theorizing, however, is beyond the scope of this study, even though such factors are explored in the Bolivian case in Chapter 4.

Citizens, meanwhile, are apt to find populists attractive when they are angry. When individuals feel a sense of injustice, particularly as a result of both procedural and distributive inequities, they seek resolution. They will want to punish the groups responsible and make changes to improve fairness. Over the last two decades or so, perceptions of widespread corruption and evidence of disadvantage have produced voter anger. Corrupt political practices are common enough, but at times corruption can be used to the material benefit of constituents. These circumstances typically do not produce anger because the procedural injustice (corrupt practice) produces a favorable distribution. The latter might be unfair to others, but those on the receiving end may be willing to overlook those inconsistencies. However, when corruption comes at the expense of ordinary citizens, anger is often the result. As the empirical analysis bears out, the signals of disadvantage in recent years have been inadequate government social spending and excessive foreign economic influence. The Bolivian country study clearly illustrates the latter of these.

Because of data limitations, the empirical studies can only evaluate the period since 1996. For this reason, I do not assume the theory applies equally well to populism in other periods. Still, there are strong reasons to assume the logic holds, even if the specific triggers vary. In other words, one can reasonably expect both supply and demand conditions regardless of time period (assuming an electoral setting). For a politician to see an advantage in the use of a populist strategy, the leading political parties must be facing problems. Likewise, for voters to find populism (as opposed to either the status quo or other kinds of political alternatives) attractive, they must be sufficiently motivated to take risks. And, as the psychology literature explains, anger provides just such a motivation.

Many questions about populism remain. One set of issues I gloss over is that of leadership and personality. There is an art to politics; it takes a relatively rare skill to cultivate a mass base of supporters. As discussed previously, many associate populism with charisma, as the charismatic personality may be well suited to attract a broad following. Perhaps, too, sufficiently skilled populists can overcome unfavorable circumstances, like relatively well-institutionalized party systems. Not every electoral cycle produces candidates of this caliber. If they did, could a populist strategy have worked in 2003, in the aftermath of Argentina's economic crisis? Not every politician, additionally, realizes the benefits of using populism in even relatively welcoming circumstances. Bolivia's party system had not yet collapsed, but would Morales have won the 2002 elections had he used a populist strategy? Charisma and other personality traits, though, remain difficult to define and assess. "I know it when I see it" might be accurate, but it is not terribly helpful for comparative analysis. In specifying the distinctive attributes of individual populists, moreover, one runs the risk of making each and every case unique, again undermining comparative analysis. Despite such difficulties, these factors should not be ignored. In fact, unless we want to interpret theories like the one offered here in deterministic terms, the role of agency must be considered. More research, in short, is required.

Additionally, more comparative analysis is needed. The strong suit of the populist literature has been its rich, detailed studies of single cases. Despite their illuminating details and multiple lessons, ample room remains for multicase and multicountry empirical analyses. In this book, I offer one such take, but I only examine a set of Latin American countries within one time period. The literature would benefit from more research, using multiple methodologies, that compares classic, neopopulist, and third-era populists. The same point applies to cross-regional work. Our understanding of the similarities and differences of European and Latin American populists is at best nascent, despite important recent contributions along these lines (e.g., de la Torre 2015; Mudde and Rovira Kaltwasser 2012, 2013).

To reiterate an earlier point, research along these lines is not only a matter of academic debate. As both historic and recent populists in Latin America have demonstrated, the phenomenon has been consequential for the polities of the region. However, populism may currently be on the wane in the region. Chávez has died and his successor has little public support, Morales currently appears to be limited to three terms, and Correa is set to leave office in 2017. More conservative candidates appear to be gaining support, additionally, which challenges the current version of populism. Nevertheless, as the history of the region demonstrates, and if the theory articulated here is correct, populism is likely to return. Several countries have long-term party system difficulties and problems with corruption. If these factors combine with the sense among ordinary citizens that they are being disadvantaged, then the conditions again would be ripe for populism. For that reason, further research into this fascinating and confounding subject is certainly in order.

Notes

1. PAIS stands for Patria Altiva i Soberana, which translates to "Proud and Sovereign Fatherland." *País* is also the Spanish word for "country."
2. Hugo Chávez was known for explicitly referencing Rousseau (Hawkins 2010).
3. If the appeals were based only on policy issues, then their advocates would be members of the loyal, not semiloyal, opposition. Those articulating antiestablishment appeals are, by definition, not members of the loyal opposition since they oppose the power elite. Yet they are not antisystem (e.g., opposed to democracy) and thus should not be considered members of the disloyal opposition.

APPENDIX 1

Party System Institutionalization Index

THE PSI HAS ITS ROOTS IN MAINWARING AND SCULLY'S (1995) FOUR-dimension model and more immediately follows Jones's (2005) index, which uses a number of indicators to measure each of the four dimensions. Each of these measures, however, is static in that it captures the quality of the party system at a given point in time, not over time. As such, the comparative utility of the measures is limited because the character of party systems can change, sometimes quickly and dramatically (e.g., Dietz and Myers 2007; Morgan 2011; Seawright 2012). One option often used is to measure party system institutionalization through the proxy of electoral volatility. Volatility (typically measured using the Pedersen index) readily offers a view across time. However, a number have raised serious questions with this one indicator (e.g., Luna and Altman 2011; Mainwaring and Torcal 2006), noting that it measures only one dimension of the concept and does not necessarily track with the others. Because party system institutionalization is a complex, multidimensional concept, room exists for variation among the indicators, particularly since no single indicator is perfect (see Luna and Altman 2011). The complexity of what one is trying to measure is all the more reason to try to use a variety of indicators across each of the dimensions and average them out.

Though the present index closely follows Jones's (2005), his relies on a few indicators for which data can be found at only one or a few points in time. A few substitutions are therefore made to provide enhanced time coverage. Gaps remain, however, for some indicators in some years. As discussed below, steps are taken to moderate the impact of the imperfect data. The country scores (see Table 5.2) are composites of the ten indicators used to evaluate the four dimensions of party system institutionalization: interparty competition, roots in society, legitimacy of parties and elections, and party organization.

The first dimension is interparty competition. Values for interparty competition are the average of presidential and lower house vote volatilities, subtracted from 100 so that higher values represent greater competition. Jones uses the average of lower house vote and lower house seat volatility, but by his own admission these data vary little, reducing the utility of using both measures. Additionally, since all of the cases under review are presidential systems and because the topic of study concerns presidential elections, the index replaces lower house seat volatility with presidential vote volatility. Election data come from Payne, Zovatto G., and Díaz (2007) and Psephos: Adam Carr's Elections Archive (psephos.adam-carr.net). Calculations of volatility use the Pedersen measure: the percentage of votes won by each party in an election is subtracted from its share in the previous election, the absolute value of this result is added to that of every other party, and the sum is divided by two. Following Karen L. Remmer (1991), a 5 percent rule is utilized to deal with small parties: all parties receiving less than 5 percent of the vote in either the baseline or subsequent election are treated collectively, with their total vote share in one election subtracted from their total vote share in the previous election, and the absolute value thereof added to that of the larger parties. The calculation does not attempt to unpack name changes and alliances; each such alteration adds to the volatility. Some criticize this method for overstating the actual level of volatility. However, changing names and alliances is in itself a type of volatility. Additionally, the use of the 5 percent rule moderates the results. As with all of the indicators, when data are unavailable in a given year, the value comes from the closest available year or the average values of two equidistant years.

The second dimension is the extent of party roots in society. The index measures this dimension by taking the average of two indicators: the percentage of the population that identifies with a party and the extent of citizen involvement in parties. The first draws from the Latinobarómetro surveys (question A504301) for the years 1996, 1997, and 2003—all of the years the question appeared—and from Vanderbilt University's LAPOP survey for 2006 and 2008 (question vb10). The Latinobarómetro question asked respondents to choose "very close," "somewhat close," "just a sympathizer," or "not close to any political party" when asked: "With respect to political parties, how do you feel?" The sum of the first three options indicates a positive response and is equivalent in the index to the "yes" response to LAPOP's question, "In this moment, do you sympathize with any political party?" Combining questions from different surveys presents certain risks, but in this case the similarity of the questions and the advantages associated with extending the time series outweigh the costs.

The data for extent of citizen involvement come from the University of Salamanca's Iberoamerican Institute and its project on Latin American Parliamentary Elites (Elites Parlamentarias de América Latina [PELA]). In its survey of legislators, question 19 asks, "How would you characterize popular participation in the life of the parties of your country: scarce and marginal, scarce and marginal except in elections, or intense and constant?"[1] The data here reflect the results for "intense and constant." Jones (2005) uses a different, though similar, question as his indicator; question 19, however, appears in more PELA surveys, thus offering better time coverage.

The third dimension concerns the legitimacy of parties and elections and has two subcomponents, each of which has two indicators. The value for party legitimacy is the average of the scores for citizens who have confidence in parties and those who feel parties are necessary for democracy. The confidence data come from Latinobarómetro's question A60201D; it uses the sum of those who respond "a lot of confidence" and "some confidence" when asked "How much confidence do you have in political parties?" The source for the party necessity indicator is Latinobarómetro's question A504309, specifically the percentage of respondents who agree with this statement: "Without parties there can be no democracy." Jones uses an indicator of whether parties are considered indispensible; this index uses an alternative to achieve better coverage over time.

Electoral legitimacy is measured by taking the average of the values for those who believe in the importance of elections and those who believe that elections are clean, not rigged. For the former, the index uses the results of Latinobarómetro's question A504402, which asks: "Some people say that the way you vote can change the way things will be in the future. Others say that no matter how you vote, things will not improve in the future. Which statement is closest to your way of thinking?" The values represent the percentage of respondents who say, "The way you vote can change the way things will be in the future." I use this question as an alternative to Jones's original indicator for elections representing a real choice, which Latinobarómetro asked on fewer occasions. To measure the extent to which citizens believe elections are clean, the index draws again from the Latinobarómetro. It uses the percentage of respondents who answer "are clean" to question A504501: "Generally speaking, do you think that the elections in this country are clean or rigged?" Jones uses a similar question that asked respondents to rank the cleanliness of elections; however, it appeared only in the 2000 survey. The average of the scores for party legitimacy and election legitimacy constitutes the value for the legitimacy of parties and elections.

The final dimension is party organization. The value for this component is the average of the scores of two indicators, party age and party continuity. Following Jones, the index calculates party age by taking the percentage of parties winning at least 10 percent of the seats in the lower house that have been in existence for at least ten years, adding the percentage of those same parties that have been in existence for at least twenty-five years, and dividing by two. The dates of the parties' founding come from Georgetown's Political Database of the Americas and, where that source was incomplete, party literature, secondary sources, media accounts, and, when absolutely necessary, Wikipedia. The data account for name changes and alliances. Party continuity uses the percentage of legislators who believe their parties are continuous between elections (PELA's question 22). Each country's score on the PSI is the average of its values for the four categories in each year.

As a point of comparison, by averaging the annual scores for each country, the division between those with weakly institutionalized and well-institutionalized systems (where 51 is the cutoff, as is discussed in Appendix 2) is similar to the results of Jones's static index. Countries with weakly institutionalized party systems for the entire period include Peru, Ecuador, Venezuela, Colombia, Bolivia, and Argentina. Mexico sits right on the threshold. Countries with well-institutionalized systems include Brazil, Paraguay, Chile, and Uruguay. Argentina and Brazil switch places between the two indices. However, by considering only the data closest to 2005, Jones misses Argentina's crisis years when massive protests rocked the country and citizens' faith in their parties plummeted. Similarly, his index misses Brazil's steady improvement in recent years, clearly pulling it away from its legacy of electoral volatility. In the present index, Brazil's score grew from 53.73 in 2005 to 59.19 in 2010. Changes and fluctuations like these highlight the limitations of cross-national but static measures.

Note

1. The data for Brazil can be found at http://americo.usal.es/oir/Elites/eliteca .htm. Those for all other countries can be found at http://americo.usal.es/oir/Elites /series_temporales.htm.

APPENDIX 2

A Note on Coding in Chapter 5

KEY ASPECTS OF QCA ARE THE OPERATIONALIZATION OF CONCEPTS AS sets and the relationship among factors as set relations. Membership in the relevant sets is based on theory, substantive knowledge, and available data. The crisp set version of QCA (csQCA) uses only dichotomized factors: either the case is a full member in the set or it is a nonmember of that set. For instance, cases are either members of the set of countries experiencing a crisis of corruption or not members of that set. Where substantive knowledge and data suggest that a dichotomization would result in the loss of information, fuzzy sets and fsQCA can be used instead.[1] Coded data in fuzzy sets have a range of values between 0 and 1. These scores do not merely represent a rank order of instances relative to one another but are used to attempt to capture states of qualitative differences. Rather than being either in or out of the set of countries with a crisis of corruption, cases might occupy some middle ground, neither fully in nor fully out of the other conditions.

The above example would be a simple three-value fuzzy coding, where 1 would represent observations that definitely have a crisis, 0 would represent those that definitely do not, and 0.5 would represent the middle ground. Increasing the number of values increases the nuance. A six-value set, for instance, would have classifications along these lines: fully in, mostly but not fully in, more or less in, more or less out, mostly but not fully out, and fully out. One can also use continuous coding, in which criteria are established for the fully in category and the fully out category, as well as the "crossover" point of greatest uncertainty. Observations can have scores anywhere between 0 and 1 (see Ragin 2009). The identification of appropriate thresholds for this and every other indicator stems from country knowledge as well as the means, medians, and distributions of the observations, using, among other techniques, the threshold setter from the TOSMANA software (Cronqvist 2007), which helps locate groupings of examples separated by gaps in the data.

To measure the outcome—populists' electoral success (*POP*)—I use three different coding schema. Finding consistent or comparable results for all versions is more challenging than just for one version. In addition, by using three options, one compensates for any weaknesses specific to individual coding options. Each of the three versions uses electoral results for populist candidates, specifically the cumulative results for all populists receiving at least 5 percent of the vote in a given first-round presidential election. As discussed in the text, electoral victory is not the issue and can be misleading. Instead, the idea is to determine when "significant" support for populists is present. Given that the elections in question are first round, typically several candidates run and the vote total for each one can be relatively low. Hence, the dichotomous, crisp set version uses 25 percent as the threshold. Those elections in which populist candidates collectively received 25 percent or more of the vote are considered full members (coded 1) of the positive outcome, and those elections where the populist vote total is less than 25 percent are nonmembers (coded 0).

The dichotomous version potentially masks important differences among elections. For instance, there might be a qualitative difference between elections in which populists receive well over 50 percent of the vote and those with a total of less than half that amount. To compensate, I also use two different fuzzy codings. The first relies on a five-value schema: 1 refers to elections in which populists received at least 50 percent of the vote; 0.75 for a 25 percent to 50 percent share; 0.50 for 10 percent to 25 percent; 0.25 for 5 percent to 10 percent; and 0 for 0 percent to 5 percent. This version allows one to recognize the overwhelming successes of those receiving an absolute majority in the first round while still acknowledge the significance of vote shares over 25 percent. The second fuzzy coding is continuous. This version strikes something of a middle ground between the other two, in that full membership in the positive outcome is set at 40 percent of the vote. The crossover point is 20 percent, which represents the point of greatest uncertainty whether this percentage should be considered a substantial share of the vote or not. Instances that are fully out have less than 10 percent of the vote. To translate the raw electoral results into continuous fuzzy coding, I used the direct calibration function found on the fsQCA software (Ragin, Drass, and Davey 2006). The relevant raw and coded data appear in Table A2.1.

Prior to evaluating the populists' vote shares, one must first identify the populist candidates themselves. To operationalize this concept one must consider the behavior of individual politicians. A determination that a

Table A2.1 Populists' Electoral Results and Coded Data

Election	Vote Share (%)	Dichotomous	Five-Value	Continuous
ARG1999	0	0	0	0.02
ARG2003	0	0	0	0.02
ARG2007	0	0	0	0.02
BOL1997	16.11	0	0.50	0.31
BOL2002	5.51	0	0.25	0.05
BOL2005	53.74	1	1	0.99
BOL2009	64.22	1	1	1
BRA1998	0	0	0	0.02
BRA2002	0	0	0	0.02
BRA2006	0	0	0	0.02
BRA2010	0	0	0	0.02
CHI1999	0	0	0	0.02
CHI2005	0	0	0	0.02
CHI2009	0	0	0	0.02
COL1998	0	0	0	0.02
COL2002	0	0	0	0.02
COL2006	0	0	0	0.02
COL2010	0	0	0	0.02
ECU1998	26.19	1	0.75	0.72
ECU2002	49.68	1	1	0.99
ECU2006	49.67	1	1	0.99
ECU2009	63.39	1	1	1
MEX2000	0	0	0	0.02
MEX2006	35.33	1	0.75	0.91
PAR1998	0	0	0	0.02
PAR2003	0	0	0	0.02
PAR2008	21.90	0	0.50	0.57
PER2001	0	0	0	0.02
PER2006	25.69	1	0.75	0.70
URU1999	0	0	0	0.02
URU2004	0	0	0	0.02
URU2009	0	0	0	0.02
VEN1998	56.20	1	1	1
VEN2000	60.30	1	1	1
VEN2006	62.84	1	1	1

politician used both antiestablishment appeals and plebiscitarian linkages means the individual should be included in the populist category. Because this study is primarily interested in the electoral fortunes of populists, the focus must be on behavior during electoral campaigns. If one were more interested in, say, a given president, then the time frame under consideration would be different.

In this case, the antiestablishment appeals need to represent a primary—though not necessarily exclusive—theme for the candidate. If the appeals are based only on policy issues or opposition to a single administration, then their advocates should be considered members of the loyal, not semiloyal, opposition. Those articulating antiestablishment appeals are, by definition, not members of the loyal opposition since they oppose the group that holds power. Yet they are not antisystem (i.e., opposed to democracy) and thus should not be considered members of the disloyal opposition.

The operationalization of plebiscitarianism considers the kind of linkage the politician attempts to use as the primary means of connecting with supporters. Evidence in government can include the frequent use of actual plebiscites, the use of mass rallies to demonstrate power or gain support for policies, and even the use of public opinion surveys for the same purposes. In electoral campaigns, these linkages can be more difficult to ascertain since all candidates attempt to speak before large crowds and convince them of their personal qualifications. Nevertheless, one can indirectly determine these linkages through the claims about leadership qualities and opinions of legal norms and formal institutions. That is, a candidate who repeatedly highlights the virtues of strong, personal leadership, the need to directly "represent" the people, and the obstacles to representation created by the rules, procedures, and institutions of the current system is seen to be promoting plebiscitarian linkages.

This project covers all of the democratic presidential elections in the presidential systems of South America and Mexico from 1996 to 2010. It takes into account any candidate who received at least 5 percent of the vote, resulting in 126 such candidates. Given this high number, I relied on a qualitative assessment of each campaign based on media reports, the secondary literature, and published biographies in order to make these determinations about their use of antiestablishment appeals and plebiscitarian linkages. For the appeals, a more formal, quantitative assessment of appeals using content analysis of campaign speeches (e.g., Hawkins 2010) could be used, but doing so for so many candidates was beyond the capabilities of this project.

Turning to the causal factors, all but one (*INCHOATE*) receive continuous fuzzy coding. As discussed in the text and Appendix 1, the concept of party system institutionalization employed here stems from Mainwaring and Scully's (1995) original formulation. They and many subsequent researchers have treated party systems in a dichotomous fashion: to use Mainwaring and Scully's language, either a party system is institutionalized or it is inchoate. Following the literature, then, this indicator has codes of either 1, indicating a weak party system, or 0, indicating a well-institutionalized party system. (Positive codes are associated with conditions expected to contribute to the outcome.) The threshold is the PSI score of 51 (see Table A2.2). This number is very close to the mean (50.97) but also represents a slight gap in the distribution of the data. As mentioned in Appendix 1, this distribution of cases is similar but not identical to other evaluations in the literature. The cases that contradict common understandings, based

Table A2.2 Coding Thresholds

Causal Factor	Full Membership	Crossover	Nonmembership
INCHOATE	N/A	51	N/A
CORRUPT	3.1	3.6	5.0
DISTRUST	20	25	31
ECONMIS	24	18	15
GLOBAL	70	55	40
SOCIAL	11	13	17

on average scores for the entire period, include Argentina, Brazil, and Mexico. However, such views sometimes rest on either historically based perceptions or static indicators. An examination of each country reveals that national circumstances can affect the extent of party system institutionalization, and these can change from one period to another. The threshold chosen not only accommodates most understandings of the quality of party systems in the region but also permits variation over time that can be explained with reference to case information.

The causal factor of corruption (*CORRUPT*) is measured using Transparency International's CPI (using a 10-point scale). Citizens in most of the countries under consideration perceive corruption to be a common problem, so the coding must separate crisis situations from politics/corruption as usual. Hence, countries experiencing an acute corruption problem are those with a CPI score of 3.1 or lower (the lower the score, the worse the corruption). Those with 5.0 or higher are fully out of the crisis-of-corruption cases. These points correspond with gaps in the data and commonsense understandings. For instance, the only countries that appear in the fully out category are Chile and Uruguay, which most observers would agree are the least corrupt within Latin America. Almost half of the countries appear in the fully in category. Though this fact does not reflect an equitable distribution, it is sadly in keeping with the prevalence of corruption throughout the region.

The causal factor of distrust in political institutions (*DISTRUST*) is measured by an index, the values for which come from averaging the results of three Latinobarómetro questions (A60201C, A60201B, and A60201D) that ask about citizens' confidence in the judiciary, congress, and political parties. The threshold for full inclusion in the set of countries that have a crisis of confidence is 20, and that for the set of countries fully without a crisis of confidence is 31 (the data range from 7.47 to 46.13). Again, context is important: a score of 31 is not terribly high, but the regional norm is to have little confidence in institutions. The issue is determining where there is an actual crisis of confidence. Scores over 31 do not necessarily mean that citizens have very high levels of trust in their governments, only that they cannot be considered to have an acute problem. Consider for instance Bolivia: its score for the 1997 elections (which come from the 1996 survey because a one-year lag is used for all data) puts it just above the crisis category. Around this time, many international institutions credited the Bolivian administration with implementing important and positive reforms, such as decentralization and capitalization. The citizens, on the other hand, were not quite as convinced and were beginning to become dissatisfied with their government, but certainly the situation could not yet be classified as a crisis. Circumstances deteriorated significantly under the administration that entered in 1997 (in part because of coca eradication policies) and continued the downward slide (in part because of neoliberal policies) until after the election of Evo Morales (the first indigenous president in a majority indigenous country), when many, though certainly not all, began to change their opinions of the political system. Bolivia's score on this index fell from 21.37 in 1997 to 16.70 in 2002 and slid further to 15.40 before bouncing back up to 19.43 for the 2009 election. The data and the thresholds, to put it simply, are in keeping with the case histories.

The code *ECONMIS* represents the causal factor of economic misery, which is measured by an index. As discussed in Chapter 5, this index is calculated by subtracting per capita GDP growth from the sum of the inflation and unemployment rates, all of which are five-year averages. The threshold for membership in the set of countries that experience economic misery is 24, and the threshold for full nonmembership in that set is 15 (the data range from 7.48 to 822.43).[2] A score of 24 represents a country that, for five years, has had high levels of inflation or unemployment, or both, that have not been moderated by gains in income. To illustrate the utility of this threshold, consider Argentina prior to its 2003 and 2007 elections. For the former, its economic misery index score was 24.49, making it a full member of the set of countries experiencing economic distress. At this point the country was still feeling the effects of its 1998–2002 depression, during which declining government revenues led to default on international debt obligations in December of 2001. The economic conditions also spurred massive demonstrations and the resignation of President Fernando de la Rúa. Compare this to Argentina's next election in 2007: though unemployment and inflation continued to be substantial, its per capita GDP growth was impressive, hitting 8.22 percent in 2005. President Néstor Kirchner enjoyed the credit for the improving economic circumstances and his wife, Cristina Fernández de Kirchner, won in the first round. Argentina's economic misery index score for this election is 22.33, below the cutoff for full membership. The threshold for full nonmembership (15), meanwhile, places Argentina's 1999 election in this category. This period came before the breakdown of economic stability that had been present under President Carlos Menem (the data are lagged one year). The country had enjoyed several years of very low inflation and moderate but positive per capita income growth, though its unemployment averaged 15 percent. As a result, its economic misery index score was 14.16. As with the other factors, the nonmembership set does not equate with wonderful circumstances but simply the absence of crisis or significant problems. In this instance, Argentina may not have experienced an unmitigated economic miracle, but it certainly was not an example of a country in economic distress.

The indicator for globalization (*GLOBAL*) uses a measure of trade exposure: imports of goods and services as a percentage of GDP plus exports of goods and services as a percentage of GDP. For countries with high scores, their exposure to international market forces is great compared to the value of domestic production. The data range from 15.84 to 103.25, with a mean of 51.16. The thresholds are 70 for full membership in the set of globalized economies and 40 for full nonmembership. Relatively few observations (five) are full members of the category "highly globalized economies"; they include the countries Paraguay, Chile, and Bolivia. Still, a significant gap in the data can be found around the upper threshold, making for an obvious break between groups of cases, separating those with substantial international exposure from extreme examples. The same sort of distribution gap is true at the lower end. The only other somewhat reasonable—though less defensible given the regional norms—alternative upper threshold is 54, and this threshold would lead to almost half of the instances being considered full members of the set of highly globalized economies. Similarly, the only other reasonable lower threshold leaves just six as fully out of the positive set (with scores ranging from 15.82 to 26.65). Such a threshold would exclude Colombia, which for all of its elections had scores in the low to mid-30s. It is one of Latin America's largest economies and lags behind its neighbors in globalizing its economy (Reina and Zuluaga 2012). As such it should belong in the set of fully out cases, which requires the use of 40 as the lower threshold, but the middle-ranking cases would be unreasonably compressed together if the alternative upper threshold were used.

Lastly, *SOCIAL* uses data for the level of government spending on social programs as a percentage of GDP. For this factor, lower numbers represent greater problems. Hence, the threshold for full membership in the set of countries with inadequate social spending is 11; the threshold for full nonmembership is 17. Compared to advanced industrialized countries, the region as a whole spends relatively little on social programs (including health, housing, and education). The thresholds used reflect key gaps in the distribution of the data. For three elections, Ecuador fell below the 5 percent mark, far below any other case. These three elections, however, are outliers. Excluding them, one can identify three clear groupings averaging 9.09 percent, 12.12 percent, and 20.55 percent. Consider Paraguay in 2008, when it spent 9.17 percent of its GDP on social programs. This level puts it above bottom-ranked Ecuador around the same time but still makes it a full member. The United Nations considers Paraguay a "medium human development" country based on its human development index scores. By contrast, Brazil in recent years has been spending quite a lot on social programs, reaching over 27 percent in 2010, and the United Nations considers it a "high human development" country. Venezuela, as another example, spent 9.81 percent prior to Hugo Chávez's first election, when a key concern was failure of government to use oil revenues for the benefit of ordinary people. By 2006, the percentage had increased to 11.52 percent as a result of Chávez's programs targeting lower classes, which helped him generate high levels of support among those groups. With these thresholds, the country appropriately falls from a full member by the time of the 2006 election.

See a summation of all country data in Table A2.3.

Notes

1. Where substantive knowledge or the data do not lend themselves to fuzzy calibration, nevertheless, dichotomized factors may still be used alongside other factors that have fuzzy codings.

2. A larger gap in the data exists around 30. Using this (rather than 24) as an upper threshold (and 20 as the crossover and 15 as the lower threshold) produces exactly the same six-factor results for all three codings of *POP*.

Table A2.3 Coded Data for All Causal Conditions

Election	INCHOATE	CORRUPT	DISTRUST	ECONMIS	GLOBAL	SOCIAL
ARG1999	0	0.97	0.98	0.02	0	0
ARG2003	1	0.99	1	0.96	0.07	0.01
ARG2007	1	0.99	0.69	0.90	0.10	0
BOL1997	0	0.77	0.90	0.01	0.26	0.34
BOL2002	1	1	0.99	0	0.12	0.03
BOL2005	1	1	1	0	0.62	0.02
BOL2009	1	0.97	0.97	0	1	0.02
BRA1998	0	0.56	0.06	1	0	0.01
BRA2002	0	0.30	0.15	0.02	0	0
BRA2006	0	0.45	0.14	0.18	0	0
BRA2010	0	0.45	0.03	0	0	0
CHI1999	0	0	0.01	0	0.54	0.38
CHI2005	0	0	0.21	0	0.93	0.41
CHI2009	0	0	0.30	0	0.99	0.30
COL1998	0	1	0.04	1	0.02	0.64
COL2002	1	0.39	0.98	1	0.01	0.91
COL2006	1	0.30	0.03	0.35	0.02	0.56
COL2010	1	0.45	0.02	0.02	0.02	0.25
ECU1998	1	0.99	0.79	1	0.12	1
ECU2002	1	1	1	1	0.30	1
ECU2006	1	1	1	0.65	0.55	1
ECU2009	1	1	0.6	0	0.93	1
MEX2000	0	0.77	0	0.99	0.83	1
MEX2006	1	0.65	0.23	0	0.53	1
PAR1998	0	1	0.02	0.25	1	1
PAR2003	0	1	1	0.68	1	0.98
PAR2008	0	1	1	0.01	1	1
PER2001	1	0.15	0.73	0.01	0.02	1
PER2006	1	0.65	0.99	0	0.10	0.99
URU1999	0	0.18	0	1	0.02	0.01
URU2004	0	0.02	0.23	0.99	0.34	0
URU2009	0	0	0	0	0.89	0
VEN1998	1	0.99	0.09	1	0.32	0.99
VEN2000	1	1	0.13	1	0.07	1
VEN2006	1	1	0	1	0.74	0.90

APPENDIX 3

A Note on the Analysis in Chapter 5

IN THIS BOOK, I USED CHRISTOPHER REICHERT AND CLAUDE RUBINSON'S (2011) KIRQ software to conduct the fuzzy set analysis of necessary and sufficient conditions. I also double-checked all results with Charles C. Ragin, Kriss A. Drass, and Sean Davey's (2006) fsQCA software. One evaluates the results of an fsQCA analysis on the basis of consistency and coverage, which are measures of the strength of set relations. Consistency "gauges the degree to which the cases sharing a given combination of conditions (e.g., democratic dyad) agree in displaying the outcome in question (e.g., peaceful coexistence)" (Ragin 2008, 44). Coverage, on the other hand, concerns the empirical relevance by assessing "the degree to which a cause or causal combination 'accounts for' instances of an outcome" (Ragin 2008, 44). Each is measured on a 0 to 1 scale, with values closer to 1 indicating stronger set relations. The coverage and consistency scores are discussed in the text. The KIRQ software also provides the option of setting proportion thresholds, which specifies "the minimum ratio of consistent to inconsistent observations required to classify a vector space corner as consistent or inconsistent with sufficiency" (Rubinson 2013, 2858). In this case, the threshold is 0.80. Further, a frequency threshold is the rule to determine which causal combinations are relevant. For large-N studies, a relatively high frequency threshold is appropriate; for intermediate-N studies, like this one, a threshold of 1 is suitable (Ragin 2009).

The tables in this appendix display, first, the necessity results for each version of coding populists' electoral success (*POP*). Necessity consistency and coverage results are the same for both the six-factor and the four-factor models (see Table A3.1). Following that are the sufficiency results for the six-factor model, showing the parsimonious results (see Table A3.2), and the truth table (see Table A3.3). This table excludes the logical remainders for issues of space. Next come the sufficiency results for the four-factor model, showing the complex results (see Table A3.4), and the full truth table (see Table A3.5).

Table A3.1 Necessity Results

POP Coding	Term	Consistency	Coverage
Dichotomous	*INCHOATE*	1.00	0.61
Five-value fuzzy	*INCHOATE*	0.91	0.58
Continuous fuzzy	*INCHOATE*	0.90	0.58

Table A3.2 Sufficiency Results, Six-Factor Model, Parsimonious Solution

POP Coding	Combination	Consistency	Raw Coverage	Unique Coverage
Dichotomous	*INCHOATE*GLOBAL* +	0.94	0.48	0.14
	*INCHOATE*CORRUPT*SOCIAL*	0.88	0.75	0.41
	Total Solution	0.88	0.89	N/A
Five-value fuzzy	*INCHOATE*GLOBAL* +	0.96	0.47	0.15
	*INCHOATE*CORRUPT*SOCIAL*	0.86	0.70	0.37
	Total Solution	0.87	0.84	N/A
Continuous fuzzy	*INCHOATE*GLOBAL* +	0.96	0.47	0.14
	*INCHOATE*CORRUPT*SOCIAL*	0.86	0.69	0.36
	Total Solution	0.87	0.83	N/A

Note: Results based on KIRQ simplification setting 3.

Table A3.3 Truth Table for Six-Factor Model

INCHOATE	CORRUPT	DISTRUST	ECONMIS	GLOBAL	SOCIAL	Con1	Con2	Con3	Result	ObsConsist	ObsInconsist
TRUE	TRUE	FALSE	TRUE	TRUE	TRUE	0.95	0.95	1.00	TRUE	VEN2006	x
TRUE	TRUE	FALSE	TRUE	FALSE	TRUE	0.85	0.85	0.88	TRUE	VEN1998; VEN2000	x
TRUE	TRUE	TRUE	FALSE	FALSE	TRUE	0.85	0.87	0.91	TRUE	PER2006	x
TRUE	TRUE	FALSE	FALSE	TRUE	TRUE	0.93	0.94	1.00	TRUE	MEX2006	x
TRUE	TRUE	TRUE	FALSE	TRUE	TRUE	0.93	0.95	1.00	TRUE	ECU2009	x
TRUE	TRUE	TRUE	TRUE	TRUE	TRUE	0.94	0.94	1.00	TRUE	ECU2006	x
TRUE	TRUE	TRUE	FALSE	FALSE	TRUE	0.82	0.81	0.83	TRUE	ECU1998; ECU2002	x
TRUE	TRUE	TRUE	TRUE	TRUE	FALSE	0.84	0.91	0.91	TRUE	BOL2005; BOL2009	x
FALSE	FALSE	FALSE	TRUE	FALSE	FALSE	0.00	0.00	0.06	FALSE	x	URU1999; URU2004
TRUE	FALSE	TRUE	FALSE	FALSE	TRUE	0.42	0.42	0.47	FALSE	x	PER2001
FALSE	TRUE	TRUE	FALSE	TRUE	TRUE	0.00	0.48	0.55	FALSE	x	PAR2008
FALSE	TRUE	TRUE	TRUE	TRUE	TRUE	0.00	0.03	0.11	FALSE	x	PAR2003
FALSE	TRUE	FALSE	FALSE	TRUE	TRUE	0.00	0.12	0.15	FALSE	x	PAR1998
FALSE	TRUE	FALSE	TRUE	TRUE	TRUE	0.00	0.01	0.08	FALSE	x	MEX2000
TRUE	FALSE	FALSE	FALSE	FALSE	TRUE	0.01	0.01	0.06	FALSE	x	COL2010
TRUE	FALSE	FALSE	FALSE	FALSE	TRUE	0.25	0.25	0.29	FALSE	x	COL2006
FALSE	FALSE	TRUE	TRUE	FALSE	TRUE	0.03	0.03	0.14	FALSE	x	COL2002
TRUE	TRUE	FALSE	TRUE	FALSE	TRUE	0.00	0.01	0.08	FALSE	x	COL1998
FALSE	FALSE	FALSE	FALSE	TRUE	FALSE	0.00	0.04	0.07	FALSE	x	CHI1999; CHI2005; CHI2009; URU2009
FALSE	FALSE	FALSE	FALSE	FALSE	FALSE	0.00	0.04	0.10	FALSE	x	BRA2002; BRA2006; BRA2010
FALSE	TRUE	FALSE	TRUE	FALSE	FALSE	0.00	0.01	0.11	FALSE	x	BRA1998
TRUE	TRUE	TRUE	FALSE	FALSE	FALSE	0.27	0.44	0.36	FALSE	x	BOL2002
TRUE	TRUE	TRUE	TRUE	FALSE	FALSE	0.01	0.01	0.06	FALSE	x	ARG2003; ARG2007
FALSE	TRUE	TRUE	FALSE	FALSE	FALSE	0.00	0.26	0.20	FALSE	x	ARG1999; BOL1997

Notes: The results for the three methods of coding *POP* are equivalent save for the consistency scores. Con1 reports consistency levels when *POP* has a dichotomous coding. Con2 reports consistency levels when *POP* has a five-value fuzzy coding. Con3 reports consistency levels when *POP* has a continuous fuzzy coding. Because of space issues, the table is truncated, excluding the forty results for which there are no empirical referents.

Table A3.4 Sufficiency Results, Four-Factor Model, Complex Solution

POP Coding	Combination	Consistency	Raw Coverage	Unique Coverage
Dichotomous	INCHOATE*CORRUPT*GLOBAL +	0.94	0.48	0.14
	INCHOATE*CORRUPT*SOCIAL	0.88	0.75	0.41
	Total Solution	0.88	0.89	N/A
Five-value fuzzy	INCHOATE*CORRUPT*GLOBAL +	0.96	0.47	0.14
	INCHOATE*CORRUPT*SOCIAL	0.86	0.70	0.37
	Total Solution	0.87	0.84	N/A
Continuous fuzzy	INCHOATE*CORRUPT*GLOBAL +	0.96	0.46	0.14
	INCHOATE*CORRUPT*SOCIAL	0.86	0.69	0.36
	Total Solution	0.87	0.83	N/A

Note: Results based on KIRQ simplification setting 2.

Table A3.5 Truth Table for Four-Factor Model

INCHOATE	CORRUPT	GLOBAL	SOCIAL	Con1	Con2	Con3	Result	ObsConsistent	ObsInconsistent
TRUE	TRUE	TRUE	TRUE	0.97	0.98	1.00	TRUE	ECU2006; ECU2009; MEX2006; VEN2006	
TRUE	TRUE	FALSE	TRUE	0.82	0.80	0.81	TRUE	ECU1998; ECU2002; PER2006; VEN1998; VEN2000	x
TRUE	TRUE	TRUE	FALSE	0.83	0.89	0.90	TRUE	BOL2005; BOL2009	x
FALSE	TRUE	TRUE	TRUE	0.00	0.19	0.23	FALSE	x	MEX2000; PAR1998; PAR2003; PAR2008
TRUE	FALSE	FALSE	FALSE	0.02	0.02	0.09	FALSE	x	COL2010
TRUE	FALSE	FALSE	TRUE	0.24	0.24	0.27	FALSE	x	COL2002; COL2006; PER2001
FALSE	TRUE	FALSE	TRUE	0.00	0.29	0.32	FALSE	x	COL1998
FALSE	FALSE	TRUE	FALSE	0.00	0.07	0.11	FALSE	x	CHI1999; CHI2005; CHI2009; URU2009
FALSE	FALSE	FALSE	FALSE	0.00	0.05	0.10	FALSE	x	BRA2002; BRA2006; BRA2010; URU1999; URU2004
TRUE	TRUE	FALSE	FALSE	0.12	0.19	0.16	FALSE	x	ARG2003; ARG2007; BOL2002
FALSE	TRUE	FALSE	FALSE	0.00	0.13	0.12	FALSE	x	ARG1999; BOL1997; BRA1998
TRUE	FALSE	TRUE	TRUE	N/A	N/A	N/A	Rem		x
TRUE	FALSE	TRUE	FALSE	N/A	N/A	N/A	Rem		x
FALSE	TRUE	TRUE	FALSE	N/A	N/A	N/A	Rem		x
FALSE	FALSE	TRUE	TRUE	N/A	N/A	N/A	Rem		x
FALSE	FALSE	FALSE	TRUE	N/A	N/A	N/A	Rem		x

Notes: The results for the three methods of coding *POP* are equivalent save for the consistency scores. Con1 reports consistency levels when *POP* has a dichotomous coding. Con2 reports consistency levels when *POP* has a five-value fuzzy coding. Con3 reports consistency levels when *POP* has a continuous fuzzy coding.

APPENDIX 4

A Note on Chapter 6

IN THE FSQCA ANALYSIS IN CHAPTER 6, I ATTEMPT TO DETERMINE THE causes of electoral support for challenge politics (*CHALLENGE*) and electoral support for those using antiestablishment appeals (*ANTI*). Coding these outcomes requires, first, the classification of all candidates in the elections from 1996 to 2010 in the eleven countries under consideration. Counting each candidacy separately (e.g., Chávez counts as three candidates because he competed in 1998, 2000, and in 2006), the thirty-five elections in this period had a total of 126 candidates who received at least 5 percent of the vote. Given this high number, I relied on a qualitative assessment of each campaign based on media reports, the secondary literature, and published biographies in order to categorize each politician.

The determination of outsider candidates stems from the individual's relationship with the country's effective parties prior to the election in question. If the party was one of the effective parties (measured by number of seats in the lower house) in the year of the previous presidential election, then it is an insider party. If not, then it is an outsider party and its candidate would be an outsider politician.

Data for effective parties comes from the Effective Number of Parliamentary Parties (NEPP) scores in Manuel Alcántara (2012), Appendix 3. The NEPP score for a given electoral cycle and the percentage of seats won by the party are rounded. If the party's ranked size is equal to or lower than the NEPP score, it is an insider party. For instance, if the NEPP score is 4.66—rounded to 5—and party A is the fifth largest in terms of seats, then it is an insider party. If party B's ranking is sixth, then it is an outsider party. For example, Carlos Gaviria ran for president of Colombia in 2006 after having served as senator with the Frente Social y Político (Social and

Political Front). In the elections of 2002 (the year of the prior presidential election), his party became the tenth largest by number of seats held in the lower house. As there were 6.88 effective parties as a result of those elections, his could not be considered an insider party. Thus, though he had political experience before his run in 2006, he was an outsider candidate. One should note an exception here: if an outsider wins the presidency, this experience supersedes the role of party effectiveness, and the individual subsequently would be considered an insider.

Second, this analysis requires coding each candidate by his or her share of the vote. Thus, although a candidate's membership in the category of *CHALLENGE* or *ANTI* is dichotomous (e.g., the person either uses antiestablishment appeals or does not), the coding used for the analysis is fuzzy. Values approaching 1 represent *CHALLENGE* or *ANTI* candidates who received a great deal of electoral support, whereas values approaching 0 represent such candidates who received very little electoral support. For *CHALLENGE*, the level of electoral support is the sum of the percentage of the vote earned by each candidate classified as either an outsider, newcomer, or antiestablishment politician plus one-half of the vote share for mavericks. As explained in Chapter 6, mavericks do not represent as clear a challenge to the status quo, and thus their impact on the score is reduced by half. Candidates with multiple classifications are counted only once. If one has multiple classifications including that of maverick, the candidate receives the full value of the vote. For *ANTI*, the level of electoral support is the sum of the vote share for all candidates in a given election classified as using antiestablishment appeals. Table 6.1 provides the raw data.

The analysis uses the fsQCA software to determine the continuous fuzzy values (see Table A4.1). Thresholds for *CHALLENGE* are 42 percent, 25 percent, and 15 percent of the vote. As a result, individuals classified as challenge candidates receiving 42 percent or more of the vote are "fully in" the category of those receiving substantial electoral support. Those receiving 15 percent or less are "fully out" of that category (they are not receiving significant electoral support). The 25 percent figure represents the level of greatest uncertainty. For *ANTI*, the thresholds are 40 percent, 20 percent, and 9 percent. The thresholds in each case are based on both substantive knowledge and the distribution of the data. Regarding the latter point, the top and bottom cutoffs fall within gaps in the empirical data, which helps account for the different thresholds for these two outcomes.

Regarding the causal factors, in the analysis, I use continuous fuzzy coding for each one save party system weakness (*INCHOATE*). Following Mainwaring and Scully (1995) and Jones (2005), and in light of shortcomings in the data, this factor has a dichotomous coding. See Appendix 2 for details and data on each of the causal factors.

Table A4.1 Fuzzy Coding for *CHALLENGE* and *ANTI*

Elections	*CHALLENGE*	*ANTI*
ARG1999	0	0
ARG2003	0.97	0.92
ARG2007	0.86	0.61
BOL1997	0.06	0.26
BOL2002	0.99	0.99
BOL2005	1	0.99
BOL2009	1	1
BRA1998	0.01	0.08
BRA2002	0.23	0.10
BRA2006	0	0.03
BRA2010	0.01	0
CHI1999	0	0
CHI2005	0	0
CHI2009	0.01	0
COL1998	0.59	0.74
COL2002	0.88	0.02
COL2006	0.32	0
COL2010	0.73	0.83
ECU1998	0.97	0.96
ECU2002	1	0.99
ECU2006	0.99	0.99
ECU2009	1	1
MEX2000	0.01	0
MEX2006	0.88	0.92
PAR1998	0	0
PAR2003	0.67	0
PAR2008	1	0.57
PER2001	0.98	0.06
PER2006	0.73	0.83
URU1999	0	0
URU2004	0	0
URU2009	0	0
VEN1998	1	1
VEN2000	1	1
VEN2006	1	1

The parsimonious results for the sufficiency tests of both *CHALLENGE* and *ANTI* appear in Chapter 6, as do the complex results for *ANTI*. The complex results for *CHALLENGE* appear in this appendix in Table A4.2.

In Chapter 6, I briefly discuss the necessity results for *CHALLENGE* and *ANTI*. The full results, using the thresholds of 0.85 and 0.55 for consistency and coverage, respectively, appear in Table A4.3 and Table A4.4.

Table A4.2 Sufficiency Results for *CHALLENGE*, Complex Solution

Combination	Consistency	Raw Coverage	Unique Coverage
*INCHOATE*CORRUPT*DISTRUST*global* +	1.00	0.35	0.08
*INCHOATE*corrupt*distrust*econmis*global* +	0.82	0.08	0.03
*INCHOATE*CORRUPT*DISTRUST*econmis* +	1.00	0.27	0.09
*CORRUPT*DISTRUST*GLOBAL*SOCIAL* +	0.88	0.21	0.09
*INCHOATE*CORRUPT*ECONMIS*SOCIAL* +	1.00	0.33	0.12
*INCHOATE*DISTRUST*global*SOCIAL* +	0.96	0.26	0.05
*INCHOATE*CORRUPT*GLOBAL*SOCIAL*	1.00	0.20	0.03
Total Solution	0.94	0.87	N/A

Note: Results based on KIRQ's simplification setting 2.

Table A4.3 Necessity Results for *CHALLENGE*

Combination	Consistency	Coverage
ECONMIS+GLOBAL+SOCIAL *	0.90	0.62
DISTRUST+GLOBAL+econmis *	0.86	0.57
SOCIAL+global *	0.90	0.58
INCHOATE *	0.86	0.91
ECONMIS+GLOBAL+corrupt *	0.85	0.57
DISTRUST+ECONMIS *	0.89	0.68
DISTRUST+global *	0.89	0.61
CORRUPT *	0.90	0.74
SOCIAL+econmis *	0.91	0.59
DISTRUST+SOCIAL	0.95	0.73
Total Solution	0.31	1.00

Table A4.4 Necessity Results for *ANTI*

Combination	Consistency	Coverage
DISTRUST+SOCIAL *	0.95	0.61
CORRUPT *	0.95	0.65
INCHOATE *	0.89	0.78
DISTRUST+ECONMIS	0.88	0.57
Total Solution	0.75	0.92

Acronyms

ADN	Acción Democrática Nacionalista (Nationalist Democratic Action)
APC	Alianza Patriótica por el Cambio (Patriotic Alliance for Change)
APR	Acción por la República (Action for the Republic)
APRA	Alianza Popular Revolucionaria Americana (American Popular Revolutionary Alliance)
ARI	Alternativa para una República de Iguales (Alternative for a Republic of Equals)
ASP	Asamblea por la Soberanía de Los Pueblos (Assembly for the Sovereignty of the Peoples)
CC-ARI	Coalición Cívica-Alternativa para una República de Iguales (Civil Coalition Alternative for a Republic of Equals)
CEPAL	Comisión Económica para América Latina (Economic Commission for Latin America and the Caribbean)
COB	Central Obrera Boliviana (Bolivian Workers Central)
CONDEPA	Conciencia de Patria (Conscience of the Fatherland)
COPEI	Comité de Organización Política Electoral Independiente (Independent Political Electoral Organization Committee)
COR	Central Obrera Regional (Regional Labor Central)
CPI	Corruption Perceptions Index
CSUTCB	Confederación Sindical Única de Trabajadores Campesinos de Bolivia (Trade Union Confederation of Bolivian Peasant Workers)

FIM	Frente Independiente Moralizador (Independent Moralizing Front)
FEJUVE	Federación de Juntas Vecinales (Federation of Neighborhood Boards)
GDP	gross domestic product
ILO	International Labor Organization
IMF	International Monetary Fund
ISI	import substitution industrialization
ISPS	Instrumento Político por la Soberanía de los Pueblos (Political Instrument for the Sovereignty of the Peoples)
JUL	Justicia, Unión y Libertad (Justice, Union, Liberty)
LAPOP	Latin American Public Opinion Project
MAS	Movimiento al Socialismo (Movement Toward Socialism)
MCNP	Movimiento Ciudadano Nuevo País (Citizen's Movement for a New Country)
MIP	Movimiento Indígena Pachakutik (Pachakutik Indigenous Movement)
MIR	Movimiento de la Izquierda Revolucionaria (Movement of the Revolutionary Left)
MIRA	Movimiento Independiente para una República Auténtica (Independent Movement for an Authentic Republic)
MNR	Movimiento Nacionalista Revolucionario (Nationalist Revolutionary Movement)
MPQ	Movimiento Patria Querida (Beloved Fatherland Movement)
MVR	Movimiento V [Quinta] República (Fifth Republic Movement)
NFR	Nueva Fuerza Republicana (New Republican Force)
OECD	Organisation for Economic Co-operation and Development
PAIS	Patria Altiva i Soberana (Proud and Sovereign Fatherland)
PAN	Partido Acción Nacional (National Action Party)
PDA	Polo Democrático Alternativo (Alternative Democratic Pole)
PDI	Polo Democrático Independiente (Independent Democratic Pole)
PH	Partido Humanista (Humanist Party)
PJ	Partido Justicialista (Justicialist Party)

PNP	Partido Nacionalista Peruano (Peruvian Nationalist Party)
PODEMOS	Poder Democrático Social (Social Democratic Power)
PP	Perú Posible (Possible Peru)
PPS	Partido Popular Socialista (Popular Socialist Party)
PRD	Partido de Revolución Democrática (Party of the Democratic Revolution)
PRE	Partido Roldosista Ecuatoriano (Ecuadorian Roldosist Party)
PRI	Partido Revolucionario Institucional (Institutional Revolutionary Party)
PRIAN	Partido Renovador Institucional de Acción Nacional (Institutional Renewal Party of National Action)
PSB	Partido Socialista Brasileiro (Brazilian Socialist Party)
PSI	party system institutionalization index
PSOL	Partido Socialismo e Liberdade (Party of Socialism and Freedom)
PSP	Partido Sociedad Patriótica (Patriotic Society Party)
PV	Partido Verde (Green Party)
QCA	qualitative comparative analysis
RECREAR	Recrear para el Crecimiento (Recreate for Growth)
UCR	Unión Cívica Radical (Radical Civic Union)
UCS	Unidad Cívica Solidaridad (Civic Solidarity Union)
UDP	Unidad Democrática y Popular (Democratic and Popular Union)
UN	Unidad Nacional (National Unity)
UNA	Una Nación Avanzada (An Advanced Nation)
UNACE	Unión Nacional de Ciudadanos Éticos (National Union of Ethical Citizens)
UNT	Un Nuevo Tiempo (A New Era)

References

Abente-Brun, Diego. 2009. "Paraguay: The Unraveling of One-Party Rule." *Journal of Democracy* 20(1): 143–156.

Abts, Koen, and Stefan Rummens. 2007. "Populism Versus Democracy." *Political Studies* 55(2): 405–424.

Adams, J. Stacy. 1965. "Inequity in Social Exchange." In *Advances in Experimental Social Psychology*, Vol. 2, edited by Leonard Berkowitz, pp. 267–299. New York: Academic.

Albin, Cecilia, and Daniel Druckman. 2012. "Equality Matters: Negotiating an End to Civil Wars." *Journal of Conflict Resolution* 56(2): 155–182.

Alcántara, Manuel. 2012. "Elections in Latin America 2009–2011: A Comparative Analysis." Kellogg Institute Working Paper no. 386. Notre Dame, IN: Helen Kellogg Institute for International Studies.

Aldrich, John. 1995. *Why Parties? The Origin and Transformation of Political Parties in America*. Chicago: University of Chicago Press.

Almeida, Paul D. 2007. "Defensive Mobilization: Popular Movements Against Economic Adjustment Policies in Latin America." *Latin American Perspectives* 34(3): 123–139.

Althusser, Louis. 1971. "Ideology and Ideological State Apparatuses (Notes Towards an Investigation)." In *Lenin and Philosophy and Other Essays*, translated by Ben Brewster, pp. 127–186. London: New Left.

Anria, Santiago. 2013. "Social Movements, Party Organization, and Populism: Insights from the Bolivian MAS." *Latin American Politics and Society* 55(3): 19–46.

Ansell, Christopher K., and M. Steven Fish. 1999. "The Art of Being Indispensable: Noncharismatic Personalism in Contemporary Political Parties." *Comparative Political Studies* 32(2): 283–312.

Arce, Moisés. 2008. "The Repoliticization of Collective Action After Neoliberalism in Peru." *Latin American Politics and Society* 50(3): 37–62.

———. 2010. "Parties and Social Protest in Latin America's Neoliberal Era." *Party Politics* 16(5): 669–686.

Arce, Moisés, and Roberta Rice. 2009. "Societal Protest in Post-Stabilization Bolivia." *Latin American Research Review* 44(1): 88–101.

Arditi, Benjamin. 2008. "Arguments About the Left Turns in Latin America: A Post-Liberal Politics?" *Latin American Research Review* 43(3): 59–81.

Arnson, Cynthia J., and Carlos de la Torre. 2013. "Conclusion: The Meaning and Future of Latin American Populism," In *Latin American Populism in the Twenty-First Century*, edited by Carlos de la Torre and Cynthia J. Arnson, pp. 351–376. Baltimore: Johns Hopkins University Press/Woodrow Wilson Center Press.

Assies, Willem. 2003. "David vs. Goliath in Cochabamba: Water Rights, Neoliberalism, and the Revival of Social Protest in Bolivia." *Latin American Perspectives* 30(3): 14–36.

Assies, Willem, and Ton Salman. 2003. "Crisis in Bolivia: The Elections of 2002 and Their Aftermath." Institute of Latin American Studies Research Paper no. 56. London: University of London.

———. 2005. "Ethnicity and Politics in Bolivia." *Ethnopolitics* 4(3): 269–297.

Austin, William, and Elaine Walster. 1974. "Reactions to Confirmations and Disconfirmations of Expectancies of Equity and Inequity." *Journal of Personality and Social Psychology* 30(2): 208–216.

Azzi, Assaad E. 1992. "Procedural Justice and the Allocation of Power in Intergroup Relations: Studies in the United States and South Africa." *Personality and Social Psychology Bulletin* 18(6): 736–747.

———. 1993. "Implicit and Category-Based Allocations of Decision-Making Power in Majority-Minority Relations." *Journal of Experimental Social Psychology* 29(3), 203–228.

Bailey, John, and Pablo Paras. 2006. "Perceptions and Attitudes About Corruption and Democracy in Mexico." *Mexican Studies* 22(1): 57–82.

Baker, Andy, and Kenneth F. Greene. 2011. "The Latin American Left's Mandate: Free Market Policies and Issue Voting in New Democracies." *World Politics* 63(1): 43–77.

Bale, Tim, Stijn van Kessel, and Paul Taggart. 2011. "Thrown Around with Abandon? Popular Understandings of Populism as Conveyed by the Print Media: A UK Case Study." *Acta Politica* 46(2): 111–131.

Banks, Arthur S., and Kenneth A. Wilson. 2015. Cross-National Time-Series Data Archive. Databanks International. Jerusalem, Israel.

Barr, Robert R. 2005. "Bolivia: Another Uncompleted Revolution." *Latin American Politics and Society* 47(3): 69–90.

———. 2009. "Populists, Outsiders, and Anti-Establishment Politics." *Party Politics* 15(1): 29–48.

Barro, Robert J. 1996. *Getting It Right: Markets and Choices in a Free Society.* Boston: MIT Press.

Barros, Sebastián. 2005. "The Discursive Continuities of the Menemist Rupture." In *Populism and the Mirror of Democracy*, edited by Francisco Panizza, pp. 250–273. London: Verso.

Basset, Yann. 2003. "Neoliberalismo v el Neopopulismo: Un Nuevo Eje del Sistema Partidario para la Bolivia de los Años 1990?" In *La Región Andina: Entre los Nuevos Populismos y la Movilización Social*, edited by Carlos Vilas. Bogotá: Observatorio Andino.

Basurto, Jorge. 1999. "Populism in Mexico: From Cárdenas to Cuauhtémoc." In *Populism in Latin America*, edited by Michael L. Conniff, pp. 75–96. Tuscaloosa: University of Alabama Press.

Bechle, Karsten. 2010. "Neopatrimonialism in Latin America: Prospects and Promises of a Neglected Concept." GIGA Working Papers no. 153. Hamburg: German Institute of Global and Area Studies.

Bellinger, Paul T., Jr., and Moisés Arce. 2011. "Protest and Democracy in Latin America's Market Era." *Political Research Quarterly* 64(3): 688–704.

Berg-Schlosser, Dirk, and Gisèle de Meur. 2009. "Comparative Research Design: Case and Variable Selection." In *Configurational Comparative Methods: Qualitative Comparative Analysis (QCA) and Related Techniques*, edited by Benoît Rihoux and Charles C. Ragin, pp. 19–32. Los Angeles: Sage.

Berg-Schlosser, Dirk, Gisèle de Meur, Benoît Rihoux, and Charles C. Ragin. 2009. "Qualitative Comparative Analysis (QCA) as an Approach." In *Configurational Comparative Methods: Qualitative Comparative Analysis (QCA) and Related Techniques*, edited by Benoît Rihoux and Charles C. Ragin, pp. 1–18. Los Angeles: Sage.

Bermeo, Nancy. 2009. "Does Electoral Democracy Boost Economic Equality?" *Journal of Democracy* 20(4): 21–35.

Best, Samuel J., and Brian S. Krueger. 2011. "Government Monitoring and Political Participation in the United States: The Distinct Roles of Anger and Anxiety." *American Politics Research* 39(1): 85–117.

Bethell, Leslie. 2013. "Populism, Neopopulism, and the Left in Brazil: From Getúlio to Lula." In *Latin American Populism in the Twenty-First Century*, edited by Carlos de la Torre and Cynthia J. Arnson, pp. 179–202. Baltimore: Johns Hopkins University Press/Woodrow Wilson Center Press.

Blanco, Louisa, and Robin Grier. 2013. "Explaining the Rise of the Left in Latin America." *Latin American Research Review* 48(1): 68–90.

Bojanic, Antonio. 2009. "The Impact of Tin on the Economic Growth of Bolivia." *Coyuntura Económica* 39(2): 171–183.

Brader, Ted. 2005. "Striking a Responsive Chord: How Political Ads Motivate and Persuade Voters by Appealing to Emotions." *American Journal of Political Science* 49(2): 388–405.

———. 2006. *Campaigning for Hearts and Minds: How Emotional Appeals in Political Ads Work*. Chicago: University of Chicago Press.

Bratton, Michael, and Nicolas van de Walle. 1994. "Neopatrimonial Regimes and Political Transitions in Africa." *World Politics* 46(4): 453–489.

Braumoeller, Bear F., and Gary Goertz. 2002. "Watching Your Posterior: Comment on Seawright." *Political Analysis* 10(2): 198–203.

Brewer, Marilynn B., and Wendy Gardner. 1996. "Who Is This 'We'? Levels of Collective Identity and Self Representations." *Journal of Personality and Social Psychology* 71(1): 83–93.

Brewer, Marilynn B., and Roderick M. Kramer. 1986. "Choice Behavior in Social Dilemmas: Effects of Social Identity, Group Size, and Decision Framing." *Journal of Personality and Social Psychology* 50: 543–549.

Brickman, Philip, Robert Folger, Erica Goode, and Yaacov Schul. 1981. "Microjustice and Macrojustice." In *The Justice Motive in Social Behavior*, edited by Melvin J. Lerner and Sally C. Lerner, pp. 173–202. New York: Plenum.

Brugnoni, Pablo. 2009. "Paraguay 2008: Estruendosos Cambios, Silenciosas Permanencias." *Revista de Ciencia Política* 29(2): 565–590.

Bruhn, Kathleen, and Kenneth F. Greene. 2007. "Elite Polarization Meets Mass Moderation in Mexico's 2006 Elections." *PS: Political Science and Politics* 40(1): 33–38.

Brusco, Valeria, Marcelo Nazareno, and Susan C. Stokes. 2004. "Vote Buying in Argentina." *Latin American Research Review* 39(2): 66–88.

Bunker, Kenneth, and Patricio Navia. 2013. "Latin American Political Outsiders Revisited: The Case of Marco Enríquez-Ominami in Chile, 2009." *Journal of Politics in Latin America* 5(2): 3–25.

Burgess, Katrina, and Steven Levitsky. 2003. "Adaptation in Latin America: Environmental and Organizational Determinants of Party Change in Argentina,

Mexico, Peru, and Venezuela." *Comparative Political Studies* 36(8): 881–911.

Bussmann, Margit, and Gerald Schneider. 2007. "When Globalization Discontent Turns Violent: Foreign Economic Liberalization and Internal War." *International Studies Quarterly* 51(1): 79–97.

Cameron, Maxwell A. 2009. "Latin America's Left Turns: Beyond Good and Bad." *Third World Quarterly* 30(2): 331–348.

Campbell, Keith. 1965. "Family Resemblance Predicates." *American Philosophical Quarterly* 2(3): 238–244.

Canache, Damarys, and Michael E. Allison. 2005. "Perceptions of Political Corruption in Latin American Democracies." *Latin American Politics and Society* 47(3): 91–111.

Canovan, Margaret. 1981. *Populism*. New York: Harcourt, Brace, Jovanovich.

———. 1999. "Trust the People! Populism and the Two Faces of Democracy." *Political Studies* 47(1): 2–16.

———. 2002. "Taking Politics to the People: Populism as the Ideology of Democracy." In *Democracies and the Populist Challenge*, edited by Yves Mény and Yves Surel, pp. 25–44. New York: Palgrave.

Carreras, Miguel. 2012. "The Rise of Outsiders in Latin America, 1980–2010: An Institutionalist Perspective." *Comparative Political Studies* 45(12): 1451–1482.

Carrión, Julio. 2009. "The Persistent Attraction of Populism in the Andes." In *Latin American Democracy: Emerging Reality or Endangered Species?*, edited by Richard L. Millett, Jennifer S. Holmes, and Orlando Pérez, pp. 233–251. New York: Routledge.

Castañeda, Jorge. 2006. "Latin America's Left Turn." *Foreign Affairs* 85(3): 28–43.

Centellas, Miguel. 2008. "From 'Parliamentarized' to 'Pure' Presidentialism: Bolivia After October 2003." *Latin Americanist* 52(3): 5–30.

Chong, Alberto, Ana L. de la O, Dean Karlan, and Leonard Wantchekon. 2011. "Looking Beyond the Incumbent: The Effects of Exposing Corruption on Electoral Outcomes." NBER Working Paper no. 17679. Cambridge, MA: National Bureau of Economic Research.

Chong, Dennis, and James M. Druckman. 2007. "Framing Theory." *Annual Review of Political Science* 10: 103–126.

Clapham, Christopher, ed. 1982. *Private Patronage and Public Power: Political Clientelism in the Modern State*. New York: St. Martin's.

Clayton, Susan, and Susan Opotow. 2003. "Justice and Identity: Changing Perspectives on What Is Fair." *Personality and Social Psychology Review* 7(4): 298–310.

Collier, David, and Robert Adcock. 1999. "Democracy and Dichotomies: A Pragmatic Approach to Choices About Concepts." *Annual Review of Political Science* 2: 537–565.

Collier, David, and Steven Levitsky. 1997. "Democracy with Adjectives: Conceptual Innovation in Comparative Research." *World Politics* 49(3): 430–451.

———. 2009. "Democracy: Conceptual Hierarchies in Comparative Research." In *Concepts and Method in the Social Sciences: The Tradition of Giovanni Sartori*, edited by David Collier and John Gerring. London: Routledge.

Collier, David, and James E. Mahon, Jr. 1993. "Conceptual 'Stretching' Revisited: Adapting Categories in Comparative Analysis." *American Political Science Review* 87(4): 845–855.

Collier, David, James Mahoney, and Jason Seawright. 2004. "Claiming Too Much: Warnings About Selection Bias." In *Rethinking Social Inquiry: Diverse Tools,*

Shared Standards, edited by Henry E. Brady and David Collier, pp. 85–102. Lanham, MD: Rowman and Littlefield.

Conaghan, Catherine M. 2000. "The Irrelevant Right: Alberto Fujimori and the New Politics of Pragmatic Peru." In *Conservative Parties, the Right, and Democracy in Latin America*, edited by Kevin J. Middlebrook, pp. 255–284. Baltimore: Johns Hopkins University Press.

———. 2008. "Ecuador: Correa's Plebiscitary Presidency." *Journal of Democracy* 19(2): 46–60.

———. 2011. "Rafael Correa and the Citizens' Revolution." In *The Resurgence of the Latin American Left*, edited by Steven Levistky and Kenneth M. Roberts, pp. 260–282. Baltimore: Johns Hopkins University Press.

Conaghan, Catherine M., and Carlos de la Torre. 2008. "The Permanent Campaign of Rafael Correa: Making Ecuador's Plebiscitary Presidency." *International Journal of Press/Politics* 13(3): 267–284.

Conniff, Michael L. 1982. "Introduction: Toward a Comparative Definition of Populism." In *Latin American Populism in Comparative Perspective*, edited by Michael L. Conniff, pp. 3–30. Albuquerque: University of New Mexico Press.

———. 1999. "Introduction." In *Populism in Latin America*, edited by Michael L. Conniff, pp. 1–21. Tuscaloosa: University of Alabama Press.

Coppedge, Michael. 2005. "Explaining Democratic Deterioration in Venezuela Through Nested Inference." In *The Third Wave of Democratization in Latin America: Advances and Setbacks*, edited by Frances Hagopian and Scott P. Mainwaring, pp. 289–318. New York: Cambridge University Press.

Corrales, Javier. 2008. "Latin America's Neocaudillismo: Ex-Presidents and Newcomers Running for President . . . and Winning." *Latin American Politics and Society* 50(3): 1–35.

Correa, Rafael. 2007. "Discurso de Posesión del Presidente de la República, Economista Rafael Correa Delgado en la Mitad del Mundo." Inaugural Address, Quito, January 15. Online.

Crabtree, John. 1998. "Neo-Populism and the Fujimori Phenomenon." In *Fujimori's Peru: The Political Economy*, edited by John Crabtree and Jim Thomas, pp. 7–23. London: Institute of Latin American Studies, University of London.

Crisp, Brian F. 2000. *Democratic Institutional Design: The Powers and Incentives of Venezuelan Politicians and Interest Groups*. Stanford, CA: Stanford University Press.

Cronqvist, Lasse. 2007. TOSMANA—Tool for Small-N Analysis [Version 1.3]. Software. Marburg, Germany. Online.

Cropanzano, Russell, and Maureen L. Ambrose. 2001. "Procedural and Distributive Justice Are More Similar Than You Think: A Monistic Perspective and a Research Agenda." In *Advances in Organizational Justice*, edited by Jerald Greenberg and Russell Cropanzano, pp. 119–151. Stanford, CA: Stanford University Press.

Crosby, Faye. 1976. "A Model of Egoistical Relative Deprivation." *Psychological Review* 83(2): 85–113.

Dahl, Robert. 1991. *Modern Political Analysis*, 5th ed. Englewood Cliffs, NJ: Prentice Hall.

Damasio, Antonio R. 1994. *Descartes' Error: Emotion, Reason, and the Human Brain*. New York: G. P. Putnam's Sons.

de la Torre, Carlos. 2007. "The Resurgence of Radical Populism in Latin America." *Constellations* 14(3): 384–397.

————. 2010. *Populist Seduction in Latin America,* 2nd ed. Athens: Ohio University Press.

————. 2013. "In the Name of the People: Democratization, Popular Organizations, and Populism in Venezuela, Bolivia, and Ecuador." *European Review of Latin American and Caribbean Studies* 95: 27–48.

————, ed. 2015. *The Promise and Perils of Populism: Global Perspectives.* Lexington: University Press of Kentucky.

de la Torre, Carlos, and Cynthia J. Arnson. 2013. "Introduction: The Evolution of Latin American Populism and the Debates Over Its Meaning." In *Latin American Populism in the Twenty-First Century*, edited by Carlos de la Torre and Cynthia J. Arnson, pp. 1–36. Baltimore: Johns Hopkins University Press/ Woodrow Wilson Center Press.

Demmers, Jolle, Alex E. Fernández Jilberto, and Barbara Hogenboom. 2001a. "Preface." In *Miraculous Metamorphoses: The Neoliberalization of Latin American Populism*, edited by Jolle Demmers, Alex E. Fernández Jilberto, and Barbara Hogenboom, pp. xi–xiii. London: Zed.

————. 2001b. "The Transformation of Latin American Populism: Regional and Global Dimensions." In *Miraculous Metamorphoses: The Neoliberalization of Latin American Populism*, edited by Jolle Demmers, Alex E. Fernández Jilberto, and Barbara Hogenboom, pp. 1–21. London: Zed.

Deutsch, Morton. 1975. "Equity, Equality, and Need: What Determines Which Value Will Be Used as the Basis for Distributive Justice?" *Journal of Social Issues* 31(3): 137–149.

di Tella, Torcuato. 1965. "Populism and Reform in Latin America." In *Obstacles to Change in Latin America*, edited by Claudio Veliz, pp. 47–74. London: Oxford University Press.

Dibble, Ursula. 1981. "Socially Shared Deprivation and the Approval of Violence: Another Look at the Experience of American Blacks During the 1960s." *Ethnicity* 8(2): 149–169.

Dietz, Henry A., and David J. Myers. 2007. "From Thaw to Deluge: Party System Collapse in Venezuela and Peru." *Latin American Politics and Society* 49(2): 59–86.

Dion, Michelle. 2008. "Retrenchment, Expansion, and the Transformation of Mexican Social Protection Policies." *Social Policy and Administration*, 42(4): 434–450.

do Alto, Hervé. 2008. "El MAS-IPSP Boliviano, Entre Movimiento Social y Partido Político." *Análisis Político* 21(62): 25–43.

Domingo, Pilar. 2001. "Party Politics, Intermediation, and Representation." In *Towards Democratic Viability: The Bolivian Experience*, edited by John Crabtree and Laurence Whitehead. New York: Palgrave.

————. 2005. "Democracy and New Social Forces in Bolivia." *Social Forces* 83(4): 1727–1743.

Dornbusch, Rudiger, and Sebastian Edwards. 1991. "The Macroeconomics of Populism." In *The Macroeconomics of Populism in Latin America*, edited by Rudiger Dornbusch and Sebastian Edwards, pp. 7–13. Chicago: University of Chicago Press.

Doyle, David. 2011. "The Legitimacy of Political Institutions: Explaining Populism in Latin America." *Comparative Political Studies* 44(11): 1447–1473.

Drake, Paul. 1978. *Socialism and Populism in Chile.* Urbana: University of Illinois Press.

————. 1991. "Comment." In *The Macroeconomics of Populism in Latin America*, edited by Rudiger Dornbusch and Sebastian Edwards, pp. 35–40. Chicago: University of Chicago Press.

————. 1999. "Chile's Populism Reconsidered." In *Populism in Latin America*, edited by Michael L. Conniff, pp. 63–74. Tuscaloosa: University of Alabama Press.

Druckman, James M. 2004. "Political Preference Formation: Competition, Deliberation, and the (Ir)relevance of Framing Effects." *American Political Science Review* 98(4): 671–686.

Eagly, Alice H., and Shelly Chaiken. 1993. *The Psychology of Attitudes*. Fort Worth, TX: Harcourt Brace Jovanovich College.

Easterly, William. 2005. "What Did Structural Adjustment Adjust? The Association of Policies and Growth with Repeated IMF and World Bank Adjustment Loans." *Journal of Development Economics* 76(1): 1–22.

Eaton, Kent H. 2006. "Bolivia at the Crossroads: Interpreting the December 2005 Election." *Strategic Insights* 5(2): 1–8.

Edwards, Sebastian. 2010. *Left Behind: Latin America and the False Promise of Populism*. Chicago: University of Chicago Press.

Encuestas y Estudios. 2010. *Así Piensan Los Bolivianos #142: La Corrupción en Bolivia*. La Paz: Encuestas y Estudios.

Etchemendy, Sebastián, and Candelaria Garay. 2011. "Argentina: Left Populism in Comparative Perspective, 2003–2009." In *The Resurgence of the Latin American Left*, edited by Steven Levitsky and Kenneth M. Roberts, pp. 283–305. Baltimore: Johns Hopkins University Press.

Eyzaguirre Ll., Gloria. 1999. "Percepciones de la Prensa Sobre el Parlamento y la Corte Nacional Electoral." In *El Derecho a la Información y Percepciones Sobre Instituciones*, edited by Juan Cristóbal Soruco Q. and Gloria Eyzaguirre Ll., pp. 75–138. La Paz: ILDIS.

Flores-Macías, Gustavo A. 2012. *After Neoliberalism? The Left and Economic Reforms in Latin America*. New York: Oxford University Press.

Frank, Thomas. 2004. "The America That Will Vote for Bush." *Le Monde Diplomatique*, February.

Freeden, Michael. 1996. *Ideologies and Political Theory: A Conceptual Approach*. Oxford: Oxford University Press.

Freidenberg, Flavia. 2015. "¡En Tierra de Caciques! Liderazgos Populistas y Democracia en Ecuador." *OPERA* 16: 99–130.

Gamarra, Eduardo A. 1994. "Market-Oriented Reforms and Democratization in Bolivia." In *A Precarious Balance: Democracy and Economic Reforms in Latin America*, edited by Joan M. Nelson, pp. 21–94. San Francisco: Institute for Contemporary Studies.

Gamarra, Eduardo A., and James M. Malloy. 1995. "The Patrimonial Dynamics of Party Politics in Bolivia." In *Building Democratic Institutions: Party Systems in Latin America*, edited by Scott Mainwaring and Timothy R. Scully, pp. 399–433. Stanford, CA: Stanford University Press.

Geddes, Barbara. 1990. "How the Cases You Choose Affect the Answers You Get: Selection Bias in Comparative Politics." *Political Analysis* 2(1): 131–150.

George, Alexander, and Andrew Bennett. 2005. *Case Studies and Theory Development in the Social Sciences*. Cambridge, MA: MIT Press.

Gerlach, Allen. 2003. *Indians, Oil, and Politics: A Recent History of Ecuador*. Wilmington, DE: Scholarly Resources.

Germani, Gino. 1974. *Politica y Sociedad en una Epoca de Transicion*, 5th ed. Buenos Aires: Paidos.

———. 1978. *Authoritarianism, Fascism, and National Populism*. New Brunswick, NJ: Transaction.

Giavazzi, Francesco, and Guido Tabellini. 2005. "Economic and Political Liberalizations." *Journal of Monetary Economics* 52(7): 1297–1330.

Gibson, James L. 2002. "Truth, Justice, and Reconciliation: Judging the Fairness of Amnesty in South Africa." *American Journal of Political Science* 46(3): 540–556.

Gidron, Noam, and Bart Bonikowski. 2013. "Varieties of Populism: Literature Review and Research Agenda." Weatherhead Center Working Paper no. 13-0004. Cambridge: Weatherhead Center for International Affairs.

Gingerich, Daniel W. 2009. "Corruption and Political Decay: Evidence from Bolivia." *Quarterly Journal of Political Science* 4(1): 1–34.

Goertz, Gary. 2006a. "Assessing the Trivialness, Relevance, and Relative Importance of Necessary or Sufficient Conditions in Social Science." *Studies in Comparative International Development* 41(2): 88–109.

———. 2006b. *Social Science Concepts: A User's Guide*. Princeton, NJ: Princeton University Press.

González Roda, Jorge. 2005. "Bolivia." In *Global Corruption Report*, edited by Diana Rodriguez, Gerard Waite, and Toby Wolfe, pp. 106–109. London: Pluto/Transparency International.

Goodman, Amy. 2005. "Leftist Union Leader Evo Morales Poised to Become First Indigenous President of Bolivia." *Democracy Now*, December 19. Online.

Goodwin, Jeff, James M. Jasper, and Francesca Polletta, eds. 2001. *Passionate Politics: Emotions and Social Movements*. Chicago: University of Chicago Press.

Gratius, Susanne. 2007. "The 'Third Wave of Populism' in Latin America." FRIDE Working Paper no. 45. Madrid: Fundación para las Relaciones Internacionales y el Diálogo Exterior.

Grayson, George W. 2007. *Mexican Messiah: Andrés Manuel López Obrador*. University Park: Pennsylvania State University Press.

Green, Duncan. 2003. *Silent Revolution: The Rise and Decline of Market Economics in Latin America*, 2nd ed. London: Latin American Bureau.

Greenberg, Jerald. 1982. "Approaching Equity and Avoiding Inequity in Groups and Organizations." In *Equity and Justice in Social Behavior*, edited by Jerald Greenberg and Ronald L. Cohen, pp. 389–435. New York: Academic Press.

———. 1987. "Reactions to Procedural Injustice in Payment Distributions: Do the Ends Justify the Means?" *Journal of Applied Psychology* 72(1): 55–61.

Greene, Kenneth F. 2009. "Images and Issues in Mexico's 2006 Presidential Election." In *Consolidating Mexico's Democracy: The 2006 Presidential Campaign in Comparative Perspective*, edited by Jorge I. Domínguez, Chappell Lawson, and Alejandro Moreno, pp. 246–267. Baltimore: Johns Hopkins University Press.

Griffin, Nicholas. 1974. "Wittgenstein, Universals and Family Resemblances." *Canadian Journal of Philosophy* 3(4): 635–651.

Grigorescu, Alexandru. 2006. "The Corruption Eruption in East-Central Europe: The Increased Salience of Corruption and the Role of Intergovernmental Organizations." *East European Politics and Societies* 20(3): 516–549.

Grofman, Bernard, and Mark Gray. 2000. "Geopolitical Influences on Trade Openness in Thirty-One Long-Term Democracies, 1960–1995." Unpublished manuscript. University of California, Irvine.

Groppo, Alejandro. 2009. *The Two Princes: Juan D. Perón and Getulio Vargas: A Comparative Study of Latin American Populism*. Villa María, Argentina: Eduvim.

Gunther, Richard, and Larry Diamond. 2003. "Species of Political Parties: A New Typology." *Party Politics* 9(2): 169–199.

Gutiérrez, Oscar. 2004. "Entrevista con Evo Morales" *Progreso Weekly*, April 29–May 05. Online.

Hawkins, Kirk A. 2009. "Is Chávez Populist? Measuring Populist Discourse in Comparative Perspective." *Comparative Political Studies* 42(8): 1040–1067.

———. 2010. *Venezuela's Chavismo and Populism in Comparative Perspective*. Cambridge: Cambridge University Press.

Hawkins, Kirk A., Scott Riding, and Cas Mudde. 2012. "Measuring Populist Attitudes." Committee on Concepts and Methods Working Paper no. 55. Mexico City: International Political Science Association, Center for Economic Research and Teaching.

Hennessy, Alistair. 1969. "Latin America." In *Populism: Its Meaning and National Characteristics*, edited by Ghita Ionescu and Ernest Gellner, pp. 28–61. New York: Macmillan.

Herrera, Eduardo Wills, Nubia Urueña Cortés, and Nick Rosen. 2003. "South America." In *Global Corruption Report*, edited by Robin Hodess, Jessie Banfield, and Toby Wolfe, pp. 103–114. Berlin: Transparency International.

Hetherington, Kregg. 2011. *Guerrilla Auditors: The Politics of Transparency in Neoliberal Paraguay*. Durham, NC: Duke University Press.

Hewitt, J. Joseph, and Gary Goertz. 2005. "Conceptualizing Interstate Conflict: How Do Concept-Building Strategies Relate to Selection Effects?" *International Interactions* 31(2): 163–182.

Hodess, Robin, and Marie Wolkers. 2004. *Report on the Transparency International Global Corruption Barometer 2004*. Berlin: Transparency International.

Horowitz, Joel. 1999. "Populism and Its Legacies in Argentina." In *Populism in Latin America*, edited by Michael L. Conniff, pp. 22–42. Tuscaloosa: University of Alabama Press.

Huddy, Leonie, Stanley Feldman, and Erin Cassese. 2007. "On the Distinct Political Effects of Anxiety and Anger." In *The Affect Effect: Dynamics of Emotion in Political Thinking and Behaviour*, edited by W. Russell Neuman, George E. Marcus, Ann N. Crigler, and Michael MacKuen, pp. 202–230. Chicago: University of Chicago Press.

Hunt, Scott A., Robert D. Benford, and David A. Snow. 1994. "Identity Fields: Framing Processes and the Social Construction of Movement Identities." In *New Social Movements: From Ideology to Identity*, edited by Enrique Laraña, Hank Johnston, and Joseph R. Gusfield, pp. 185–208. Philadelphia: Temple University Press.

Hutchinson, Francis, Tom Lavers, and Marie Wolkers. 2005. *Report on the Transparency International Global Corruption Barometer 2005*. Berlin: Transparency International.

Hylton, Forrest, and Sinclair Thomson. 2007. *Revolutionary Horizons: Past and Present in Bolivian Politics*. London: Verso.

Ignazi, Piero. 1992. "The Silent Counter-Revolution. Hypotheses on the Emergence of Extreme-Right Wing Parties in Europe." *European Journal of Political Research* 22(1–2): 3–34.

———. 1996. "The Intellectual Basis of Right-Wing Anti-Partyism." *European Journal of Political Research* 29(3): 279–296.

Instituto Interuniversitario de Iberoamérica. 2010. *Estudios 09, 10, 47 y 62: Bolivia.* Salamanca: Universidad de Salamanca. http://americo.usal.es/oir/elites/series %20temporales/Bolivia.pdf.

International Institute for Democracy and Electoral Assistance (IDEA). 2015. *Voter Turnout Data for Bolivia.* Stockholm: IDEA. Online.

International Labor Organization (ILO). 2014. *Key Indicators of the Labour Market.* Geneva: ILO. Online.

International Monetary Fund (IMF). 2006. "Bolivia: Selected Issues." IMF Country Report no. 6/273. Washington, DC: IMF.

Jasper, James M. 2011. "Emotions and Social Movements: Twenty Years of Theory and Research." *Annual Review of Sociology* 37: 285–303.

Jiménez Pozo, Wilson, Fernando Landa Casazola, and Ernesto Yañez Aguilar. 2005. "Bolivia." In *Indigenous People, Poverty, and Human Development in Latin America 1994–2004*, edited by Gillette Hall and Harry Anthony Patrinos, pp. 40–66. New York: Palgrave Macmillan.

Jones, Mark P. 2005. "The Role of Parties and Party Systems in the Policymaking Process." Paper presented at the Inter-American Development Bank Workshop "State Reform, Public Policies, and Policymaking Processes," Washington, DC, April 3.

Jost, John T., Brett W. Pelham, Oliver Sheldon, and Bilian Ni Sullivan. 2003. "Social Inequality and the Reduction of Ideological Dissonance on Behalf of the System: Evidence of Enhanced System Justification Among the Disadvantaged." *European Journal of Social Psychology* 33(1): 13–36.

Kahneman, Daniel, and Amos Tversky, eds. 2000. *Choice, Values, and Frames.* New York: Cambridge University Press.

Kapstein, Ethan B. 2008. "Fairness Considerations in World Politics: Lessons from International Trade Negotiations." *Political Science Quarterly* 123(2): 229–245.

Kaufman, Daniel, Aart Kraay, and Massimo Mastruzzi. 2010. "The Worldwide Governance Indicators: Methodology and Analytical Issues." World Bank Policy Research Working Paper no. 5430. Washington, DC: World Bank.

Kaufman, Robert R., and Alex Segura-Ubiergo. 2001. "Globalization, Domestic Politics, and Social Spending in Latin America: A Time-Series Cross-Section Analysis, 1973–97." *World Politics* 53(4): 553–587.

Kay, Bruce H. 1996. "'Fujipopulism' and the Liberal State in Peru, 1990–1995." *Journal of Interamerican Studies and World Affairs* 38(4): 55–98.

Kenney, Charles D. 1998. "Anti-Politicians, Outsiders and Party Politics: New Conceptual Strategies and Empirical Evidence from Peru." *Party Politics* 4(1): 57–75.

Keren, Michael. 2000. "Political Perfectionism and the 'Anti-System' Party." *Party Politics* 6(1): 107–116.

King, Gary, Robert O. Keohane, and Sidney Verba. 1994. *Designing Social Inquiry: Scientific Inference in Qualitative Research.* Princeton, NJ: Princeton University Press.

Klašnja, Marko, Joshua Tucker, and Kevin Deegan-Krause. 2014. "Pocketbook vs. Sociotropic Corruption Voting." *British Journal of Political Science*, available on CJO2014. doi:10.1017/S0007123414000088.

Knight, Alan. 1998. "Populism and Neo-Populism in Latin America, Especially Mexico." *Journal of Latin American Studies* 30(2): 223–248.

Kohl, Benjamin. 2006. "Challenges to Neoliberal Hegemony in Bolivia." *Antipode* 38(2): 304–326.

Kohl, Benjamin, and Linda Farthing. 2006. *Impasse in Bolivia: Neoliberal Hegemony and Popular Resistance*. London: Zed.

———. 2012. "Material Constraints to Popular Imaginaries: The Extractive Economy and Resource Nationalism in Bolivia." *Political Geography* 31(4): 225–235.

Kostadinova, Tatiana. 2009. "Abstain or Rebel? Corruption Perceptions and Voting in East European Elections." *Politics and Policy* 37(4): 691–714.

Kurtz-Phelan, Daniel. 2005. "Bolivia, After the Election." *Slate*, December 22. Online.

Laclau, Ernesto. 1977. *Politics and Ideology in Marxist Theory*. London: Verso.

———. 2005a. *On Populist Reason*. London: Verso.

———. 2005b. "Populism: What's in a Name?" In *Populism and the Mirror of Democracy*, edited by Francisco Panizza, pp. 32–49. London: Verso.

Laserna, Roberto. 2007. "El Caudillismo Fragmentado." *Nueva Sociedad* 209: 100–117.

Laserna, Roberto, Jesús Ortego, and Douglas Chacón. 2006. *Conflictividad Sociolaboral en Bolivia: Estudios y Reflexiones*. La Paz: Organización de los Estados Americanos, Departamento de Prevención de Crisis y Misiones Especiales.

Lasswell, Harold D., and Abraham Kaplan. 1950. *Power and Society: A Framework for Political Inquiry*. New Haven, CT: Yale University Press.

Lawson, Kay. 1980. "Political Parties and Linkage." In *Political Parties and Linkage: A Comparative Perspective*, edited by Kay Lawson, pp. 3–24. New Haven, CT: Yale University Press.

———. 1988. "When Linkage Fails." In *When Parties Fail: Emerging Alternative Organizations*, edited by Kay Lawson and Peter H. Merkl, pp. 13–38. Princeton, NJ: Princeton University Press.

Laycock, David. 1990. *Populism and Democratic Thought in the Canadian Prairies, 1910 to 1945*. Toronto: University of Toronto Press.

———. 2002. *The New Right and Democracy in Canada*. Oxford: Oxford University Press.

Leaman, David. 2004. "Changing Faces of Populism in Latin America: Masks, Makeovers, and Enduring Features." *Latin American Research Review* 39(3): 313–326.

Ledebur, Kathryn. 2005. "Bolivia: Clear Consequence." In *Drugs and Democracy in Latin America: The Impact of U.S. Policy*, edited by Coletta A. Youngers and Eileen Rosin, pp. 143–184. Boulder, CO: Lynne Rienner.

Leighley, Jan E., and Jonathan Nagler. 1992. "Socioeconomic Class Bias in Turnout, 1964–1988: The Voters Remain the Same." *American Political Science Review* 86(3): 725–736.

Lerner, Jennifer S., Roxana M. Gonzalez, Deborah A. Small, and Baruch Fischhoff. 2003. "Effects of Fear and Anger on Perceived Risks of Terrorism: A National Field Experiment." *Psychological Science* 14(2): 144–150.

Lerner, Jennifer S., and Dacher Keltner. 2000. "Beyond Valence: Toward a Model of Emotion-Specific Influences on Judgement and Choice." *Cognition and Emotion* 14(4): 473–493.

———. 2001. "Fear, Anger, and Risk." *Journal of Personality and Social Psychology* 81(1): 146–159.

Lerner, Melvin J. 1981. "The Justice Motive in Human Relations: Some Thoughts on What We Know and Need to Know About Justice." In *The Justice Motive in Social Behavior*, edited by Melvin J. Lerner and Sally C. Lerner, pp. 11–35. New York: Plenum.

Leventhal, Gerald S. 1980. "What Should Be Done with Equity Theory? New Approaches to the Study of Fairness in Social Relationships." In *Social Exchange: Advances in Theory and Research*, edited by Kenneth J. Gergen, Martin S. Greenberg, and Richard H. Willis, pp. 27–55. New York: Plenum Press.

Levitsky, Steven. 2003. "From Labor Politics to Machine Politics: The Transformation of Party-Union Linkages in Argentine Peronism, 1983–1999." *Latin American Research Review* 38(3): 3–36.

Levitsky, Steven, and Maxwell A. Cameron. 2003. "Democracy Without Parties? Political Parties and Regime Change in Fujimori's Peru." *Latin American Politics and Society* 45(3): 1–33.

Levitsky, Steven, and James Loxton. 2013. "Populism and Competitive Authoritarianism in the Andes." *Democratization* 20(1): 107–136.

Levitsky, Steven, and María Victoria Murillo. 2008. "Argentina: From Kirchner to Kirchner." *Journal of Democracy* 19(2): 16–30.

Li, Quan, and Rafael Reuveny. 2003. "Economic Globalization and Democracy: An Empirial Analysis." *British Journal of Political Science* 33(1): 29–54.

Lijphart, Arend. 1997. "Unequal Participation: Democracy's Unresolved Dilemma." *American Political Science Review* 91(1): 1–14.

Lind, E. Allen, Carol T. Kulik, Maureen Ambrose, and Maria V. de Vera Park. 1993. "Individual and Corporate Dispute Resolution: Using Procedural Fairness as a Decision Heuristic." *Administrative Science Quarterly* 38(2): 224–251.

Linz, Juan J. 1994. "Presidential or Parliamentary Democracy: Does It Make a Difference?" In *The Failure of Presidential Democracy: Comparative Perspectives,* Vol. 1, edited by Juan J. Linz and Arturo Valenzuela, pp. 3–87. Baltimore: Johns Hopkins University Press.

Lipset, Seymour Martin. 1960. *Political Man: The Social Bases of Politics.* Garden City, NY: Doubleday.

López Montaño, Cecilia, ed. 1997. *El Impacto de la Ayuda Externa en América Latina.* Bogotá: TM Editores.

Lowi, Theodore. 1985. *The Personal President: Power Invested, Promise Unfulfilled.* Ithaca, NY: Cornell University Press.

Luna, Juan Pablo, and David Altman. 2011. "Uprooted but Stable: Chilean Parties and the Concept of Party System Institutionalization." *Latin American Politics and Society* 53(2): 1–28.

Luna, Juan Pablo, and Fernando Filgueira. 2009. "The Left Turns as Multiple Paradigmatic Crises." *Third World Quarterly* 30(2): 371–395.

Luzzani, Telma. 2001. "South America." In *Global Corruption Report 2001,* edited by Robin Hodess, Jessie Banfield, and Toby Wolfe, pp. 168–184. Berlin: Transparency International.

Mackie, Diane M., Thierry Devos, and Eliot R. Smith. 2000. "Intergroup Emotions: Explaining Offensive Action Tendencies in an Intergroup Context." *Journal of Personality and Social Psychology* 79(4): 602–616.

MacRae, Donald. 1969. "Populism as an Ideology." In *Populism: Its Meaning and National Characteristics,* edited by Ghita Ionescu and Ernest Gellner, pp. 153–179. New York: Macmillan.

Madrid, Raúl L. 2005. "Indigenous Parties and Democracy in Latin America." *Latin American Politics and Society* 47(4): 161–179.

———. 2008. "The Rise of Ethnopopulism in Latin America." *World Politics* 60(3): 475–508.

————. 2011. "Bolivia: Origins and Policies of the Movimiento al Socialismo." In *The Resurgence of the Latin American Left*, edited by Steven Levitsky and Kenneth M. Roberts, pp. 239–259. Baltimore: Johns Hopkins University Press.

————. 2012. *The Rise of Ethnic Politics in Latin America*. New York: Cambridge University Press.

Madrid, Raúl L., Wendy Hunter, and Kurt Weyland. 2010. "The Policies and Performance of the Contestory and Moderate Left." In *Leftist Governments in Latin America: Successes and Shortcomings*, edited by Kurt Weyland, Raúl L. Madrid, and Wendy Hunter, pp. 140–180. New York: Cambridge University Press.

Mahoney, James, and Gary Goertz. 2004. "The Possibility Principle: Choosing Negative Cases in Comparative Research." *American Political Science Review* 98(4): 653–669.

Mainwaring, Scott. 2006a. "The Crisis of Representation in the Andes." *Journal of Democracy* 17(3): 13–27.

————. 2006b. "State Deficiencies, Party Competition, and Confidence in Democratic Representation in the Andes." In *The Crisis of Democratic Representation in the Andes*, edited by Scott Mainwaring, Ana María Bejarano, and Eduardo Pizarro Leongómez, pp. 295–346. Stanford, CA: Stanford University Press.

Mainwaring, Scott, Ana María Bejarano, and Eduardo Pizarro Leongómez, eds. 2006. *The Crisis of Democratic Representation in the Andes*. Stanford, CA: Stanford University Press.

Mainwaring, Scott, and Timothy R. Scully. 1995. *Building Democratic Institutions: Party Systems in Latin America*. Stanford, CA: Stanford University Press.

————. 2008. "Latin America: Eight Lessons for Governance." *Journal of Democracy* 19(3): 113–237.

Mainwaring, Scott, Timothy R. Scully, and Jorge Vargas Cullell. 2010. "Measuring Success in Democratic Governance." In *Democratic Governance in Latin America*, edited by Scott Mainwaring and Timothy R. Scully, pp. 11–51. Stanford, CA: Stanford University Press.

Mainwaring, Scott, and Mariano Torcal. 2006. "Party System Institutionalization and Party System Theory After the Third Wave of Democratization." In *Handbook of Political Parties*, edited by Richard S. Katz and William Crotty, pp. 204–227. London: Sage.

Mainwaring, Scott, and Edurne Zoco. 2007. "Political Sequences and the Stabilization of Interparty Competition: Electoral Volatility in Old and New Democracies." *Party Politics* 13(2): 155–178.

Mair, Peter. 2008. "Concepts and Concept Formation." In *Approaches and Methodologies in the Social Sciences: A Pluralist Perspective*, edited by Donatella della Porta and Michael Keating, pp. 177–197. New York: Cambridge University Press.

Major, Brenda. 1994. "From Social Inequality to Personal Entitlement: The Role of Social Comparisons, Legitimacy Appraisals and Group Membership." *Advances in Experimental Social Psychology*, Vol. 26, edited by Mark P. Zanna, pp. 293–355. San Diego, CA: Academic Press.

Malloy, James. 1977. "Authoritarianism and Corporatism in Latin America: The Modal Pattern." In *Authoritarianism and Corporatism in Latin America*, edited by James Malloy, pp. 3–19. Pittsburgh: University of Pittsburgh Press.

————. 1991. "Democracy, Economic Crisis and the Problem of Governance: The Case of Bolivia." *Studies in Comparative International Development* 26(2): 37–57.

Manzetti, Luigi, and Carol J. Wilson. 2007. "Why Do Corrupt Governments Maintain Political Support?" *Comparative Political Studies* 40(8): 949–970.

March, Luke. 2007. "From Vanguard of the Proletariat to Vox Populi: Left Populism as a 'Shadow' of Contemporary Socialism." *SAIS Review of International Affairs* 27(1): 63–77.

Marcus, George E., and Michael B. MacKuen. 1993. "Anxiety, Enthusiasm, and the Vote: The Emotional Underpinnings of Learning and Involvement During Presidential Campaigns." *American Political Science Review* 87(3): 672–685.

Mark, Melvin M., and Robert Folger. 1984. "Responses to Relative Deprivation: A Conceptual Framework." *Review of Personality and Social Psychology* 5: 192–218.

Marsteintredet, Leiv. 2007. "Graded Conceptual Membership: Linking Radial Concepts and Fuzzy Sets in the Study of Democracy." Committee on Concepts and Methods Working Paper no. 19. Mexico City: International Political Science Association, Center for Economic Research and Teaching.

Martin, Joanne. 1986. "The Tolerance of Injustice." In *Relative Deprivation and Social Comparison: The Ontario Symposium*, Vol. 4, edited by James M. Olson, C. Peter Herman, and Mark P. Zanna, pp. 217–242. Hillsdale, NJ: Lawrence Erlbaum.

Mayorga, Fernando. 2003. "Neopopulismo y Democracia in Bolivia." *Revista de Ciencia Política* 23(3): 99–118.

———. 2006. "El Gobierno de Evo Morales: Entre Nacionalismo e Indigenismo." *Nueva Sociedad* 206: 4–13.

Mayorga, Fernando, and Eduardo Córdova. 2008. *El Movimiento Antiglobalización en Bolivia: Procesos Globales e Iniciativas Locales en Tiempo de Crisis y Cambio*. La Paz: Plural Editores/UNRISD/CESU-UMSS.

Mayorga, René Antonio. 1995. *Antipolítica y Neopopulismo*. La Paz: CEBEM.

———. 1997. "Bolivia's Silent Revolution." *Journal of Democracy* 8(1): 142–156.

———. 2006. "Outsiders and Neopopulism: The Road to Plebiscitarian Democracy." In *The Crisis of Democratic Representation in the Andes*, edited by Scott Mainwaring, Ana María Bejarano, and Eduardo Pizarro Leongómez, pp. 132–167. Stanford, CA: Stanford University Press.

McCann, James A., and Jorge I. Domínguez. 1998. "Mexicans React to Electoral Fraud and Political Corruption: An Assessment of Public Opinion and Voting Behavior." *Electoral Studies* 17(4): 483–503.

McCoy, Jennifer. 2010. "Venezuela Under Chávez: Beyond Liberalism." In *Latin America's Left Turns: Politics, Policies, and Trajectories of Change*, edited by Maxwell A. Cameron and Eric Hershberg, pp. 81–100. Boulder, CO: Lynne Rienner.

Mello, Patrick A. 2012. "A Critical Review of Applications in QCA and Fuzzy-Set Analysis and a 'Toolbox' of Proven Solutions to Frequently Encountered Problems." Paper presented at the annual meeting of the American Political Science Association, New Orleans, August 30–September 2.

Mishler, William, and Richard Rose. 2001. "What Are the Origins of Political Trust? Testing Institutional and Cultural Theories in Post-Communist Societies." *Comparative Political Studies* 34(1): 30–62.

Møller, Jørgen, and Svend-Erik Skaaning. 2010. "Beyond the Radial Delusion: Conceptualizing and Measuring Democracy and Non-Democracy." *International Political Science Review* 31(3): 261–283.

Montada, Lee. 1991. "Coping with Life Stress: Injustice and the Question 'Who Is Responsible?'" In *Social Justice in Human Relations*, Vol. 2, edited by Herman Steensung and Riël Vermunt, pp. 9–30. New York: Springer.

Montes, J. Esteban, Scott Mainwaring, and Eugenio Ortega. 2000. "Rethinking the Chilean Party System." *Journal of Latin American Studies* 32(3): 795–824.

Montúfar, César. 2013. "Rafael Correa and His Plebiscitary Citizens' Revolution." In *Latin American Populism in the Twenty-First Century*, edited by Carlos de la Torre and Cynthia J. Arnson, pp. 295–323. Baltimore: Johns Hopkins University Press/Woodrow Wilson Center Press.

Morales, Evo. 2002. "Interview with Evo Morales." Centro de Medios Independientes, October 28. http://ecuador.indymedia.org/es/2002/10/515.shtml.

Morales, Juan Antonio, and Jeffrey D. Sachs. 1990. "Bolivia's Economic Crisis." In *Developing Country Debt and Economic Performance*, Vol. 2, edited by Jeffrey D. Sachs, pp. 157–259. Chicago: University of Chicago Press.

Morgan, Jana. 2011. *Bankrupt Representation and Party System Collapse*. University Park: Pennsylvania State University Press.

Morris, Stephen D. 1991. *Corruption and Politics in Contemporary Mexico*. Tuscaloosa: University of Alabama Press.

———. 2009. *Political Corruption in Mexico: The Impact of Democratization*. Boulder, CO: Lynne Rienner.

Moser, Robert G. 1999. "Electoral Systems and the Number of Parties in Postcommunist States." *World Politics* 51(3): 359–384.

———. 2001. *Unexpected Outcomes: Electoral Systems, Political Parties, and Representation in Russia*. Pittsburgh, PA: University of Pittsburgh Press.

Mouzelis, Nicos. 1985. "On the Concept of Populism: Populist and Clientelist Modes of Incorporation in Semiperipheral Polities." *Politics and Society* 14(3): 329–348.

Mudde, Cas. 2004. "The Populist Zeitgeist." *Government and Opposition* 39(4): 541–563.

———. 2007. *Populist Radical Right Parties in Europe*. Cambridge: Cambridge University Press.

Mudde, Cas, and Cristóbal Rovira Kaltwasser. 2011. "Voices of the Peoples: Populism in Europe and Latin America Compared." Kellogg Institute Working Paper no. 378. Notre Dame, IN: Helen Kellogg Institute for International Studies.

———. 2012. "Populism and (Liberal) Democracy: A Framework for Analysis." In *Populism in Europe and the Americas: Threat or Corrective for Democracy*, edited by Cas Mudde and Cristóbal Rovira Kaltwasser. New York: Cambridge University Press.

———. 2013. "Exclusionary vs. Inclusionary Populism: Comparing Contemporary Europe and Latin America." *Government and Opposition* 48(2):147–174.

Mutz, Diana C., and Jeffery J. Mondak. 1997. "Dimensions of Sociotropic Behavior: Group-Based Judgements of Fairness and Well-Being." *American Journal of Political Science* 41(1): 284–308.

Naím, Moisés. 2001. "The Real Story Behind Venezuela's Woes." *Journal of Democracy* 12(2): 17–31.

Navia, Patricio, and Ignacio Walker. 2010. "Political Institutions, Populism and Democracy in Latin America." In *Democratic Governance in Latin America*, edited by Scott Mainwaring and Timothy R. Scully, pp. 245–265. Stanford, CA: Stanford University Press.

Norris, Pippa. 2005. *Radical Right: Voters and Parties in the Electoral Market*. Cambridge: Cambridge University Press.

Nun, José. 1994. "Populismo, Representación y Menemismo." *Sociedad* 5: 93–119.

O'Donnell, Guillermo. 1973. *Modernization and Bureaucratic-Authoritarianism.* Berkeley: University of California Press.

———. 1994. "Delegative Democracy." *Journal of Democracy* 5(1): 55–69.

———. 1998. "Horizontal Accountability in New Democracies." *Journal of Democracy* 9(3): 112–126.

Okun, Arthur M. 1962. "Potential GNP: Its Measurement and Significance." In *Proceedings of the Business and Economics Statistics Section of the American Statistical Association,* pp. 98–104. Washington, DC: American Statistical Association.

Olivera, Óscar, and Tom Lewis. 2004. *Cochabamba: Water War in Bolivia.* Cambridge, MA: Southend.

O'Neill, Kathleen 1999. "Decentralization in the Andes: Power to the People or Party Politics?" Ph.D. dissertation, Harvard University.

Ortiz, David G., and Sergio Béjar. 2013. "Participation in IMF-Sponsored Economic Programs and Contentious Collective Action in Latin America, 1980–2007." *Conflict Management and Peace Science* 30(5): 492–515.

Ostiguy, Pierre. 2009. "The High and the Low in Politics: A Two-Dimensional Political Space for Comparative Analysis and Electoral Studies." Kellogg Institute Working Paper no. 360. Notre Dame, IN: Helen Kellogg Institute for International Studies.

Oviedo Obarrio, Fernando. 2010. "Evo Morales and the Altiplano: Notes for an Electoral Geography of the Movimiento al Socialismo, 2002–2008." *Latin American Perspectives* 37(3): 91–106.

Panfichi, Aldo. 1997. "The Authoritarian Alternative: 'Anti-Politics' in the Popular Sectors of Lima." In *The New Politics of Inequality in Latin America: Rethinking Participation and Representation,* edited by Douglas A. Chalmers, Carlos M. Vilas, Katharine Hite, Scott B. Martin, Kerianne Piester, and Monique Segarra, pp. 217–236. Oxford: Oxford University Press.

Panizza, Francisco. 2000. "Neopopulism and Its Limits in Collor's Brazil." *Bulletin of Latin American Research* 19(2): 177–192.

———. 2005. "Introduction: Populism and the Mirror of Democracy." In *Populism and the Mirror of Democracy,* edited by Francisco Panizza, pp. 1–31. London: Verso.

———. 2013. "What Do We Mean When We Talk About Populism?" In *Latin American Populism in the Twenty-First Century,* edited by Carlos de la Torre and Cynthia J. Arnson, pp. 85–116. Baltimore: Johns Hopkins University Press/Woodrow Wilson Center Press.

Panizza, Francisco, and Romina Miorelli. 2009. "Populism and Democracy in Latin America." *Ethics and International Affairs* 23(1): 39–46.

Pappas, Takis S. 2012. "Populism Emergent: A Framework for Analyzing Its Contexts, Mechanics, and Outcomes." EUI Working Paper RSCAS 2012/01. Florence: European University Institute, Robert Schuman Centre for Advanced Studies.

Paramio, Ludolfo. 2006. "La Izquierda y el Populismo." In *La "Izquierda" en América Latina,* edited by Pedro Pérez Herrero, pp. 21–46. Madrid: Editorial Pablo Iglesias.

Pauwels, Teun. 2011. "Measuring Populism: A Quantitative Text Analysis of Party Literature in Belgium." *Journal of Elections, Public Opinion and Parties* 21(1): 97–119.

Payne, J. Mark, Daniel Zovatto G., and Mercedes Mateo Díaz. 2007. *Democracies in Development.* Washington, DC: Inter-American Development Bank.

Perreault, Thomas. 2006. "From the *Guerra Del Agua* to the *Guerra Del Gas*: Resource Governance, Neoliberalism and Popular Protest in Bolivia." *Antipode* 38(1): 150–172.

Peters, John G., and Susan Welch. 1978. "Political Corruption in America: A Search for Definitions and a Theory." *American Political Science Review* 72(3): 974–984.

Posada-Carbó, Eduardo. 2005. "Language and Politics: On the Colombian 'Establishment.'" Kellogg Institute Working Paper no. 320. Notre Dame, IN: Helen Kellogg Institute for International Studies.

Postero, Nancy Grey. 2004. "Articulation and Fragmentation: Indigenous Politics in Bolivia." In *The Struggle for Indigenous Rights in Latin America,* edited by Nancy Grey Postero and Leon Zamosc, pp. 189–216. Brighton, England: Sussex Academic.

Quintana Taborga, Juan Ramón. 2005. "Bolivia, Entre el Crisis y el Caos: Existe una Salida Negotiada?" Análise de Conjuntura no. 11. Rio de Janiero: Observatório Político Sul-America.

Ragin, Charles C. 2000. *Fuzzy Set Social Science.* Chicago: University of Chicago Press.

———. 2006. "Set Relations in Social Research: Evaluating Their Consistency and Coverage." *Political Analysis* 14(3): 291–310.

———. 2008. *Redesigning Social Inquiry: Fuzzy Sets and Beyond.* Chicago: University of Chicago Press.

———. 2009. "Qualitative Comparative Analysis Using Fuzzy Sets (fsQCA)." In *Configurational Comparative Methods: Qualitative Comparative Analysis (QCA) and Related Techniques,* edited by Benoît Rihoux and Charles C. Ragin, pp. 87–122. Los Angeles: Sage.

Ragin, Charles C., Kriss A. Drass, and Sean Davey. 2006. *Fuzzy-Set/Qualitative Comparative Analysis 2.0.* Tucson: Department of Sociology, University of Arizona.

Reichert, Christopher, and Claude Rubinson. 2011. *Kirq.* Houston, TX: University of Houston–Downtown.

Reina, Mauricio, and Sandra Zuluaga. 2012. "The Impact of Globalization on Latin America: The Case of Colombia." The Impact of Globalization on Latin America Task Force Working Paper, September 11. Miami, FL: University of Miami, Center for Hemispheric Policy.

Remmer, Karen L. 1991. "The Political Impact of Economic Crisis in Latin America in the 1980s." *American Political Science Review* 85(3): 777–800.

———. 2012. "The Rise of Leftist–Populist Governance in Latin America: The Roots of Electoral Change." *Comparative Political Studies* 45(8): 947–972.

Resnick, Danielle. 2015. "Varieties of African Populism in Comparative Perspective." In *The Promise and Perils of Populism: Global Perspectives,* edited by Carlos de la Torre, pp. 317–348. Lexington: University Press of Kentucky.

Rigobon, Roberto, and Dani Rodrik. 2005. "Rule of Law, Democracy, Openness, and Income." *Economics of Transition* 13(3): 533–564.

Rihoux, Benoît, and Gisèle de Meur 2009. "Crisp Set Qualitative Comparative Analysis." In *Configurational Comparative Methods: Qualitative Comparative Analysis (QCA) and Related Techniques,* edited by Benoît Rihoux and Charles C. Ragin, pp. 33–68. Los Angeles: Sage.

Rihoux, Benoît, and Charles C. Ragin, eds. 2009. *Configurational Comparative Methods: Qualitative Comparative Analysis (QCA) and Related Techniques.* Los Angeles: Sage.

Roberts, Kenneth M. 1995. "Neoliberalism and the Transformation of Populism in Latin America." *World Politics* 48(1): 82–116.

————. 2002. "Party-Society Linkages and Democratic Representation in Latin America." *Canadian Journal of Latin American and Caribbean Studies* 27(53): 9–34.

————. 2003. "Populist Mobilization and Political Organization in Latin America: Historical and Contemporary Variations." Paper presented at the annual meeting of the Latin American Studies Association, Dallas.

————. 2006. "Populism, Political Conflict, and Grass-Roots Organization in Latin America." *Comparative Politics* 38(2): 127–148.

————. 2007. "Latin America's Populist Revival." *SAIS Review* 27(1): 3–15.

————. 2008. "The Mobilization of Opposition to Economic Liberalization." *Annual Review of Political Science* 11: 327–349.

————. 2012. "Market Reform, Programmatic (De)alignment, and Party System Stability in Latin America." *Comparative Political Studies* 46(11): 1422–1452.

————. 2013. "Parties and Populism in Latin America." In *Latin American Populism in the Twenty-First Century*, edited by Carlos de la Torre and Cynthia J. Arnson, pp. 37–60. Baltimore: Johns Hopkins University Press/Woodrow Wilson Center Press.

Roberts, Kenneth M., and Erik Wibbels. 1999. "Party Systems and Electoral Volatility in Latin America: A Test of Economic, Institutional, and Structural Explanations." *American Political Science Review* 93(3): 575–590.

Robinson, William I. 2008. *Latin America and Global Capitalism: A Critical Globalization Perspective*. Baltimore: Johns Hopkins University Press.

Rodríguez, Pedro L., José R. Morales, and Francisco J. Monaldi. 2012. "Direct Distribution of Oil Revenues in Venezuela: A Viable Alternative?" Center for Global Development Working Paper no. 306. Washington, DC: Center for Global Development.

Rooduijn, Matthijs, Sarah L. de Lange, and Wouter van der Brug. 2014. "A Populist *Zeitgeist*? Programmatic Contagion by Populist Parties in Western Europe." *Party Politics* 20(4): 563–575.

Rose, Richard, and William Mishler 2007. "Explaining the Gap Between the Experience and Perception of Corruption." Studies in Public Policy no. 432. Aberdeen, Scotland: University of Aberdeen, Centre for the Study of Public Policy.

Roxborough, Ian. 1984. "Unity and Diversity in Latin American History." *Journal of Latin American Studies* 16(1): 1–26.

Rubinson, Claude. 2013. "Contradictions in fsQCA." *Quality and Quantity* 47(5): 2847–2867.

Rudolph, Thomas J., Amy Gangl, and Dan Stevens. 2000. "The Effects of Efficacy and Emotions on Campaign Involvement." *Journal of Politics* 62(4): 1189–1197.

Rudra, Nita, and Stephan Haggard. 2005. "Globalization, Democracy, and Effective Welfare Spending in the Developing World." *Comparative Political Studies* 38(9): 1015–1049.

Rundquist, Barry S., and Susan B. Hansen. 1976. "On Controlling Official Corruption: Elections vs. Laws." Unpublished manuscript.

Rundquist, Barry S., Gerald S. Strom, and John G. Peters. 1977. "Corrupt Politicians and Their Electoral Support: Some Experimental Observations." *American Political Science Review* 71(3): 954–963.

Sachs, Jeffrey D. 1990. *Social Conflict and Populist Politics in Latin America*. San Francisco: ICS Press.

Salman, Ton. 2007. "Bolivia and the Paradoxes of Democratic Consolidation." *Latin American Perspectives* 34(6): 111–130.

Sanchez, Omar. 2008. "Transformation and Decay: The De-Institutionalization of Party Systems in South America." *Third World Quarterly* 29(2): 315–337.

———. 2009. "Party Non-Systems: A Conceptual Innovation." *Party Politics* 15(4): 487–520.

Sartori, Giovanni. 1970. "Concept Misinformation in Comparative Politics." *American Political Science Review* 64(4):1033–1053.

———. 1984. "Guidelines for Concept Analysis." In *Social Science Concepts: A Systematic Analysis*, edited by Giovanni Sartori, pp. 15–85. Beverly Hills, CA: Sage.

Scarrow, Susan E. 1996. "Politicians Against Parties: Anti-Party Arguments as Weapons for Change in Germany." *European Journal of Political Research* 29(3): 297–317.

Schamis, Hector E. 2006. "Populism, Socialism, and Democratic Institutions." *Journal of Democracy* 17(4): 20–34.

———. 2013. "From the Peróns to the Kirchners: 'Populism' in Argentine Politics." In *Latin American Populism in the Twenty-First Century*, edited by Carlos de la Torre and Cynthia J. Arnson, pp. 145–178. Baltimore: Johns Hopkins University Press/Woodrow Wilson Center Press.

Schedler, Andreas. 1996a. "Anti-Political Establishment Parties." *Party Politics* 2(3): 291–312.

———, ed. 1996b. *The End of Politics? Explorations into Modern Antipolitics*. New York: St. Martin's.

———. 2007. "The Mobilization of Distrust." *Journal of Democracy* 18(1): 88–102.

Schneider, Carsten Q., and Claudius Wagemann. 2010. "Standards of Good Practice in Qualitative Comparative Analysis (QCA) and Fuzzy Sets." *Comparative Sociology* 9(3): 397–418.

Seawright, Jason. 2012. *Party-System Collapse: The Roots of Crisis in Peru and Venezuela*. Stanford, CA: Stanford University Press.

Seligson, Mitchell A. 2002. "The Impact of Corruption on Regime Legitimacy: A Comparative Study of Four Latin American Countries." *Journal of Politics* 64(2): 408–433.

———. 2006. "The Measurement and Impact of Corruption Victimization: Survey Evidence from Latin America." *World Development* 34(2): 381–404.

———. 2007. "The Rise of Populism and the Left in Latin America." *Journal of Democracy* 18(3): 81–95.

Seligson, Mitchell A., Abby Cordova, Juan Carlos Donoso, Daniel Moreno Morales, Diana Orcés, and Vivian Schwarz Blum. 2006. "Democracy Audit: Bolivia 2006 Report." Nashville, TN: Latin American Public Opinion Project.

Seligson, Mitchell A., and Dominique Zéphyr. 2008. "The Americas Barometer 2006: Report on Corruption." In *Global Corruption Report 2008: Corruption in the Water Sector*, edited by Dieter Zinnbauer and Rebecca Dobson, pp. 312–315. New York: Cambridge University Press.

Shils, Edward. 1956. *The Torment of Secrecy: The Background and Consequences of American Security Policies*. London: Heinemann.

Shirk, David A. 2005. *Mexico's New Politics: The PAN and Democratic Change*. Boulder, CO: Lynne Rienner.

Shultz, Jim. 2003. "Bolivia: The Water War Widens." *NACLA Report on the Americas* 36(4): 34–37.

Silva, Eduardo. 2009. *Challenging Neoliberalism in Latin America.* New York: Cambridge University Press.

Singer, Matthew M. 2007. "The Presidential and Parliamentary Elections in Bolivia 2005." *Electoral Studies* 26(1): 200–205.

Singer, Matthew M., and Kevin M. Morrison. 2004. "The 2002 Presidential and Parliamentary Elections in Bolivia." *Electoral Studies* 23(1): 172–182.

Skocpol, Theda, and Margaret Somers. 1980. "The Uses of Comparative History in Macrosocial Inquiry." *Comparative Studies in Society and History* 22(2): 174–197.

Smith, Heather J., Tracey Cronin, and Thomas Kessler. 2008. "Anger, Fear, or Sadness: Faculty Members' Emotional Reactions to Collective Pay Disadvantage." *Political Psychology* 29(2): 221–246.

Smith, Heather J., and Daniel J. Ortiz. 2002. "Is It Just Me? The Different Consequences of Personal and Group Relative Deprivation." In *Relative Deprivation: Specification, Development, and Integration,* edited by Iain Walker and Heather J. Smith, pp. 91–115. New York: Cambridge University Press.

Smith, Heather J., Thomas F. Pettigrew, Gina M. Pippin, and Silvana Bialosiewicz. 2012. "Relative Deprivation: A Theoretical and Meta-Analytic Review." *Personality and Social Psychology Review* 16(3): 203–232.

Sosa, Manuel Robles. 2005. "Entrevista con el Candidato Presidencial Evo Morales." Prensa Latina, December 13. www.rebelion.org/noticia.php?id=24101.

Springer, Natalia. 2005. "Bolivia: A Situation Analysis." Geneva: United Nations High Commissioner for Refugees, Protection Information Section.

Stanley, Ben. 2008. "The Thin Ideology of Populism." *Journal of Political Ideologies* 13(1): 95–110.

Stavrakakis, Yannis. 2004. "Antinomies of Formalism: Laclau's Theory of Populism and the Lessons from Religious Populism in Greece." *Journal of Political Ideologies* 9(3): 253–267.

Stefanoni, Pablo, and Hervé do Alto. 2006. *La Revolución de Evo Morales: de la Coca al Palacio.* Buenos Aires: Capital Intelectual.

Stein, Ernesto, Mariano Tommasi, Koldo Echebarría, Eduardo Lora, and Mark Payne, eds. 2006. *The Politics of Policies: Economic and Social Progress in Latin America.* Washington, DC: Inter-American Development Bank.

Stein, Steve. 1980. *Populism in Peru: The Emergence of the Masses and the Politics of Social Control.* Madison: University of Wisconsin Press.

Stokes, Susan C. 2005. "Perverse Accountability: A Formal Model of Machine Politics with Evidence from Argentina." *American Political Science Review* 99(3): 315–326.

———. 2009. *Globalization and the Left in Latin America.* Unpublished manuscript. New Haven, CT: Yale University.

Stoner-Weiss, Kathryn. 2001. "The Limited Reach of Russia's Party System: Underinstitutionalization in Dual Transitions." *Politics and Society* 29(3): 385–414.

Taggart, Paul. 2002. "Populism and the Pathology of Representative Politics." In *Democracies and the Populist Challenge,* edited by Yves Mény and Yves Surel, pp. 62–80. New York: Palgrave.

Tarrow, Sidney. 1998. *Power in Movement: Social Movements and Contentious Politics,* 2nd ed. Cambridge: Cambridge University Press.

Tavits, Margit. 2007. "Clarity of Responsibility and Corruption." *American Journal of Political Science* 51(1): 218–229.

Taylor, Donald M., and Fathali M. Moghaddam. 1994. *Theories of Intergroup Relations: International Social Psychological Perspectives,* 2nd ed. Westport, CT: Praeger.

Thibaut, John W., and Laurens Walker. 1975. *Procedural Justice: A Psychological Analysis.* Hillsdale, NJ: Lawrence Erlbaum.

Thoumi, Francisco E. 2003. *Illegal Drugs, Economy, and Society in the Andes.* Baltimore: Johns Hopkins University Press/Woodrow Wilson Center Press.

Torcal, Mariano, Richard Gunther, and José Ramón Montero. 2002. "Anti-Party Sentiments in Southern Europe." In *Political Parties: Old Concepts and New Challenges,* edited by Richard Gunther, José Ramón Montero, and Juan J. Linz, pp. 257–290. New York: Oxford University Press.

Tyler, Tom R. 1988. "What Is Procedural Justice? Criteria Used by Citizens to Assess the Fairness of Legal Procedures." *Law and Society Review* 22(1): 103–135.

———. 1990. *Why People Obey the Law: Procedural Justice, Legitimacy, and Compliance.* New Haven, CT: Yale University Press.

———. 2001. "A Psychological Perspective on the Legitimacy of Institutions and Authorities." In *The Psychology of Legitimacy,* edited by John T. Jost and Brenda Major, pp. 416–436. New York: Cambridge University Press.

Tyler, Tom R., and Steven Blader. 2000. *Cooperation in Groups: Procedural Justice, Social Identity, and Behavioral Engagement.* Philadelphia: Psychology Press.

Tyler, Tom R., Kenneth A. Rasinski, and Kathleen M. McGraw. 1985. "The Influence of Perceived Injustice on the Endorsement of Political Leaders." *Journal of Applied Social Psychology* 15(8): 700–725.

Tyler, Tom R., and Heather J. Smith. 1998. "Social Justice and Social Movements." In *The Handbook of Social Psychology,* Vol. 2, 4th ed., edited by Daniel T. Gilbert, Susan T. Fiske, and Gardner Lindzey, pp. 595–629. New York: McGraw-Hill.

US Department of State. 2008. *Bolivia: Human Rights Report.* Washington, DC: US Department of State.

US Embassy, La Paz. 2007. "Clone Wars: MAS 'Parallelism' in Action." Wikileaks: Wikileaks Cable 07LAPAZ3062_a. Online.

van Cott, Donna Lee. 2003. "From Exclusion to Inclusion: Bolivia's 2002 Election." *Journal of Latin American Studies* 35(4): 751–775.

———. 2005. *From Movements to Parties in Latin America: The Evolution of Ethnic Politics.* New York: Cambridge University Press.

———. 2007. "Latin America's Indigenous Peoples." *Journal of Democracy* 18(4): 127–142.

van Zomeren, Martijn, Russell Spears, Agneta H. Fischer, and Colin Wayne Leach. 2004. "Put Your Money Where Your Mouth Is! Explaining Collective Action Tendencies Through Group-Based Anger and Group Efficacy." *Journal of Personality and Social Psychology* 87(5): 649–664.

Vilas, Carlos M. 1992–1993. "Latin American Populism: A Structural Approach." *Science and Society* 56(4): 389–420.

———. 2005. "¿Populismos Reciclados o Neoliberalismo A Secas? El Mito del Neopopulismo Latinoamericano." *Estudios Sociales* 26(1): 27–51.

Wagner, Markus. 2014. "Fear and Anger in Great Britain: Blame Assignment and

Emotional Reactions to the Financial Crisis Political Behavior." *Political Behavior* 36(3): 683–703.

Walker, Iain, and Heather J. Smith. 2002. *Relative Deprivation: Specification, Development, and Integration*. New York: Cambridge University Press.

Walker, Ignacio. 2008. "Democracy and Populism in Latin America." Kellogg Institute Working Paper no. 347. Notre Dame, IN: Helen Kellogg Institute for International Studies.

Walster, Elaine, G. William Walster, and Ellen Berscheid. 1978. *Equity: Theory and Research*. Boston: Allyn and Bacon.

Weber, Max. 1978. *Economy and Society: An Outline of Interpretive Sociology*, edited by Guenther Roth and Claus Wittich. Berkeley: University of California Press.

Weiss, Howard M., Kathleen Suckow, and Russell Cropanzano. 1999. "Effects of Justice Conditions on Discrete Emotions." *Journal of Applied Psychology* 84(5): 786–794.

Welch, Susan, and John R. Hibbing. 1997. "The Effects of Charges of Corruption on Voting Behavior in Congressional Elections, 1982–1990." *Journal of Politics* 59(1): 226–239.

Wenzel, Michael. 2002. "What Is Social About Justice? Inclusive Identity and Group Values as the Basis of the Justice Motive." *Journal of Experimental Social Psychology* 38(3): 205–218.

———. 2004. "The Social Side of Sanctions: Personal and Social Norms as Moderators of Deterrence." *Law and Human Behavior* 28(5): 547–567.

Weyland, Kurt. 1996. "Neo-Populism and Neo-Liberalism in Latin America: Unexpected Affinities." *Studies in Comparative International Development* 32(3): 3–31.

———. 1999. "Neoliberal Populism in Latin America and Eastern Europe." *Comparative Politics* 31(4): 379–401.

———. 2001. "Clarifying a Contested Concept: Populism in the Study of Latin American Politics." *Comparative Politics* 34(1): 1–22.

———. 2003. "Economic Voting Reconsidered: Crisis and Charisma in the Election of Hugo Chávez." *Comparative Political Studies* 36(7): 822–848.

———. 2013. "Populism and Social Policy in Latin America." In *Latin American Populism in the Twenty-First Century*, edited by Carlos de la Torre and Cynthia J. Arnson, pp. 117–144. Baltimore: Johns Hopkins University Press/Woodrow Wilson Center Press.

Wibbels, Erik. 2006. "Dependency Revisited: International Markets, Business Cycles, and Social Spending in the Developing World." *International Organization* 60(2): 433–468.

Wiesehomeier, Nina, and David Doyle. 2013. "Discontent and the Left Turn in Latin America." *Political Science Research and Methods* 1(2): 201–221.

Wiles, Peter. 1969. "A Syndrome, Not a Doctrine: Some Elementary Theses on Populism." In *Populism: Its Meaning and National Characteristics*, edited by Ghita Ionescu and Ernest Gellner, pp. 166–179. New York: Macmillan.

Williams, Sue. 1999. "The Globalization of the Drug Trade." *UNESCO Sources* 111: 4–5.

Wittgenstein, Ludwig. 1953. *Philosophical Investigations*. London: Macmillan.

Wood, Elisabeth Jean. 2003. *Insurgent Collective Action and Civil War in El Salvador*. New York: Cambridge University Press.

Worsley, Peter. 1969. "The Concept of Populism." In *Populism: Its Meaning and National Characteristics*, edited by Ghita Ionescu and Ernest Gellner, pp. 212–250. New York: Macmillan

Yashar, Deborah J. 1999. "Democracy, Indigenous Movements, and Postliberal Challenge in Latin America." *World Politics* 52(1): 76–104.

———. 2005. *Contesting Citizenship in Latin America: The Rise of Indigenous Movements*. New York: Cambridge University Press.

Zakaria, Fareed. 2016. "Populism on the March." *Foreign Affairs* 95(6): 9–15.

Zibechi, Raúl. 2005. "New Challenges for Radical Social Movements." *NACLA Report on the Americas* 38(5): 14.

Zuboff, Shoshana. 2008. "Obama's New Peer Populism." *BusinessWeek*, August 21.

Index

academic literature, 23–24, 25(table)
Acción Democrática Nacionalista
(ADN), 80–81, 87, 107
accountability, plebiscitarianism limiting,
176–177
Africa, explaining populist successes in,
59
agency, 78(n4), 169–170
agrarian movements, 52
Alianza Popular Revolucionaria
Americana (APRA), 11, 197
amateurs, 170(n3)
anger. *See* emotions
antiestablishment appeals: Bolivia's
party system decline, 87; causal
factors of populist emergence, 4–5;
challenge politics, 149; choosing
populist candidates or other
alternatives, 72–73; classifying
mavericks, 156–157; cumulative
effects of populism, 174–175;
defining populism, 44; defining "the
establishment," 48–49; demand-side
factors, 66; explaining electoral
success, 162–165; explanations for
populism, 58–59; identifying and
categorizing populist candidates, 16,
116–117, 151–152, 155–157, 192–
194; logical consequences of
populism, 175–177; mass movements
as response, 74–76; Morales' 2005

campaign strategy, 104–105, 107–
108; Morales' election strategy, 99–
102; Néstor Kirchner, 155; party
system institutionalization, 64; as
political strategy, 6; symbols of
populism, 45–46; weak party
institutionalization and, 167–168
antiestablishment personalist leadership,
147
appeals: linkages and, 56(n17). *See also*
antiestablishment appeals
Argentina: clientelism, 56(n21); coded
data for all causal conditions,
199(table); economic misery, 196–
197; explaining populist successes,
59; gains under populism, 10–11;
Menem's victory and policies, 2;
populists' electoral results and coded
data, 193(table); PSI index,
122(table); trust analysis, 124; use of
challenge politics, 150, 160
Asamblea por la Soberanía de los
Pueblos (ASP), 101
authoritarianism: centralization of power
in the executive, 13–14; executive
power and the conflict between
populism and democracy, 179–180;
first era populist figures, 11;
Mexico's legacy, 140
autonomy, group, 51–52
Avalos, Isaac, 103

239

About the Book

LATIN AMERICA HAS RECENTLY EXPERIENCED A POWERFUL RESURGENCE OF populism, a phenomenon that has had an outsized influence on the region's politics. What explains this resurgence? And what is distinctive about this new populist era? Answering these questions, Robert Barr offers a refined conceptualization of populism and an intriguing explanation of its recent electoral successes across the continent.

Robert R. Barr is associate professor of political science at the University of Mary Washington.